REVIEW OF NATIONAL LITERATURES is a forum for scholars and critics concerned with literature as the expression of national character and as the repository of national culture in its most vital and most readily communicable form. The editors recognize the validity of the critical perspective of recent decades when, as a corrective against the excesses of an exclusively nationalist orientation, it has seemed important to emphasize internationalist and even anti-nationalist tendencies in the study of literature. But they also recognize the validity of Professor René Wellek's strictures against deliberate cultivation of an internationalist point of view which has the effect, as he says, of encouraging "an indiscriminate smattering, a vague, sentimental cosmopolitanism" that often mistakes the poverty of national literatures for their wealth. Professor Wellek has remarked correctly that in the comparative study of what is sometimes called world literature, it is "the problem of 'nationality' and of the distinct contributions of the individual nations to this general literary process which should be realized as central."

On the assumption so ably expressed by a distinguished statesman of the 20th century that "it would be reactionary to abolish those distinctions of language, literature, and art, which give to the human mind its infinite variety," REVIEW OF NATIONAL LITERATURES undertakes to encourage a continuing reassessment of the wealth of national literatures – from the earliest to the most recent – as a prerequisite for the understanding and diffusion of "world literature" in its profoundest sense.

Each issue focuses on a national culture, or, more particularly, on a representative theme, author, literary movement, or critical tendency, in an effort to provide substantial and concentrated materials for comparative study. To insure competent presentation of highly specialized or novel topics – such as contemporary literary developments in a new or emerging nation – the regular editors, when necessary, enlist the collaboration of "special editors."

Review of National Literatures and World Report

General Editor: Anne Paolucci

Published by Council on National Literatures

ITALY: FICTION, THEATER, POETRY, FILM SINCE 1950

Special Editor: Robert S. Dombroski

Distributed by Griffon House Publications

Copyright © 2000 by Council on National Literatures
New Series: III

ISSN: 1521-7337
ISBN: 0-918680-90-5

Published by
COUNCIL ON NATIONAL LITERATURES
68-02 Metropolitan Avenue
Middle Village, NY 11379

Contents

Robert S. Dombroski
Foreword — 7

Joseph Farrell
Making Theater in Italy — 9

Peter Hainsworth
Literature and Society 1950-2000 — 29

Charles Klopp
Rallying Points: Literary and Cultural Journals, 1945 to the Present — 53

John Picchione
Major Trends in Italian Poetry: From the Post-War Years to the Present — 72

Rinaldina Russell
Coming of Age: An Overview of Women's Writing in Italy in the Last Half Century — 90

Joseph Francese
The Italian Postmodern: A Comparative Perspective — 111

Ellen Nerenberg
Pulp Fiction, "Italian Style" — 127

Peter Bondanella
Italian Cinema from the 1950s to the Present — 146

ROBERT S. DOMBROSKI

Foreword

Since the Second World War, Italian culture has gained wide circulation in Europe and the Americas, as can be seen in the prestige enjoyed by Italian design and cinema and by the numerous translations of Italian literary works. The authors that gained prominence in the second half of the century are numerous, but their work for the most part builds on that that of earlier generations. It would be hard to imagine a Sciascia without a Verga or a Pirandello, a Consolo without a Gadda, a Calvino or a Tabucchi without a Svevo; nor can we separate completely the various forms of experimental poetry from the great tradition of early twentieth century verse which culminates in Montale. What sets the last fifty years apart from the earlier century is an increase in the intensity and consistency of literary activity at a level that could be called at once 'high' and 'popular.' The essential reason for this is that, with the defeat of fascism and the liberalization of Italian social and political institutions, Italy has become a nation, not just in principle, but in fact. Gramsci's ideal of a 'national-popular' literature, a reality in England and France since the early nineteenth century, has to a large measure now been realized in Italy.

Each of the essays collected here addresses a general theme. Peter Hainsworth discusses literature from the standpoint of its place in society: the social issues raised by literary works and the effect of the changes in society on imaginative writing. Joseph Farrell's essay focuses on the general problems in the development of contemporary Italian theater within the framework of the age-old conflict between writer and actor. The important role played by literary magazines in the development of literary ideologies is then surveyed by Charles Klopp; it is followed by John Picchione's detailed review of the rich history of recent Italian poetry. The problems facing women authors in the creation of a feminine voice are the subject of Rinaldina Russell's informative essay. Joseph Francese explores the responses of Italian writing to postmodernism, while Ellen Nerenberg introduces us to Italy's most recent trend of pulp fiction. The final essay by Peter Bondanella surveys the development of Italian cinema.

R.S.D.
Graduate School/CUNY

JOSEPH FARRELL

Making Theater in Italy

In his introduction to *Six Characters in Search of an Author,* Pirandello himself provided his readers with a shadow manifesto for his own theater, or at least for that complex of ideas which became known as "Pirandellismo" and which, according to Leonardo Sciascia, merits the modest description of "half-philosophy" rather than philosophy. (Sciascia, 1128) The characters of the play, writes Pirandello, "without knowing, without wishing to," nevertheless became the vehicles for the expression of the "torments of my own spirit." These torments were three: "the deception of mutual understanding based irremediably on the empty abstraction of words; the multiple personality of each individual according to all the possibilities of being which are to be found in each one of us, and finally the tragic, immanent conflict between life which is continually moving and form which fixes it, immutably." (Pirandello, 1921, 60)

The play-within-the-play is, among other things, an examination of these conflicts and an exposition of this half-philosophy, but historians of Italian theater will find their attention drawn to other conflicts mentioned more casually in the framework play. The unfortunate fictional director inside that work had already run into difficulties with the rehearsals even before the six characters presented themselves to throw everything completely off course. The play his company should have been performing was another work by Pirandello, *The Rules of the Game,* but the enigmas and subtleties of character and plot were beyond the grasp of the cast. The director was sympathetic. "What am I to do," he exploded with exasperation, "if there is not even one good play sent from France, and we find ourselves reduced to staging Pirandello?" (Pirandello, 1921, 103)

This conflict between Italian and foreign, or between living and "classical," writers for access to the stage, or between directors and writers for pre-eminence, is still unresolved in theater in Italy. Were Pirandello to walk around the streets of Milan or Rome today, he would find the situation he described with such high irony scarcely improved a century later. Any visitor to Paris or London hoping to familiarize himself with the health of French or British theater would have no difficulty in locating theaters staging the most recent works by playwrights from those countries, but a tourist in Italy intending to take the pulse of Italian theater would be hard put to find venues featuring Italian authors, whether new or established. Plays advertised on the hoardings today would be more probably be British or American than French, but they are as unlikely to be Italian.

It is not merely a question of nationality. Behind the sarcasm of Pirandello"s words, there lay a deeper bitterness over this neglect of the writer as such in Italian theater where, to have his role and voice recognized, the playwright has historically faced struggles of a type unknown to his counterparts in other European cultures. "Italy, ever as poor in drama as she is rich in theatricality," wrote Eric Bentley in the 1950s (Bentley, 1968), drawing attention to the central anomaly of Italian dramaturgy, which can be simply stated: Italy has always been rich in theater but beggarly in playwrights. The country's contribution to the development of European theater has been enormous, but the number of writers it has produced has been limited. There is no Shakespeare, Calderon, Racine or Goethe, no gilded period in the history of Italian playwriting to correspond to the Elizabethan age in Britain, the Golden Century in Spain, the Classical Age in France or the Romantic Moment in Germany. Only Pirandello and Goldoni can be said to have entered the international theater canon, and the position is scarcely better among moderns. Among twentieth century playwrights, Eduardo De Filippo and Dario Fo are widely performed, and probably more respected abroad than at home, but that is a poor harvest compared to the list of writers which other countries could produce.

This is not to say that theater in Italy is moribund, or that it is wholly dependent on imports, but it is to assert that Italian dramaturgy is *sui generis,* and that any history of theater in Italy has to be more polycentric than is conventionally the case elsewhere. The author is not the protagonist. In Italy, theater has always been actor-centered, not author-centered. This lowly status of the writer has deep roots, perhaps as deep as *commedia dell'arte,* the principal theatrical tradition native to Italy. The touring companies in *commedia* days, and their descendants until the days when cinema and television forced them out of business, found themselves able to dispense altogether with the author as independent figure, and to give pride of place to the *capocomico*, literally the head-actor. Franca Rame, one of Italy"s leading actresses and wife of Dario Fo, comes from such a family of strolling players, and has recounted how her father or uncle would summon the family-company together, hammer out the details of a plot from a tale or legend associated with the town they were visiting, pin up entrances and exits on the back of the stage door, and allow the cast to improvise from an accumulated store of memories and acquired skills. The author was *de trop*. In the eighteenth century, Carlo Goldoni's reform was multi-faceted, but one aspect was the attempt to impose a written script on the actor, and so grant dominance to the author. The success of his reform was profound and lasting in other respects, but in its attempt to give priority to the author, it was a failure.

Any history of Italian dramaturgy in any century which pays heed only to the writers would be as worthless as a history of music which examined composers without reference to conductors, wind and string players, patrons or even public tastes. Plainly the terms of this theatrical anomaly can be overstated, since it is clear that theater is everywhere and invariably a collaborative activity, which involves the talents of writer, performer, director, producer, set designer, lighting designer, prompter and perhaps also of usher and ticket-seller. Theater is never pure literature, but a mongrel genre generated by a multiplicity of forces. Every dramatist has to learn the lesson that his primary function is to provide material for recitation and acting, but the lesson that theater-making is collaborative, and that the writer, if he has a role at all, can aspire to be no more than *primus inter pares,* is more deeply woven into the experience of theater-makers in Italy than elsewhere. Nevertheless, since the division of labor in Italian theater has never been as crisp as in countries North of the Alps, the history of theater in the cities of the Italian peninsula, in the twentieth century as much as in previous ages, is a history of conflicts or power struggles, between categories who elsewhere lived in harmony because they recognized boundaries. In Italy theater, as distinct from dramatic literature, emerges from competition between the writer, the actor and director.

No one better expresses this conflictual relationship than Luigi Pirandello himself, particularly in his theater-in-theater trilogy. At least until the foundation in 1925 of the Arts Theater in Rome, at which point he took on the tasks of producer and director, he had little love for the actor. The actor's ability to create a new identity seemed a threat to him as writer. In an essay of 1908, *Illustrators, Actors and Translators,* he puts into the same category as actors those illustrators of works of fiction who were, he writes, always prone to draw from their own imagination images which are "a poor interpretation of the images expressed by the poet." He invites sympathy for any writer who has had the misfortune "to have a novel or short story published in an illustrated review." The playwright deserves the same compassion over his need to employ the services of actors. As he wrote: "And in another context and in another field, anyone who has written for the theater can tell of the impossibility, or near impossibility, of a faithful interpretation. Because in dramatic art, what is the scene if not a great, live vignette in action? What are actors if they are not also illustrators? But here necessary illustrators, unfortunately." (Pirandello, 1908, 213)

It is hard to imagine a more demeaning presentation of the actor's function. The ideal of the actor is the puppet. All independence, all ability to define or redefine, to burrow into emotional memory in order to create character, as Stanislavsky wished, is denied them. That final adverb "unfortunately" is revealing, and can be taken as the assertion of a philosophy which refuses to contemplate theater as collaboration. The writer would be king. "However much the actor strives to penetrate the intentions of the author," Pirandello insists, "it will always be hard for him to see as the author has seen, to feel the character as the author has felt him, to render him on the stage as the author wished." (*Ibid*. 215) For Pirandello, this intrinsic inability to convey in their crystalline purity the intentions of the author is pure loss. The "unfortunately" necessary collaboration, the acceptance of the skills of other craftsmen, be they actors or directors, who could intervene between the author's words and those audience perception, was viewed by him as at best a necessary evil. Having no respect for the category "actor," he seems, especially in his early days in the theater, to have feared that their intrusion would coax or coerce the audience into interpreting the work in ways other than those intended by the author. His distrust of actors is a factor in *Six Characters in Search of an Author,* where the characters are openly derisive when they are invited by the director to step aside and allow trained actors to strive to reproduce the feelings and pain which drive them on. The actors' expertise or tricks of the trade are no more than a cheap distortion of the life the characters themselves endure and which they strain to convey — even if by the vehicle of the "empty abstractions of words" — to a watching humanity.

This criticism of fellow theater-makers is developed in the other parts of the theater-in-theater trilogy. *Each in His Own Way* (1924) overtly satirizes theater critics and even audiences in their attempts to interpret, or to extract meaning from, the author's dramatic efforts. The plot is complex, and uncompleted, but the on-stage action involves a dinner party where Donna Livia expresses worry about her son who has seemingly fallen in love with a scheming *femme fatale*. There are quintessentially Pirandellian debates over the facts of the case, and even over the shifting nature of truth itself, but in the stalls, Amalia Moreno, who is significantly an actress, believes she recognizes herself in the scarlet woman, slaps the leading lady on the face and eventually makes such a fuss that the performance has to be aborted. In addition to the two acts, there two "choral intermezzi" where anxious critics and members of the audience, given no names but identified as An Old Failed Author, Those For, Those Against, A Literary Man Who Is Above Writing, The Angry Spectator and the Peaceable Spectator congregate in the foyer in a futile effort to assess and interpret what they have witnessed. Their inability to agree on meaning is in part a statement that there can be no sharing of something as hazy and personal as truth, but there is an uncomfortable clash between the respect Pirandello accords his own creations on the stage in their genuine groping for understanding, and his scornful satire of the caricatures in the foyer engaged on the same quest. Perhaps it was this clash which led the director Luigi Squarzina to state *vis à vis* his own 1961 production of the play: "the stage was being blasphemed and desecrated — and therefore it too was denounced as part of reality rather than as a temple devoted to some mysterious ritual." (Bassnett, 1989, 57)

Tonight We Improvise (1930) is a more penetrating look at authors and actors, but is particularly scathing on that troubling newcomer to Italian theater, the director. It is no accident that the fictional director, Dr. Hinkfuss, has a German-sounding name. Pirandello's biographer, Gaspare Giudice, records that the play was written during the writer's stay in Berlin in 1929, and that while there Pirandello went frequently to see productions mounted by Max Reinhardt. He remained ambiguous about Reinhardt's achievements, more skeptical than awed or impressed, and although the play is dedicated to Reinhardt, the director must have received it as gingerly as a man opening a letter-bomb. Susan Bassnett suggests that his doubts over Reinhardt arose from his perception that under the guidance of such a director "the spectacle could become an end in itself, resulting in a diminution of the text" (Bassnett, 65). In these terms, the director was, like the actor, a rival or an obstacle. Dr. Hinkfuss, pompous, self-important and contemptuous of the others, is a caricature as much as the derided audience figures of *Each in His Own Way*. Significantly, Hinkfuss's aim is to dispense with the writer, and to devise a script based on improvised lines created by himself and fed to the actors in rehearsal. He views himself as the complete dictator, whose notion of theater leaves no role for any other figure. His proposed work is set in Sicily but has the grand scale of an expressionist spectacle, involving religious processions and an airplane show in an airfield, but he finds himself facing a rebellion from the actors. "Your idea of theater is merely giving people something showy to stare at," the leading actor tells him, as they unite in defiance to chase him off the set. *Tonight We Improvise* is a meditation on the process of theater-making, with the Hinkfuss vision clearly and unambiguously rejected.

Actors have already been shown as an "unfortunate" necessity, and in all his writing on theater, Pirandello never produces any theory of acting in any way equivalent to those created by Stanislavski or Brecht. It is true that he softened his views in later years, when he wrote such works as *Diana and Tuda* (1926) or *As You Desire Me* (1930) for the actress Marta Abba, and when he himself directed various plays of his own and of other writers for his Arts Theater. Nevertheless, the figure of the director still caused him difficulties. Pirandello was not alone. From the time of his, relatively late, appearance, the director was a threatening and disturbing presence to entrenched interests in Italian theater.

Many critics suggested that the director was essential to any process of renovation of theater. There was agreement over the nature of the problem. Cesare Molinari has suggested that the nineteenth century can be regarded as the century of the actor. (Ferrone, 76) There were two successive generations, known picturesquely as the "great actor" and the "*mattatore,*" the latter term taken, for reasons no one understands, from the Spanish *matador*. Thinkers such as Piero Gobetti and Antonio Gramsci, whose prime interest was politics but who saw cultural matters as means of taking the health of the body politic, attacked the power of the "great actor," with his restricted focus on the display of his own *bravura*, and his inability to impose the wider vision which theater needed. When the director began to make a tentative appearance, his influence was resented by actors. Molinari suggests that he makes some appearance in the 1870s (Ferrone, 80), but most commentators put his arrival much later. There was not even an agreed title until well into the twentieth century. Various terms such as *corago, direttore artistico* or even *regisore* had enjoyed some vogue, until in a celebrated article in the review *Scenario* in February 1932, the philologist Bruno Migliorini suggested that the French word be adapted and that this new figure be termed the *regista*. (Puppa, 1990, 6)

Several early *registi* in twentieth-century Italy were foreigners, notably Tatiana Pavlova, while Reinhardt and Jacques Copeau both directed epoch-making productions at the *maggio musicale* in Florence in 1933. Silvio D'Amico, who had been advocating the introduction of the director as the most effective means of renovating Italian theater, took advantage of this visit to proclaim the aesthetic advantages of the directorial system, and to advocate the preservation of the Italianness of theater not by inviting directors from abroad to work in Italy but by sending actors abroad to study techniques. (D'Amico, 134-138) The proposal was not taken up, and D'Amico found himself reiterating the need for the director all throughout the Fascist era, and restating that case at a conference held shortly after the Liberation, when the call went up for the abolition of the director, because "directing is a Fascist invention!" (D'Amico, 79). The exclamation mark is his.

The core of the dispute concerned tradition and power. There never had been any offstage figure granted the discretion to interpret a text, impose a vision, coach and coax the actors to conform with that vision, decide on design and costume and develop the style which would bring all these elements into harmony. In the post-war years, the director inherited his kingdom. His well-established position in other countries was a factor, as was the growth in popularity of cinema, where the director had been the linchpin from the outset. The case was clinched by the establishment in the 1940s of *teatri stabili* in all the principal cities of Italy. The two innovations, the imposition of the director over actor and author, and the replacement of the touring company by the "stable" theater went hand in hand. Both revolutionized Italian theater more deeply than any author has done.

The touring company had been the backbone of Italian theatrical life since the emergence of *commedia dell'arte* in the mid sixteenth century, and had not died with Goldoni's reform. The Rame family of traveling players, who operated in Lombardy, can be taken as representative. They traced their ancestry back to the seventeenth century, originally as puppeteers, but in the early twentieth century they decided cinema was a threat, so at a family council around 1920 they switched to what they termed *teatro di persona*, person theater, as distinct from puppet theater. All the scenery, devices, plots and mastery of the craft they had accumulated over decades were transferred into a completely new category of theater, allowing the family-company to survive until the 1950s, when they finally closed down. Their skills were in traditional, improvisational theater, but they were the despair of modernisers and reformers who wished to see in Italy a theater which could compare with the French or Scandinavian. For the reformers, such a theater could only emerge with the construction of the grand theater-buildings and the "stable companies" which were common elsewhere.

The "stable theater" had had its advocates, and even practitioners, since the earliest years of the century, and with the Liberation its moment arrived. On 21 January 1947, the Milan city council approved the concession of an ex-cinema, used by the SS during the Nazi occupation, to act as the site of a new theater, the *Piccolo Teatro*. According to the manifesto published in Elio Vittorini's magazine *Politecnico*, the new theater was to be "not an experimental theater, not a theater for the out-of-the-ordinary, not a closed theater for a circle of initiates, but an arts theater for all." The program was to be popular and accessible, so as to realize the underlying vision of theater as celebration and community activity. "The theater will remain what it has always been in the deepest intentions of its founders — a place where a community, freely gathered together, reveals itself to itself, where the community listens to words which it will accept or reject." In the word then current, theater was to be viewed as a "public service," like transport or education. (Bertani, 194-8; Hirst, 23-7)

The manifesto does not debate the role of the director as such, but the establishment of the *Piccolo*, soon imitated in other Italian cities, made the dominance of the director a *fait accompli*. The various *stabili* became identified not with the resident actors, nor with a particular writer or writing style, but with the aesthetics and philosophy of the director who was now fully empowered to choose the repertoire and impose his own distinctive imprint on the entire workings of the theater. The matter was clinched with the emergence of three directors of undisputed genius — Luchino Visconti (1906-76), Giorgio Strehler (1921 - 1999) and Luigi Squarzina (1922 -). The *Piccolo* was controlled by Strehler, the *Stabile di Genova* by Squarzina as was, later, the *Stabile di Torino* by Luca Ronconi.

This first generation of directors established the parameters for the *regista*'s role. Unlike their counterparts in France or Britain, none saw it as incumbent on them to encourage and foster new Italian playwrights, or to make the staging of new plays an integral part of their professional duty. The repertoire remained essentially classical, or "experimental" and the director's role was viewed as concerned with reshaping, rereading, reassessing the script in accordance with his own vision. The main creative energy was to spring from the director. This convention gave many second-rate directors license to present versions of plays which were unrecognizable but which could be justified in the name of experimentation, but with the best of directors, this tendency led to some highly applauded, insightful productions.

With his productions of Goldoni, Brecht and Pirandello, Strehler freshened and invigorated Italian acting and directing skills. In his celebrated productions of Goldoni"s *Harlequin, Servant of Two Masters*, he sought a fusion of *commedia dell'arte* techniques and modern physical theater, while with his successive versions of Pirandello's late myth, *The Mountain Giants*, he found a key to make a demanding literary work a piece of captivating visual theater. He can also claim the credit for changing the nature of political theater by introducing Brecht to Italian audiences with his 1956 production of *Threepenny Opera*, and with his subsequent productions of *Galileo*.

Visconti was equally at home in theater and cinema, and brought to both a professional rigor, a cult of the image and a dialectic between the pull of *verismo* and of decadentism. His 1945 production of Jean Cocteau's *Les enfants terribles* was a watershed in post-war theater. More than any other director, Visconti was bent on exercising total control over the actors. The performers were made to take their part in an ensemble which left little to their individual flair. In the late 40s, Visconti, who did relent later, went so far as to compare actors to horses, both requiring firm handling.

Squarzina made strenuous efforts to renew the somewhat stale standard repertory and to lead a move from the introspection of much Italian theater, introducing a strong social and political component to his productions, especially of Brecht and Goldoni. He encountered difficulties with his political paymasters in Rome, where he moved in 1976, unlike Strehler, who found an accommodation with the Socialist rulers in Milan. All directors of *teatri stabili* were obliged to tolerate, sometimes with morally and aesthetically ruinous consequences, the party political power and *lottizzazione* (political spoils system) which had become an accepted part of public life in Italy.

The implications of this concept of the director's role was, for Italian playwrights, calamitous. Experimentation, workshops, laboratory techniques and *avant-garde* were voguish terms which justified the inclination of directors to restructure known works by Shakespeare, Pirandello, Alfieri or Aeschylus rather than undertake the messy labor of collaborating with living authors. Massimo Castri, a noted exponent of the *avant-garde,* staged a version of *Right You Are (If You Think So!)* in which he deleted all the lines spoken by Laudisi, and reduced the character to a piano player seated at the back of the stage. Foreign writers rebelled against this excessive power of the *regista.* (Puppa, 1980) Harold Pinter was outraged at what he regarded as a travesty his work, *The Caretaker,* by Luchino Visconti. (Billington, 56) Meanwhile, Italian writers, such as Giuseppe Manfridi, Umberto Santino or Vittorio Franceschi who would have dominated the national stage in any other country have been denied outlets.

The low standing of the writer can be measured in inverse proportion to the regular output of tracts and manifestos calling for the appearance of an *authors'* theater. Once again, Silvio D'Amico was to the fore. In 1937, we find him advocating "a theater which, alongside the theater of actors, of singers, of instrumentalists, of painters and *virtuosi* of every stamp, will be a theater *of authors."* (D'Amico, 171-2) He would scarcely have been mollified had he known that historians saw the Fascist era, when he was writing, as one of the few periods when the playwright had exercised a kind of "dictatorship" in theater. (Tessari,

1996, p.95) This tyranny, if such it was, did not survive the Liberation, and in 1959 Eduardo De Filippo wrote a public *Letter to the Minister for the Arts* drawing attention to the "paradoxical condition in which the playwright is held in Italy." Eduardo explained that while the "normal position of the playwright in theater is the position of dominance," in Italy the author has been kept "in a position of inferiority, surrounded by indifference and indeed by contempt . . . ." (Bergonzini, 149)

The paradox is that the century had opened not only with a ferment of theatrical activity in general but also with the appearance of more, and more self-assertive, writers than Italy had previously known. In 1911, that quintessential iconoclast, F.T. Marinetti, championed the playwright in his *Manifesto of the Futurist Dramatists.* (De Maria, 46-52) The emphasis on *dramatists* is quirky, particularly since Marinetti had no wish to argue for a narrow text-bound literary theater, but was groping for a style of total theater, controlled by a central, coordinating figure. On the other hand, Marinetti, who was a more enigmatic and ambiguous figure than his bombastic reputation suggests, viewed himself as primarily a man of letters, and no doubt it was partly this self-image which caused him to grant that decisive role to the writer. Equally, he may simply be that he was unaware that in Germany that function he sought was already being bestowed on the director. (Lapini, 47)

Marinetti had grand aspirations for theater, but little regard for theater practitioners, other than the playwright. The Futurists had made their own debut with an Italianized version of Marinetti's *Poupées électriques* in the Teatro Regio in Turin, and had initiated their subversive "Futurist *soirées*" in various venues. He believed that among "all the forms of literary activity, it is unquestionably the theatrical work which could have a futurist impact." (Lapini, 44) The problem was the non-futurist attitudes which abounded. The audience was a bourgeois beast worthy only of contempt. The first point of the Manifesto uncompromisingly advocated "Contempt of the Audience," which "having no other desire than to digest enjoyably in the theater, cannot approve, disapprove or correct anything in a work of art." For the visionary, there was, he wrote, a "voluptuousness in being booed," which was to be cultivated, with the one qualification "that everything which is booed in theater is not necessarily beautiful or new." Even if Marinetti saw theater, rather than painting or sculpture, as the ideal means for the expression of his new aesthetic of speed and power, he still viewed actors, "animals of the stage," as being too much in thrall to the immediate audience, too easily cowed by the allegiance to their traditional training. As such, they were unlikely to be open to the subtle delights of being heckled or booed. Innovation could not come from them.

Two years later, Marinetti published his *Manifesto of Variety Theater*, a work which complements the earlier tract but was also of greater foresight and importance than was realized at the time, even by the author. The tract has that braggadocio, swagger and even harlequinade which are inseparable from all futurist productions. Marinetti writes that his disgust with bourgeois theater had led him to attend assiduously "Variety Theater (music hall, café concerto or equestrian circus) which today offers the only spectacle worthy of a truly futurist spirit." He was moved by "the rhythms of the sketches, by the mingling of genres and by their anti-academic, primitive and ingenuous spirit." (De Maria, 70) The manifesto is a sustained polemic against naturalism, and Lia Lapini makes the shrewd point that it anticipates the outlook not only of futurist theater, but also of many aspects of the entire, multiform, heterogeneous theatrical *avant-garde*. She identifies these points of identification as lying in "synthetic action, dynamism of form and color, simultaneous movement, illogicality and improbability," and in particular an attention "to intelligence on the brink of madness." (Lapini, 49-50)

What was less appreciated at the time was the approval contained in the manifesto of popular culture and in the so-called minor genres. It is true that *commedia dell'arte*, circus, clowns and even music hall attracted the attention of modernist directors, or the new proponents of political theater, including Meyerhold, Brecht and Mayakovsky, but Marinetti seems to have been drawn to Variety in itself, its stage techniques, the physical quality of production and entertainment, the vitality of performance and the rejection of barriers. He found an alternative to the tame repertoire favored by commercial theater, which he abominated, in the sturdy fare offered in vaudeville. When he spoke of his delight at the involvement of the audience, "which does not remain static like a brainless *voyeur*," his enthusiasm could have been underwritten by Dario Fo, whose appreciation of the absence of the fourth wall in popular theater was equal to Marinetti's. Marinetti was one of the first to recognize that a renovation of theater could spring from a proper appreciation of popular culture, and that a division between high and low culture was the fruit of snobbishness, not of aesthetics. It may have taken decades to flower, but Marinetti's tract sowed the seeds for a re-evaluation of popular culture.

The desire to renovate theater was one of the principal aims of the playwrights who became known as the *Grotesques*, contemporaries of the futurists. There was a certain overlap between the two movements, not just in a common contempt for bourgeois audiences and bourgeois theater. The author Enrico Cavacchioli, for instance, moved from the futurists to the grotesques. The birth of the movement can be given a precise date, 29 May 1916, when Luigi Chiarelli's *The Mask and the Face* was premiered in Rome. It was a writers' movement, and has as much claim to be viewed as a school as any comparable grouping of creative spirits.

In *teatro grottesco*, the dramatist claimed central place. Nothing is more striking in the output of these writers — Luigi Chiarelli (1880-1947), Rosso di San Secondo (1887-1956), Luigi Antonelli (1882-1942), Enrico Cavacchioli (1885-1954) as well as early Pirandello — than the centrality of theater as metaphor and image of life. Where the naturalists held as ideal the invisibility of the writer, the writers of the grotesque, and with them Pirandello whose early theatrical output shares their vision and inspiration, kept the writer in full view as central, conducting figure, set on creating a reality which might parallel life but was not a representation of it. The drama could not be a microcosm of an outside reality, but a conscious fiction, parable, parody or flight into a fantasy which was a meta-reality. It rested on an *ante-litteram* version of the Absurd, which explains Silvio D'Amico's lament that the humor it arouses had nothing in common with the "endearing, frank laughter of our elders." (Livio, V) Irony, deformation of known reality, the introduction of the *raisonneur* who comments from the stage on the progress of events, the overturning of expected links in plots were among the techniques most typical of these writers.

If grotesque theater now seems less innovative and much less revolutionary than it appeared at the time, that is in part due to the fact, underlined by Chiarelli himself, that they were anxious to remain linked to the Italian tradition. (Livio, VIII) Although their treatment of the classic themes of bourgeois theater, most notably the "eternal triangle," was more wry, detached and ironic than was customary, it was those themes which engrossed them. In Chiarelli's *The Face and the Mask*, the bluff husband is afraid not so much of his wife"s adultery as of the ridicule which will be his subsequent lot. He realizes that the codes of the time require him to kill her, but when he is acquitted by the courts of murder, he finds he is besieged by proposals of marriage. "Even in the most tragic moments, we are pursued by ridicule." (Livio, 63) Luigi Antonelli's play *The Man Who Met Himself* (1918) features Luciano at two stages of his life, wracked by doubts over his wife's fidelity, and taking on the guise of Gregory to betray himself. Perhaps the greatest of grotesque plays was Pirandello's *Right You Are (If You Think So)*, (1917) which the playwright himself described as "a bit of devilry." (Pirandello, 1938, 43) The irritation of the audience arose from the refusal of a tidy *dénouement*. In life and logic, the veiled lady must have one identity only, she must be *either* Signora Frola's daughter *or* Signor Ponza's second wife, since these are two opposing possibilities, but in Pirandello's fiction, which he himself describes as a "parable," she can be both.

Pirandello learned from both the futurists and the grotesques, but neither of them were decisive in his formation. Precisely what was decisive has been the subject of an unresolved debate. For Gramsci and Leonardo Sciascia, Pirandello was a product of Sicilian culture, so Pirandellismo was a transfer onto a European stage of a purely Sicilian relativism and notion of social personality. For others, such as Eric Bentley, the decisive impact was with German philosophy. Pirandello studied in Bonn in the twilight years of German idealism, and Pirandellismo was a "digest of nineteenth-century German thought." (Bentley, 1965, 133) Pirandello's thought is richly layered, and its various seams — the multiplicity of personality, the untruthfulness of truth, the relativity of identity, the barren nihilism tempered by a belief in humor as compassion — have been adequately mined, so perhaps it is sufficient here to pause over the idiosyncrasy of Pirandello's contribution to theater.

He was 43, already well established as a poet and novelist when he first came to the theater in 1910, and even after the success of *Right You are (If You think So)* (1917) he still regarded his theatrical career as a parenthesis, after which he would get back to his real business. "Pirandello did not love the theater," writes Paolo Puppa, and he may well be right. (Puppa, 1987, 78) He was encouraged by the Sicilian actor-author, Nino Martoglio, with whom he collaborated, but it appears that his interest was spurred more by his involvement in Sicilian culture than his interest in theater as such. Several of his works were staged by another great Sicilian actor, Angelo Musco, who helped shape his work. He never developed any appreciation of the actor or director, although he himself did later direct such works as Luigi Antonelli's *The Master* (1933). For the formulation, if not for the content, of "Pirandellismo," he was indebted to the critic Adriano Tilgher, an association which must be unique in literary history. Tilgher had developed his own aesthetic theories, involving the clash of Life and Form in the flux of existence, and in a famous essay of 1923 on Pirandello Tilgher applied this notion to Pirandello's drama and gave it canonical form which was subsequently accepted by the writer himself. (Tilgher, 1923) If Pirandello had found his critic, it is also true, in Sciascia's words, that "Tilgher had found his writer." (Sciascia, 1111) This notion underlies such plays as *Diana and Tuda*, and the formula was repeated in the preface to *Six Characters*, but Pirandello later resented this Tilgherian overlay on his theater, and told critics not to search for any philosophy, especially not a Tilgherian philosophy, in his work. While recent critics have sought to present a Pirandello free of Tilgher, it was the "half-philosophy," in its Tilgherian form, which has been largely responsible for Pirandello's influence abroad, especially in France, where his impact on such writers as Sartre and Anouilh has been enormous. He had less influence in Italy. There is no Italian Pirandellian school of writers to compare with the once flourishing Ibsenite school.

Fascism attempted to deal with the lack of Italian writers, and the Duce himself collaborated with Gioacchino Forzano to produce a trilogy of historical epics, including *Caesar* (1939), which were written *pour encourager les autres*. The lack of writers concerned equally the Christian Democrats who assumed power in the Republic which succeeded Fascism. The role of the state as impresario and patron had been debated throughout the century, but the problem was that when the state intervened, especially with the so-called Andreotti law of 1948, it *de iure* recognized the rights of managements of the new" stable theaters," but *de facto* arrogated to itself the power to manipulate and control. Certain playwrights, especially in the period between 1947 and 1953 when Giulio Andreotti exercised unfettered control over everything related to theater and censorship (Forgacs, 186), conquered for themselves positions of privilege. This took various forms, but if Eric Bentley was right in pointing out that in the fifties Italy found "that a profession of playwrights cannot be legislated into existence with the help of subsidies" (Bentley, 1986, 278), he was referring to genuine playwrights. Caricatures or plastic substitutes can, however, be willed into being. In 1969, the grandly titled *Annuario dell'Istituto del Dramma italiano* announced that there were a total of 569 registered playwrights in Italy. The same organ also revealed that of the works performed the previous year, 44 were products of the De Filippo family, while 20 were by Dario Fo. Few of these 569 playwrights were known to the general public, and fewer still were likely to be presented to theater audiences.

The theater writer, as the person who labored in a locked room and then presented a completed text to a director, was scarcely known in Italy until the Christian Democrat regime gave him legitimacy. The same forces gave official status to a category of writer which has no equivalent in any other country — the unperformed playwright. There are many literary prizes presented for playscripts which will never be performed on stage, and Italian publishers have shown a remarkable willingness to publish works which are supposedly dramas, but which, on account of the meandering speeches in which the characters express themselves, the introverted or abstruse subject matter of the play itself, the absence of action or development and the failure to pay heed to plotting, could never hold an audience's attention. This figure, the unperformed playwright, was derided by Dario Fo, but he too admitted, in his own idiosyncratic style, that there was a problem over playwriting in Italy: "With every year that passed, the presence of the

Living-Italian-Author on the hoardings of companies or of public theaters became more and more ephemeral . . . like the amphetamine inspired vision of some junkie high on an overdose." (Fo, 1987, p.162)

Pre-eminent among those whose work had the advantage of official benevolence was the Catholic playwright, Diego Fabbri (1911-1980). Fabbri followed public taste, and although his plays (*Inquisition*, 1950; *The Seducer*, 1951; *Jesus on Trial*, 1955), initially presented dilemmas for the Catholic conscience, he exploited to the full the 1960s vogue for nudity, especially female nudity. As the (Catholic) critic Adriana Zarri trenchantly remarked, in Fabbri's theater "first women strip, then they seek pardon by saying prayers." Fabbri had always enjoyed the patronage of the ETI, the Italian Theatrical Board, and in 1969 became its Chairman. Fabbri was a contemporary of Ugo Betti, another Catholic writer, obsessed with original sin, and an exponent with Fabbri of what became known as "Inquisition theater." Betti's characters delve ever more deeply into their inner being, before attaining a point of conversion towards some supernatural value. Betti enjoyed great popularity in the English-speaking world with such plays as *Corruption in the Palace of Justice*, *The Queen and the Rebels*, *The Burnt Flower Bed* but it has not lasted.

This weighty, literary tendency of the Italian stage has been further encouraged by the proneness of Italian theater managements to commission novelists rather than genuine playwrights, and then rely on a conspiracy of critics and directors to pretend that the results were imaginative works of theater. Alberto Moravia, Natalia Ginzburg, Enzo Siciliano, C. E. Gadda, Leonardo Sciascia, Gesualdo Bufalino and Dacia Maraini are among novelists who have disregarded the calamitous precedents of Charles Dickens and Henry James and have written for the stage. Only Maraini, who set up a feminist theater company, the *Teatro della Maddalena*, and involved herself fully with the work of production, wrote works of any lasting value. *Mary Stuart*, which treats the adventures of Mary Queen of Scots as a myth and focuses closely on her relationship with Queen Elizabeth of England, remains a splendidly panoramic work, while her most successful work is probably *The Dreams of Clytemnestra*, an updating of Aeschylus overlaid with the domestic drama of a modern Italian woman whose husband has moved to America. Criticism made of Ginzburg, that her plays are static conversation pieces where no action occurs and no development is apparent, could be applied to many of the others. Sciascia found some success in Sicily with his three plays, but then gave up playwriting, saying that although he had a deep love for the theater, he "had collided with the figure of the director." (Lajolo, 33) The only theater he, like Pirandello, would recognize, was writer's theater.

The dominance of the word was an article of faith for Pier Paolo Pasolini, novelist, essayist, poet and film-maker, who also produced modern versions of the Greek myths. In the aftermath of the events of May 1968, at exactly the moment when popular theater and an "alternative circuit" were the holy grail of the left, he drew up his own *Manifesto for a New Theater*. Pasolini dismissed the possibility of attracting a popular audience, and intended instead aiming his theater at "the progressive groups of the bourgeoisie." His new theater was to be essentially a literary theater: "Come to the performances of the 'theater of the word' with the idea of listening more than seeing (this is a necessary constraint in order to understand better the words you will hear, *and therefore the ideas, which are the real characters of this theater*)." (Pasolini's emphasis) (Ward, 181)

This concept put Pasolini at the opposite end of a huge spectrum from the two leading playwrights of post-war Italy, Eduardo De Filippo and Dario Fo. The two recognized each other as kindred spirits, to the extent that Fo wrote that "Eduardo could have been my father." (Fo, 1987, 121) Both operated within the popular tradition, both adopted broad comedy as their preferred genre, perhaps less farcical in the case of Eduardo than of Fo; both used theater as a platform for voicing social concerns which, for Eduardo if not for Fo, stopped short of specific political commitment. Eduardo came from the rich theatrical traditions of Naples, while Fo forged for himself the tradition he chose to make his own. Both eschewed the avant-garde, both belonged to the central Italian theatrical tradition, which is the tradition of the actor-author. Both, but more especially Fo, aroused passionate debates over whether the scripts they wrote had any real value in themselves or whether they were vehicles for their own talents, whose shallowness was exposed when the protagonist was absent.

The paradoxical feature of these debates is that the actor-author, who has normally also been designer, costumier and director or protodirector, has always been, in the sense Ralph Waldo Emerson used the term, the representative man of Italian theater. In Italy the distance between text and performance has been, thanks to the actor-author, narrow. If theater is everywhere the word made flesh, in Italy at least, the well-worn debate about the value of theater scripts could be rephrased so that it becomes not a writing-versus-performance dispute, but a recognition that writing-plus-performance, or writing with a view to performance, provides the only standard by which drama can be judged. Dario Fo is fond of pointing out that not only were Shakespeare's folios not published by him, but that "that's the way it was for many famous authors. Half of what we know of Ruzante was printed only after his death. The scripts of Molière were *canovacci* until some traditional authors encouraged him to have them published." (Valentini, 80)

Fo and De Filippo are descendants of the *capocomico* of *commedia dell'arte*. It is no accident that Fo's idol and icon, Ruzante, who was active in the Veneto of late Renaissance, was an actor-author, as were the principal figures in the troupes of strolling players, like the Rame family, who dominated the stage all over Italy until the post-war period. How much of his skill and his vision of theater Dario Fo learned from his wife, Franca Rame, and her family, is open to conjecture. Nineteenth-century Naples produced several such actor-author figures, including Antonio Petito, Raffaele Viviani and Eduardo Scarpetta.

In Naples, the boundaries between high and low art had always been blurred. Antonio Petito emerged from café dansant, and Eduardo Scarpetta enriched his native tradition with his many adaptations of French boulevard comedy. Eduardo De Filippo (1900-1985) belonged to a theatrical dynasty, being son of Scarpetta, brother of Peppino and Titina, and father of Luigi, all actor-authors. Eduardo was a *figlio d'arte*, born to the stage, so that his early works *(Sik-Sik, the Magician*, 1929) were light squibs written by a man creating his own performance pieces. Naples, with its poverty, its wit and wiles, its distinctive dialect, its social problems, all expressed in a comedy which has a bite and snap of its own, is a character in his theater as much as Mother Russia is said to be the protagonist of all Russian novels. When Fascism decreed the suppression of dialects, Eduardo was given special permission by Mussolini to continue performing in Neapolitan. Mussolini's admiration is puzzling, since Eduardo's theater unerringly exposes the sores of society. He insisted that his comedies should be seen as modern tragedies, adding that "humor is a more sharply pointed blade than tragedy." (De Filippo, 1986, 15). His typical protagonist is a lost, upright, confused little man, out to gain respect for himself and his family, but aware that such respect is impossible without some financial standing. Pasquale Lojacono of *These Ghosts* (1946) rents a supposedly haunted house in the hope of sub-letting it, thereby winning some measure of wealth and regaining the love of his wife, who is having an affair with a more affluent man. The family, either in the purely literal sense, as in *My Love and My Heart* (1955), or in a combined literal and metaphorical sense, as with *Napoli Milionaria!* (1945), where it also represents Italy, is the arena where all De Filippo's drama unfolds. Eduardo was an unbending, traditional moralist, who flayed private as well as public vice. Perhaps his finest work remains *Filumena Marturano* (1946), originally written for his sister, Titina, examining the plight of a woman from the slums of Naples, who is kept by a rich man, but desires to be married to him. Her tricks and ruses are unsuccessful in law, but are sufficient to bring about a change of attitude, more precisely a conversion, in him. Although he was as closely identified with Naples as Joyce with Dublin, relations between him and the city were conflictual, and he stopped writing for the theater in 1973.

The independence they won themselves as actor-authors, staging their own works and appealing to a mass audience, allowed both De Filippo and Fo to deride the theatrical establishment as roundly as they satirized the political and ecclesiastical powers-that-be. In the series of workshops which formed the basis of *Tricks of the Trade,* Fo reflected on the conduct of ETI with an irony which does not altogether mask his bitterness. His anger was occasioned by the treatment dished out to himself and Eduardo, who were the object of legislative discrimination as well as being the only two writers who were appreciated by audiences in Italy and abroad: "We had the cheek to continue to produce plays and, as if that were not enough, year after year headed the charts in terms of box office returns and of attendances. Further, we, mere actors, had the unheard-of impudence to write the plays and also to do the staging ourselves! The upshot was that these authors of established repute — unperformed — subsidized by the ministry intrigued together until they managed to persuade the minister to pass a very curious law, whose terms forbade the payment of tax rebates (the restitution of total taxes paid in the course of a season) to those authors who were simultaneously actors and directors. It worked for a year, then was withdrawn. De Filippo and I had threatened to exchange plays: he would have done mine, and I his." (Fo, 1987, 121-2)

His contempt for his unperformed, and for many performed, contemporaries was based on his vision of the need for links between theater and the society which produced it. He idealized those writers who had challenged society and especially the powers that be in society, not those who had sought an easy accommodation with authority. "I have heard the old lament on the crisis facing living authors, and on how only dead authors are performed, but I wonder if we are sure that these living authors are really alive? Rooting about in theater history in all times, I find that where authors were genuinely tied to the history of their own age, they invariably found an audience to support and encourage them." In contrast, he suggested an experiment in which researchers of the future attempted to reconstruct the history of our times from a selection of comedies and dramas which had been fired up into space. "They would find nothing but a stream of grand concepts and of words playing blind man's buff without ever finding each other; there would be nothing but characters out of time and bereft of all sense of reality. Nobody could ever manage to guess when or by whom those works had been written. Days, nights, months, eras — all without context." (Fo, 1987, 122)

Fo is known principally for the big, political farces which he wrote in his most militant phase after his break with "bourgeois theater" in 1968. In the fifties, he launched himself on theater with cabaret-style, satirical revues (*Finger in the Eye*, 1953), switched into straight comedy a decade later (*Seventh: Steal a Little Less*, 1964) during his so-called bourgeois period, which came to an end in 1968. In the "bourgeois" period, he was not only the satirist but also the amused spectator who invited Italians to observe how badly they behaved, and how appalling was the conduct of those who governed them. What disconcerted his audiences was that he also offered amusement. The two co-operative companies he established during the post-1968 militant period, *New Scene* from 1968-70, and *La Comune* from 1970-73, were touring companies whose operational principles were similar to those of the traditional troupes of strolling players. Fo's discovery was that he could combine political anger with laughter, as was demonstrated by such works as *Accidental Death of an Anarchist* (1970), a hilarious farce dealing with a tragedy, the death in custody of a railway worker suspected, wrongly, of involvement in Italy's first terrorist outrage. Fo's political commitment to the ideal of the co-operative sat uneasily with his own superlative solo acting skills, and it may be that the imbalance between his unique abilities and the more modest skills of his comrades contributed to the early break-up of the two troupes. Fo the actor was at his best in his one-man shows, most notably *Mistero buffo* (1970) and *Johan Padan Discovers America* (1991).

He was awarded the Nobel prize in 1998, but the reaction to that award inside Italy suggested that the status of the writer in Italy is unchanged. There were many supporters, but the political and literary establishment expressed horror and disbelief. The writer is still a figure without full recognition in Italian theater, but Italian theater is vibrant. The old paradox still stands.

BIBLIOGRAPHY

Bassnett, Susan. 1983. *Luigi Pirandello*, London, MacMillan.

Bentley, Eric, 1965. *The Life of the Drama*. London, Methuen.

_____1985. *Thinking About The Playwright*, London, MacMillan.

Bergonzini, Luciano and Zardi Federico 1961. *Teatro anno zero*, Florence, Parenti. (The letter by Eduardo De Filippo is republished in full in the appendix.)

Bertani, Odoardo. 1990. *Parola di Teatro*. Milan, Garzanti.

Billington, Michael. 1996. *Harold Pinter*. London, Faber.

D'Amico, Silvio. 1937. "Per un teatro degli autori," in *Rivista italiana del Dramma*, March, 1937.

_____1945. *Il teatro non deve morire*, Rome, Edizione dell'Era Nuova.

De Filippo, Eduardo. 1945. *Napoli Milionaria*, Turin, Einaudi.

_____1946. *Questi Fantasmi*, Turin, Einaudi.

_____1946. *Filumena Marturano*, Turin, Einaudi.

_____1986. *Lezioni di teatro*, Turin, Einaudi.

De Maria, Luciano. 1973. *Per conoscere Marinetti e i futuristi*, Milan, Mondadori. (The manifesto on theater is republished in the second part.)

Ferrone, Siro (editor). 1980. *Teatro dell'Italia Unita*. Milan, Il Saggiatore.

Fo, Dario, 1987, *Manuale minimo dell'attore*, Turin, Einaudi. (English translation by Joseph Farrell, *Tricks of the Trade*, London, Methuen, 1991, p.112.)

Forgacs, David, 1992. *L'industrializzazione della cultura italiana 1880-1990*, Bologna, Il Mulino.

Hirst, Davis L. 1987. *Giorgio Strehler*, Cambridge, Cambridge University Press.

Livi, Gigi (editor), 1965. *Teatro grottesco del novecento*, Milan, Mursia.

Pirandello, Luigi, 1921. *Sei personaggi in cerca d'autore*, in *Opere*, volume IV,

Maschere nude volume 1, Milan, Mondadori, 1958.

_____*Il gioco della parti*, 1919 Ibid.

_____*Illustratori, attori e traduttori*, 1908, in *Opere*, volume VI.

_____*Lettere al figlio Stefano*, in Almanacco Bompiani, 1938, reprinted as *Omaggio a Pirandello*, 1987, Milan, Bompiani.

Puppa, Paolo. 1980. *Il salotto di notte*. Milan, Multimmagine.

_____1987. *Dalle parti di Pirandello*. Rome, Bulzoni.

_____1990. *Teatro e spettacolo nel secondo novecento*. Bari, Laterza.

Sciascia, Leonardo, 1991. *Pirandello e La Sicilia*, in *Opere*, 1984-89, edited by Claude Ambroise, Milan, Bompiani.

Sciascia, Leonardo and Lajolo, Davide, 1981. *Conversazione in una stanza buia*. Milan, Sperling & Kupfer.

Tessari, Roberto, 1996. *Teatro italiano del novecento: Fenomenologie e strutture 1906-1976*. Florence, Casa Editrice Le Lettere.

Tilgher, Adriano, 1923. *Studi sul teatro contemporaneo*. Rome, Moroni.

Valentini, Chiara, *Espresso*, 23 October 1997, p.80.

Ward, David. 1995, *A Poetics of Resistance: Narrative and the Writings of Pier Paolo Pasolini*. New York, Fairleigh Dickson University Press. (Contains the text of Pasolini"s manifesto.)

PETER HAINSWORTH

Literature and Society 1950-2000

The enormous changes which have taken place in Italian society and in Italian culture (in a broad sense) since 1950 have affected what writers write about, how they write, how what they write is produced and read, how they see their role, how they intervene (or do not intervene) in public debates. At the same time there has also been a remarkable degree of continuity in literary culture[1], perhaps more than in society as a whole. Though there were revolutionary moments, most evidently the late 1960s, until about 1980 literature generally managed to absorb modernity into pre-existing practices. Modernity's main arena was television and the cinema. As during much of its history in Italy, literature remained the domain of a minority of the population, able when it wished to withdraw from immediate concerns and to focus on distinctly literary matters, even at times, with some support from educational and cultural institutions, to stand back from the market requirements that dominated other media. Conversely, though it played a part in wider political and cultural debates, it never achieved the directive role which it claimed for itself at various times or thought fell to it as its duty. In part the internal history of Italian literature from 1945 to about 1975 is the story of the evolution of the idea of *impegno*, or commitment. When that notion dies, then major changes began to emerge within literature, which coincide with a host of other significant changes, ranging from Italy's becoming a consumerist, technological society to the passing of the generation of writers who had been dominant since World War II. The new developments underway, which may indeed be occurring at a very deep level, have so far coexisted with previous practices rather than transformed them.

Two interrelated factors which have conditioned Italian literature since before the Renaissance have continued to be as important in their modern guise as they ever were. The first is regionalism. Modern Italian writers are often associated with a particular region and write about it. Ignazio Silone, for example, writes about the Abruzzi, Fulvio Tomizza about Trieste and the Italian speaking-parts of former Jugoslavia, Leonardo Sciascia about Sicily, whilst amongst the poets Andrea Zanzotto is strongly associated with the Veneto, Giorgio Caproni with Genova, Albino Pierro with Lucania. But this probably inexhaustible list includes many writers who have long moved away from their place of origin, even if it continues to occupy their imagination, and says little that is distinctive about Italian literature as opposed to other literatures. It is of much greater significance that there is no single literary center for the country as a whole comparable to Paris or London, for example. In this century, until the beginning of World War II, the city which had the most thriving literary culture in terms of ideas, discussions, reviews and the actual production of significant works of literature was Florence. Primacy, though not so noticeable and certainly not so mythologized, has since passed to Milan, where Eugenio Montale, Elio Vittorini and others moved from Florence before or soon after the war, and which as well as being the effective business and industrial capital of the country is also the seat of Mondadori and other major publishers. Other cities or regions which have continued to be or have emerged as distinctive and often important literary centers, are scattered unevenly throughout the north and center of the country — Trieste, with its Slavic and Germanic, as well as Italian, orientation; the Veneto, where dialect-poetry has flourished, in part thanks to the presence of Zanzotto; Turin, which was particularly important as an intellectual center from the 1930s to the 1950s, thanks to the publishers Einaudi, and to cultural initiatives from FIAT and other firms; Bologna, where left-wing culture has been given a modernist twist through the presence of Umberto Eco at the university since the later 1960s; and Rome, the political and religious capital, which long had a literary culture centered on Alberto Moravia and Elsa Morante, but which, as the country's film-capital, also drew figures as diverse as Pier Paolo Pasolini, the poet Attilio Bertolucci, and the script-writer turned novelist Andrea Camilleri. South of Rome the problems of the Mezzogiorno have been as perceptible in literature as in other fields, the one center of literary culture being Naples. Otherwise the writer, like the peasant or worker, has had to emigrate north. Only in Sicily has literary emigration become less the norm, largely because of the efforts and the presence of Leonardo Sciascia and the Palermo publishers

Sellerio, who have achieved a national profile and sales for the Sicilian writers they publish. In the 1970s the regions acquired greater autonomy, and since then, partly under the pressures emanating from new movements such as the Lega Nord, artistic festivals and literary prizes have multiplied remarkably. It is not clear that they have greatly altered the distribution of literary centers, though they have brought writers to the attention of a wider public, at least as personalities.

But so far as literary culture is concerned regionalism rarely means provincialism. The second enduring feature which I have in mind is the prevalence, in literature as in all forms of educated discourse, of the national language, the use of which pre-supposes in the Italian context that the cultural horizons at any given moment are national or even international. Dialect — the defining language of any particular region, town or even village, and until the 1970s the normal spoken medium of the majority of Italians — was rejected by most authors as culturally and intellectually inferior and politically divisive. In the 1940s and 50s the left struggled to break out of the narrow confines in which literature seemed imprisoned, and set a premium by the Gramscian idea of a *letteratura nazional-popolare*. But it saw the national language as the one viable medium of expression, though at the time this was anything but widely used by the workers and peasants, and the actual forms of language in ostensibly popular fiction were distinctly literary. Franco Fortini went so far as to argue that attempts at popular language, and at the popularization of inherently difficult ideas, could only be self-deluding and ineffective.[2] In practice the barriers remained almost insuperable until the 1980s, and are still by no means negligible, partly because of the orientation of literature itself. Though there have been exceptions, the most highly rated Italian fiction has been self-aware in the extreme, often modernist or experimental with its eyes on figures such as Proust, Hemingway and Virginia Woolf and the native tradition of fine writing. Conversely it has been relatively uninterested in plot, character and dialogue in a broadly realist mold. Poetry has been even more a matter for initiates. Literary criticism, including reviews on the *terza pagina* of newspapers, has tended to be rhetorically complex and abstract in thought and terminology, as has been the idiom of academic discourse in general. In the 1950s, whether the perspective was left- or right-wing, the idiom was that of idealist philosophy, derived from Croce and Gramsci, which later injections of structuralism and post-structuralism rendered more complex still. Until very recently, what has generally seemed neither feasible nor aesthetically desirable, in either literature or in intellectual discourse as a whole, has been a form of ordinary language, which — perhaps illusorily — could be felt by readers to be close to normal spoken usage. Overall literary culture has preserved a regard for high rhetoric and a hierarchy of literary values which to Northern European and Anglo-Saxon eyes seems archaic or classically Mediterranean, and which reflects the way in which other traditional cultural practices have been maintained in the country, alongside striking manifestations of modernity.

From the 1950s to the early 1960s the picture was not substantially different from what it had been in 1945 or even earlier. Even leaving aside questions of language, it was often felt that the *letterati*[3] were a caste apart. This was reinforced by a variety of other factors, ranging from the weakness of the public library system even in major cities to the fact that obligatory schooling stopped at fourteen, whilst, in the South at least, illiteracy continued to be widespread. All the same the section of the population reading and absorbing literature was not numerically or socially insignificant. It was drawn principally from the educational and civil-service sectors and from the professional classes, that is from a section of the population which either was middle-class or aspired to middle-class status and culture. This *piccola e media borghesia* was proportionately smaller in Italy than in France, Britain and Germany for most of the 20th century and politically more embattled, but it provided the cultural and economic substrate for most literature, and also its buyers, readers and interpreters, not to mention most of its actual producers. Educationally the middle or aspiring middle classes privileged the *liceo classico*, which tended to provide a "humanistic" education, that saw literature in elevated, non-utilitarian terms, and furnished the necessary social basis for taking stylistically and linguistically demanding writing as the literary norm. Obviously not all members of this social group were readers — small-scale industrialists, for instance, who were the backbone of Italy's economic miracle, were notorious for never opening a book — but the indications are that by the early 1970s the number of readers was higher than has often been claimed,[4] largely because of the tripling of the number of university-students in the late 1960s.[5] It also included (and still includes) a high proportion of "strong" readers, that is, readers who read extensively, or at the very least amass substantial personal libraries in a way that has been not the norm in countries such as Britain, where the actual number of readers is proportionately larger.[6] In this respect Italian readers have been well served since at least the early 1960s by a flexible, active book-trade, with well-stocked, up-to-date shops in all centers of any size in the center and north of the country.

From the perspective of 2000 it appears that the changes which have occurred in Italy over the last fifty years may have been intense in certain periods, but that overall they have come about without sudden interruptions or moments of revolution. However, until the later 1970s, it was widely felt that the condition of the country as a whole was anything but stable. A left- or right-wing revolution, or social and economic collapse, were regularly thought to be imminent, and to be resisted or furthered, depending on the point of view, in part through the agency of literature and literary culture. It was much harder for a writer or critic to stand back or apart from what the left saw as the movement of history, and the right as a godless threat directed largely from outside. A political discussion of historical and aesthetic aspects of literature continued in the academies, even with respect to contemporary developments, and a few resolutely apolitical critics, such as Gianfranco Contini (once active in the Resistance above Domodossola), were acknowledged as masters by both left and right. But to a large extent the discussion of contemporary literature was politicized, and commonly in polarized terms which reflected the polarized political situation inside the country and internationally. However it did so in a way that was curiously skewed. The *Democrazia cristiana* (DC) was largely without significant literary voices, even though it won the support of half or more of Italian voters in the elections of 1948, and remained the largest political party right up to the collapse of communism and the re-alignment of the Italian political map in the early 1990s. Similarly the far right, which was numerically by no means negligible since it was usually taken to include the right wing of the DC as well as the *Movimento Sociale Italiano* (MSI) and other groups with more or less Fascist affiliations, had its outlets primarily in newspapers and periodicals. The one well-known voice of conservative right-wing attitudes was Giovanni Guareschi, who made his name nationally and internationally with his ruefully comic Don Camillo stories, which pitted shrewd and kindly village-priest against misguided but not dislikeable communist mayor, to the inevitable discomfiture of the latter.

To a large extent it was the left that was dictating the political agenda for literature. Until the mid-1970s its key-notion was *impegno*, a term which had emerged under Fascism but which had been turned against Fascism and had acquired force and resonance through the Resistance. Though its implications were constantly debated and changed considerably over the years, the basic assumption was that the writer had an obligation to contribute to the historical changes assumed to be underway, often with regard to specific issues and in relation to specific political parties. Though by no means limited to the Communist Party (PCI), *impegno* tended to be couched in Marxist terminology and to imply a Marxist outlook, with the writer's stance being assessed in terms of its consistency and its objective political significance. Such a politicized approach pervaded leftist discussions of literature in newspaper articles and cultural reviews and dominated literary congresses. Thus around 1950 membership of the PCI was almost the norm for writers and intellectuals, though the span of attitudes was broad. Within a few years they were distancing themselves from the party in the wake of revelations of Stalin's atrocities and the Hungarian revolt of 1956. But the Marxist idiom remained and in some cases the commitment to revolution moved well to the left of the official party.

What center positions were assumed had an air of weakness. Even though they now seem to have conformed better to the social realities of the lives of writers and readers alike, they were difficult to hold, given the climate of the times. The reformist liberal socialism of the *Partito d'Azione*, which, in the immediate aftermath of the fall of Fascism, had attracted poets such as Montale and Zanzotto and the future academic and idiosyncratic autobiographer Luigi Meneghello, had foundered in party terms soon after the war, leaving its supporters in uncomfortable minoritarian positions for decades afterwards. Nevertheless it was plain even at the time that some of the most important writing of the post-war years did not belong to the left or to the right. A poet like Montale, who proclaimed his separateness from both, could not simply be dismissed as a voice of bourgeois reaction. The discussions of his work by Fortini and Pasolini in the 1950s and 60s are largely concerned with how to reconcile his greatness as a poet articulating the tragedy of the modern condition with his voicing of attitudes which neither found it possible to share.

The reasons behind the distinctively left-wing orientation of Italian literature in this period are largely historical. Moderate democracy had lost the support of the majority of intellectuals and *letterati* soon after unification and never recovered it. If the contemporary international division between East and West was replicated in the political division between the DC and the PCI (with associated lesser parties on either side), then literary culture was driven in effect to align itself on one side or the other, and alignment with the right was unthinkable, at least in public. Justly or unjustly, the right was associated with Fascism, which had been defeated only few years previously at the cost of what Italians see as a civil war. In the 1950s the wounds were still raw (they still remain remarkably painful in 2000), and the threat of Fascist resurgence seemed all too real. What was more, the sort of dramatic renewal that had been dreamt of when Mussolini was deposed in 1943 and which had given the Resistance its moral inspiration, had not occurred. A great deal remained from the Fascist past in terms of culture, personnel, education, even economic policies and institutions. Many of the most significant writers of the post-war period were already well known before the war or had begun their careers under Fascism. Perhaps only a few, like Giovanni Papini and Ardengo Soffici, had been out-and-out supporters of the regime, and they were now at the end of their careers. But many others had skeletons in their cupboards. The disclosure that he was the author of some anti-semitic articles led the novelist Guido Piovene, who had re-cast himself as a campaigning communist, to publish an abject self-justification in his *La coda di paglia* (1962). Others maintained a wary silence, or passed themselves off as fundamentally anti-Fascists. Giuseppe Ungaretti was able to ride out censure in the immediate post-war years and become an admired, a-political poet and something of a cult-figure at poetry festivals in the 1960s, even though he had supported Mussolini since 1919 and eventually been appointed to the Accademia d'Italia in 1942. Italy's major modernist prose-writer, Carlo Emilio Gadda, who had been a Fascist supporter almost as long, similarly suppressed his right-wing views and dated his own incipient anti-Fascism to well before the war. Only figures like Vittorini and Pratolini, who had belonged to the revolutionary wing of Fascism as young men and then made the transition to communism, were able, with a certain mixture of circumspection and courage, to look back to their Fascist pasts in public and to explore to an extent their own fundamentally consistent political trajectories. Even writers like Montale who were minimally compromised, if at all, felt obliged to draw as much of a veil as they could over their relations with the regime.

The problem was (and is) complicated by the character of the novels, essays and poetry of recognized literary value produced during the Fascist years. Most was not in any obvious way in thrall to the regime. In the immediate post-war years the left was dismissive of the political isolationism of hermetic poetry and the more exquisite prose of the period, and saw *letteratura impegnata* as breaking out of such ivory towers. But it also proved possible to argue that literature was an area in which Italian culture had maintained its dignity and its traditions at a time when the country as a whole allowed itself to be morally and politically perverted. In recent years this view has tended to become more and more the accepted one. By the 1980s Montale in particular had become the emblem of a quiet resistance to the oppressive absurdity of the regime, showing in himself the "decenza quotidiana" that he ascribed to his friend Sergio Fadin.[7] But it has proved much more difficult to probe and understand the appeal of Fascism to large swathes of Italian society. Many post-war novels looked back to the Fascist years. Pratolini's complex portrayal of 1920s Florence in *Lo scialo* (1960) is perhaps the only one which examined the issues in any depth and in at all convincing terms.

That is not to say that *Lo scialo* is a completely successful novel. Like much of Pratolini it is torn by the conflicting demands of *impegno* and literature. The debate in *Politecnico* between Vittorini and Togliatti in

1947, on the role of culture in relation to the PCI, had effectively implanted the idea that literature should not be subordinate to the dictates of the party: imaginative freedom could itself have revolutionary effects, although perhaps hidden or indirect.[8] But the many notable writers and critics who were committed members of the party were still convinced that the writer as an individual and the literary work that he produced were under an obligation to *impegnarsi* and to contribute to the struggle and eventual victory of progressive forces in society. The literary means by which this contribution should be achieved were commonly seen as some form of neo-realism, which, if some in the PCI hierarchy had had their way, would not have been substantially different from Soviet Socialist realism. In the event committed fiction of any note found itself constantly struggling to reconcile an explicit political stance and message with individual vision. The difficulties were already palpable in Calvino's early *Il sentiero dei nidi di ragno* (1947), which grafts its orthodox political statements onto an imaginatively free and potentially politically heterodox narrative by introducing a Gramscian partisan leader, Kim, in its later pages. Similar problems arise in other undoubtedly interesting novels, such as Pavese's *Il compagno* (1947) and Moravia's *La ciociara* (1955). But Pratolini was the main voice of committed fiction and the author whose work gave rise to most debate; in particular *Metello* (1955) mixed idealized representation of the struggles of the Florentine workers in pre-World War I Florence with the private life of its heroic protagonist, the result being for the prominent communist critic Carlo Muscetta too much *camera da letto* and too little *camera di lavoro*.[9] He might well have added that Pratolini and many of his contemporaries were also focused on the past: the need for *impegno* was ostensibly a present concern, but the novels were characteristically set in the earlier 20th century, particularly the Fascist and Resistance years, that is, at moments of actual struggle rather than in the uncertain stasis of 1950s Italy, with its prolonged, undramatic stand-off between left and right. To that extent 1950s committed fiction often had a nostalgic air and tended to re-iterate what had become political commonplaces.

Much of the debate over *impegno* was carried through with reference to fiction. It was the genre which seemed to offer the prospect of combining popular appeal and modernism, after the example of the American fiction which writers like Pavese and Vittorini had been reading and translating since the early 1930s. But poetry was still important. Throughout the century it had been seen as at the antipodes to bourgeois fiction — by turns popular, aristocratic and profoundly Italian. In the post-war years it was the mirage of popular poetry that held sway, that is, the mirage of a poetry expressing in lyric form the objective needs and subjective feelings of the *popolo*, whether written by the people themselves or by educated poets submerging their individual selves in the larger mass. In practice the gap between these two kinds of poetry was irreducible, as is evident from the collection of popular or folk-poems published by Pasolini as *Canzoniere italiano* in 1972. Not only are the modern poems (on workers' and peasants' struggles and World War I, for example) in dialect, but their mode is far removed from the literary lyric, whether in dialect or Italian. All the same literary poets had been attempting since the Resistance years to move to a more approachable form of writing, in contrast with the plainly exclusive manner of pre-war Hermeticism. In the case of Salvatore Quasimodo, previously amongst the most unapproachable of poets, the change was remarkable, though not quite so abrupt as was often judged. Joining the PCI after the war, and convinced that poetry was now choral rather than individual and had a public rather than a private role, Quasimodo attempted to write in an explicit, deliberately flat style, and from a broadly humanist perspective, about public issues and the moral and political choices they raised. *Giorno dopo giorno* (1947) and subsequent collections won him the Nobel prize in 1959, though it is now his earlier work which is more highly rated.

As was polemically but convincingly argued by Alberto Asor Rosa in the mid-1960s,[10] *impegno* as generally seen by writers of the 1940s and 50s was hemmed in by illusions. The *popolo* for whom and about whom they were notionally writing was ill-defined, mythicized, mostly dialect-speaking and disinclined, if it read at all, to read what were in practice complex literary texts. Even neo-realist film, which was more obviously approachable, was less popular with Italians of all political persuasions than American and Italian films of a more commercial nature.[11] Committed writers like Vittorini and Pratolini, as much as poets like Quasimodo, had begun their careers in the sophisticated hermetic environment of 1930s Florence. Their post-war work still attempted to preserve elevated literary values, even if it pretended to reach out to a wider readership and asserted a progressive ideology. In some ways the solution which accurately reflected the real quandaries of literature was that adopted by quieter poets than Quasimodo, such as Vittorio Sereni and Mario Luzi, who made their poems the locus for internal debate about their inability, or the inability of literature, to make the political commitment they felt was imperative.

All the same more concrete and sometimes more effective forms of literary *impegno* were visible in writers who have now largely vanished from view, just as many of their concerns have become remote. About 30% of Italy's working population were still peasants in 1950.[12] If the realist novel of unremitting peasant misery was now waning — the last significant example is probably Beppe Fenoglio's *La malora* (1954) —

there were now writers closely involved with particular communities. The outstanding figures were the poet and novelist Rocco Scotellaro, whose *Contadini del Sud* (published posthumously in 1954) used documentary reportage to allow his peasant protagonists to speak for themselves, and Danilo Dolci, whose work with the peasants of Trappeto and Partinico in Sicily — which led to books such as *Banditi a Partinico* (1955) — became internationally famous. The situation in the South was also highlighted by others such as Carlo Levi, though he is best-known for his account of internal exile in Lucania in the mid 1930s in *Cristo si è fermato a Eboli* (1945). But Ignazio Silone, the writer whose *Fontamara* had been distributed to Italian POWS in Britain and America for its anti-Fascism, and who was seen abroad as the voice of non-communist spiritual socialism, had a very low profile indeed in Italy itself until the later 1960s, in part because his novels about the Abruzzi took issue with both the left and the right, though also because of widespread suspicions, apparently recently confirmed, about his political untrustworthiness in the 1930s.[13]

As the 1950s went on, *impegno* as practiced or debated since the war seemed increasingly rigid and out of touch with the seismic social and economic changes taking place in the country. An urbanized and industrialized Italy was emerging, which was sweeping away peasant culture. Most dramatically Southern peasants were flooding North to Milan, Turin and Genova, though there was also extensive immigration into the cities from the Northern and Central countryside. The economic success and rampant power of modern capitalism made it apparent by the 1960s that both the committed intellectual and the traditional *letterato* standing apart from the general *mêlée* were likely to find themselves recast as operatives or technicians within the all-embracing system that was emerging. The new situation called forth a debate on literature and industry focused principally on the novel, in which Vittorini showed again his remarkable ability both to move with the times and to retain his highly literary cast of mind. What was needed, he now argued, was not representation of contemporary reality in the terms of bourgeois realism but a modernist fiction of the kind exemplified by the French *nouveau roman* (the *école du regard* as it was called more commonly in Italy).[14]

The author who was following anything like that path was Vittorini's close associate at the time, Italo Calvino, who, even before leaving the PCI in 1956, had turned away from realism with *Il visconte dimezzato* of 1952. In what became the trilogy of *I nostri antenati* (1960) he produced entertaining fantasies which seemed nonetheless to have a bearing on contemporary social and psychological realities. But Calvino's fantasies were unique, though the anti-bourgeois dynamic was sufficient to prevent realist conventions from constituting the norm. Various writers, including Calvino himself in stories such as *La nuvola di smog* (1958), documented the disorienting effects of the changes taking place, almost inevitably with quite startling bitterness and anger at the loss of humanity — the *umano* — that was widely felt to have resulted, though usually with a certain amount of grotesque humour. Almost always the settings are Northern cities, most commonly Milan: Luciano Bianciardi's *La vita agra* (1962) and Giuseppe Berto's *Il male oscuro* (1964), for instance, focus on the neuroses of the alienated intellectual; Goffredo Parise in *Il padrone* (1965) and Paolo Volponi in *Memoriale* (1962) center more on the alienated worker, reduced to a robotic figure by the modern factory or office; and Lucio Mastronardi, in his three novels about his native Vigevano, makes comedy out of the miseries of life in a small Po valley town in the throes of industrialization and social (and linguistic) confusion. There is more control in Natalia Ginzburg, who tended to be dismissed at the time as a non-literary with a domestic focus but who probed the progressive dissolution of the Italian family and its psychological consequences in a series of novels running from the late 1940s to the 1970s. Only one author of note approached the new Italy from a significantly different perspective. In his two Roman novels, *Ragazzi di vita* (1955) and *Una vita violenta* (1959), Pier Paolo Pasolini emphasized the instinctive vitalistic rebellion of the boys of the squalid *borgate* he took as his protagonists, which he contrasted with the repressiveness of both PCI orthodoxy and bourgeois thinking. But by the early 1960s Pasolini was concentrating on film rather than fiction. Certainly amongst Roman writers it was Moravia who had the greater success, both in market terms and amongst critics; in novels such as *La noia* (1960), he provided easily read critiques of bourgeois alienation, which included amounts of sexual spice that were unusual for a mainstream author at the time.

As a writer Moravia was able to adjust to the new developments almost with ease, in spite of his ideological disapproval of bourgeois society. Others who, like him, had been active in the pre-war years were as unhappy as the younger writers just mentioned with what was happening in the country. Denunciation became almost the norm, for poets as much as novelists. In the articles originally written for the *Corriere della sera* and eventually included in *Auto da fè* (1966), Montale brought a bemused, sardonic wit to bear on modern culture and society, and also on the impasse in modern thought which he saw as the underlying problem. It was a manner which he accentuated in the poetry of the 1960s that he collected in *Satura* (1971), and which he then developed still further in his last collections. The poet who is often thought of as his successor, Andrea Zanzotto, was equally scathing about modern society, though for him the immediate concern was much more the wholesale destruction of the rural Veneto society and (from the 1960s onwards) environment. For both of them, as for many other poets, the key issue became the question of whether poetry was possible at all in the modern world. In their actual verse and in their theoretical statements both indicate that, though the crisis is partly ontological, it is very much connected with the revolution in modern society and culture taking place in front of their eyes.[15]

They were of course right. Poetry had retained its prestige as a literary genre through the Fascist period. Even modern poetry had enjoyed relatively good sales,[16] especially, as had happened in other countries, during the war years. It was now becoming increasingly minoritarian and increasingly perceived as remote from more urgent realities. At the same time it was also being institutionalized. Anthologies of modern poetry were appearing with educational, not polemical purposes.[17] In a similar way criticism of modern poetry entered the universities, though it did not really become a valid area of research and academic activity until the later 1960s, when a *tradizione del Novecento* began to be constructed.[18]

Such a development leads directly to the present. So too do various other phenomena which first made themselves felt in the later 1950s. Tomasi di Lampedusa's *Il gattopardo* (1958) was the first Italian bestseller, that is, the first Italian novel to reach sales of more than 100,000 copies within a few months of publication.[19] It was quite unlike the now standard committed fiction. Its setting was 19th century Sicily, its characters mostly Sicilian aristocrats, its attitude to Italian history since unification downright skeptical, its style ironic, and the picture it created sumptuously evocative. It was almost certainly the splendor which appealed rather than the political slant, though it was the latter which most disturbed leftist critics. In any event it was not alone amongst successful books in shying away both from the immediate present and from left-wing orthodoxies. Even if the next big commercial success, Carlo Cassola's *La ragazza di Bube* (1960), was in a more neo-realist vein, it had important features in common with *Il gattopardo*, since its emphasis fell on the force of love and, politically, on the failure of the PCI to live up to its promises. Such writing, like the fantasy novels of Calvino, indirectly acknowledges contemporary politics and issues of alienation, confusion and the need to find alternative solutions to those generally proposed. Both readers and writers seem to have wanted not pure escapism but freedom from literary and political straight-jacketing. In the early 1960s Giorgio Bassani, who as an editor for Feltrinelli accepted *Il gattopardo* (turned down by Vittorini at Einaudi as regressive), seemed to achieve emotional and literary resonances denied to the committed left with *Il giardino dei Finzi-Contini* (1962) and his other elegiac novels about Jewish society in Ferrara before and after the terrible events of the war. It was also during this same period that the importance of Primo Levi was first generally recognized. *Se questo è un uomo*, which had passed unnoticed when it was first published in 1947, and re-emerged in the wake of the success of its sequel *La tregua* (1963), combined with Bassani's much more allusive fiction to set the Holocaust before the attention of the Italian public in a way that previous Italian writing had not wished or been able to achieve.

The author who best demonstrated that contemporary problems could be confronted in literature was Leonardo Sciascia. In many ways he continued on from the work of the generation of Dolci, Scotellaro and other intellectuals active in the South. He was a member of parliament as an independent on the communist list and a town-councillor in Palermo, as well as working throughout his career to revitalize Sicilian culture and to dispel the idea (deriving particularly from *Il gattopardo*) that the distinguishing features of Sicily had always been its torpor and passivity. But his Sicilian detective novels of the 1960s and early '70s were up-to-date as literature, in the way Vittorini wanted, displaying analogies with contemporary French fiction that the French themselves admired, though they were nothing like so detached. They made the Mafia a central literary theme for the first time, and configured ways of representing administrative and political corruption in Sicily and Italy as a whole that chimed with views that were already widespread in the early 1960s and by the 1970s were almost the norm in Italy as a whole. For many the culminating confirmation of how well-founded they were was the kidnapping and eventual murder of the Christian Democrat secretary, Aldo Moro, by the *Brigate rosse* in 1978. In *L'affaire Moro* (1978) Sciascia analyzed the letters Moro had been allowed to write during his imprisonment, applying techniques and ideas he had developed in his fiction. The result is a powerful and still disturbing indictment of the Italian political establishment. It is also one of the few Italian literary texts to name names, rather than proceed by allusion and abstraction.

Sciascia was an isolated figure; he now sadly seems all too worthy as a writer and even in the 1960s and 70s often sounded monotonously rational. Excitement seemed to lie with the neo-avantgarde — the poets who burst on the scene with Alfredo Giuliani's 1961 anthology *I novissimi* and then the broader *Gruppo 63* which took its name from the 1963 congress it held in Palermo. In fact the group had come into being in the later 1950s around the Milanese review *il verri*. Even before that the need for a combination of a radical political agenda and literary experimentalism had shown itself in *Officina*, the short-lived Bologna review produced by Pier Paolo Pasolini, Roberto Roversi and Francesco

Leonetti. But one of the distinguishing features of the neo-avantgarde was its ability to provoke and exploit publicity in ways that no other literary movement had done since the war. Internally in constant ferment, as regards the rest of the world it was overtly and insistently polemical, dismissing both bourgeois society and the institutionalized left represented by the PCI as ossified and repressive in cultural and political terms. A new agenda should be created and acted upon which would be up-to-date with intellectual developments in other countries, and which would be liberating, or revolutionary, in its effects, dispensing with useless rules and breaking down cultural and political barriers of all kinds. It was a totalizing agenda, which looked back to the original avantgarde ("l'avanguardia storica") of the Futurists, but which had a left-wing internationalist perspective, not that of the nationalist right.

Though much of the rhetoric was shared, there were divergences from early on about quite what kind of a revolution was being aimed at. For poets like Alfredo Giuliani, Antonio Porta and Edoardo Sanguineti the aim was to bring to bear the vitality and openness of contemporary American poetry on the restrained modernism of Montale and his generation. For critics and theorists like Umberto Eco and Renato Barilli the aim was to deprovincialize Italian culture — to make it take a trip to Chiasso, as the novelist and essayist Alberto Arbasino put it — which in practice meant getting finally beyond leftist cultural orthodoxies and taking up the possibilities offered by new combinations of Marxism, structuralism, psychoanalysis, anthropology and social theory. To some cynical outsiders it appeared that individuals like these were mainly out to make a name for themselves, and to assure themselves places in the cultural and academic establishment, as did indeed happen. But the general climate was revolutionary, and radical changes seemed to be in the offing throughout Western Europe and America. At least some members of the Italian neo-avantgarde, notably the poet and novelist Nanni Balestrini, were ready to stand by their revolutionary rhetoric and to join the students and workers in the strikes and protests of 1968, though for most of the rest this was a watershed which signaled the movement's final division and exhaustion.

Balestrini produced the only powerful novel of the protests of the late 1960s and early 1970s in his *Vogliamo tutto* (1971), which articulated the anarchic solidarity of the southern workers in the Milanese car-factories. He then carried on with the political struggle throughout the 1970s, going for some time into hiding when he was under suspicion of having connections with terrorist groups, whilst continuing in his writing his fusion of literary modernism and revolutionary politics. But he was unusual amongst creative writers. The revolutionary movements and the terrorism that followed may have been central experiences for the 1968 generation of students, and drew in a certain number of academics, for the most part philosophers and political scientists, but Italian literary culture as a whole kept its distance. Pasolini characteristically engaged in provocative dialogue with the young, arguing at one moment that the real workers were the poor Sardinians and Southerners who made up the police facing the protesting middle-class students. Franco Fortini, equally characteristically, attempted to get the students and the revolutionary groups to think through the implications of their rhetoric and their position, as did highly intellectual reviews such as *Quaderni piacentini* (1962-84). But by the late 1970s literary culture, like Italian society as a whole, had effectively acknowledged that radical social and cultural change was impossible from below, and that the political vocabulary and ideas of the left that had dominated the cultural agenda in Italy since the war had to be changed or even abandoned. Radical critical discussion continued at a fairly high level in *Alfabeta* (1979-88), the liveliest critical periodical of its time, which was largely inspired by Balestrini, but included on its editorial board figures such as Umberto Eco and the academic critic Maria Corti. Even *Alfabeta* effectively acknowledged that, whatever the cost and whether the left liked it or not, modernization was replacing revolution.

In literary culture that meant above all a new diversity, in which no single trend or stance emerged comparable to neo-realism and the political *impegno* that went with it. The most that can be said is that from the early 1980s onwards the conflicting drives to be up-to-date and to hold onto the past that had emerged in the 1960s have become even more pronounced, though now couched in increasingly consumerist terms. The bond between literary culture and the left, already seriously weakened in the 1980s, has diminished still further in the wake of the reordering of national and international political alignments in the 1990s. Writers are now more associated with ecological, conservationist, or third-world concerns than with *Rifondazione communista*, which has retained the old-style Marxism of the PCI, or even with the center-left parties which are its mainstream successors. As for many Italians in their everyday lives, the political agenda has often receded into the literary background, however much survivors from the 1950s and 60s may recoil from the new barbarism and the new indifference to political struggles of the old kind.[20] In many ways literature has come to reflect the varied concerns and interests of its readers rather than proposing for itself the goal of directing the actions of the mass of the population.

Literary trips to Chiasso were already very frequent by the mid-1970s. In fact in the larger perspective Arbasino's jibe was ill-founded; Italian literature had been sensitive to developments abroad throughout the century, in spite of Fascist attempts at literary autarchy or periods of relative indifference such as the 1950s. But now, stimulated by the internationalism of the neo-avantgarde and also of student culture, keeping up-to-date with what was going abroad became almost a frenzy, reflecting and accompanying the general perception that Italy could, and must, achieve economic parity with other leading industrialized nations. Nor did abroad simply mean Western Europe and America: interest also boomed in Eastern Europe, the Far East, Africa and South America. Italian bookshops came quickly to contain at least as much material in translation, often from hitherto exotic languages, as material originally written in Italian. Whilst Italian literature retained its remarkable sense of the Italian tradition at a linguistic and stylistic level, it became the norm for an author to look abroad as much as within Italy for ideas, techniques and affiliations of attitude and sensibility. From the later 1960s to the end of the 1970s cultural primacy was widely felt to lie in France. Calvino encapsulated a general trend when he moved to Paris in 1965, becoming part of the Oulipo group that included Georges Perec and Raymond Queneau. But the field has opened up since then. The absence of a single dominant cultural ideology (other than that of modernity in some form) has meant that the Italian writer has been able to make choices amongst European and world literatures that are the literary equivalents of the destinations available to the modern tourist.

The production and distribution of books of all kinds has also assumed the forms of modern consumerism. Until at least the mid-1960s it was possible for a major publishing firm like Einaudi to give priority to its educative ethos over its economic interests, and for Feltrinelli to be seriously committed to furthering the cause of the revolutionary left, as was signalled most spectacularly in 1972, when Gian Giacomo Feltrinelli died apparently attempting to blow up Milan's electricity grid. The orientations remain, but all publishers have had to adapt more strictly to market demands, with new successful firms appearing in the 1980s with primarily commercial aims, whilst Mondadori, already the major Italian publisher in the Fascist years, has become a one of the most important companies in the Italian economy. Whilst the traditional hard-back book has survived, increasingly as a luxury or specialized item, the market has been driven by the modern paper-back since at least the early 70s. The crucial move was Mondadori's introduction of its Oscar imprint in 1965. Oscars, initially foreign and Italian classics — the first two were Hemingway's *Farewell to Arms* and Verga's *I Malavoglia* — were sold as a periodical in newspaper kiosks. Though they subsequently also entered the book-shops, they forced other publishers to follow in the same direction of producing attractive looking, cheaply priced paperbacks. The best-seller on a quite startling scale became a real possibility, though one which it has generally proved difficult to engineer. It was one thing to give away copies of *Love Story* with boxes of Baci chocolates, another for Einaudi to persuade readers to buy Elsa Morante's anti-war and anti-authoritarian *La Storia*, which it launched in 1975 in a blaze of publicity, somewhat resented by the author, and which led to sales of 600,000 copies. The really big sellers since World War II — that is, books that sold more than 1 million copies — have in fact been curiously heterogeneous. They comprise *Il gattopardo*, and Eco's *Il nome della rosa* (1980), which were readily accepted as literature whatever controversies they gave rise to, and other books that for one reason or other were put in some other category: *Lettera a un bambino mai nato* (1975) by the journalist Oriana Fallaci on the abortion-issue, the Pope's *Varcare la soglia della speranza* (1994), the letters by schoolchildren collected by Marcello D'Orta as *Io speriamo che me la cavo* (1990), and Susanna Tamaro's *Va dove ti porta il cuore* (1994), the novel which most Italians appear to have read but which was savaged by the literary establishment.[21]

The 1970s as a whole were perceived even at the time as a period of stasis for Italian fiction in which little of real interest was produced, except for isolated novels by Calvino, Elsa Morante, Stefano D'Arrigo and one or two others. In all probability it was actually a period of adaptation to new ideological and market conditions, and a period between generations, when the writers who had emerged before the war or soon after were fading away, and another generation was still to appear. At the same time, apart from the changes in sales and publishing mentioned above, other social changes were occurring which quickly began to impinge on literature. The position of women was altering, a crucial moment being the divorce referendum of 1974, which was the strongest sign both of the success of militant Italian feminism and of the general pressures within society to move away from traditional images and practice, the persistence of which is remarkably evident in left-wing fiction of the 1950s. The position of homosexuals was also changing; it was becoming possible to be openly and assertively homosexual at least in the major cities of the center and north. And wrapped up in these developments was a re-configuration of the Italian family, which moved towards the nuclear unit of Northern Europe and America, though distinguished by an unprecedented low birth-rate. When the Italian novel began to re-assert itself in the early 1980s, the diversity which was apparent in comparison with what had come before was in part attributable to this new diversity in society.

For the first time in the history of Italian literature women writers of the last twenty years have been at least as prominent as male writers, both numerically and in terms of the quality and prestige of their writing. With few exceptions (such as Elsa Morante) their predecessors tended to have a narrow focus; more recent writers such as Rosetta Loy, Francesca Durante, Francesca Sanvitale, Paola Capriolo, Fabrizia Raimondino, Dacia Maraini, whether they concern themselves principally with women's issues or not, have an intellectual, literary and social range and a sense of contemporary realities which few male writers can show. Thankfully no writer, male or female, has attempted to produce the great novel of the modern Italian experience, though the rapidity and depth of the changes might seem to warrant one. But Italian women writers have explored and articulated facets of that experience from a variety of angles and with varying degrees of subtlety, almost always taking account of the importance of individual experience within the context of the general, rather than making the individual stand for the general, as was so often the case in neo-realist fiction. Though Italian homosexual writers have been nothing like so much in evidence numerically, at least one, Aldo Busi, was able in his first two novels — *Seminario sulla gioventù* (1984) and *Vita standard di un venditore provvisorio di collant* (1985) — to make homosexual experience in Northern Italy public, and at the same time to use it to comment on the tragi-comic strangeness of a society ostensibly given over to pure commercialism.

The revival in fiction was signalled by *Il nome della rosa* and also by Calvino's *Se una notte d'inverno un viaggiatore*, which was also published in 1979 and was also remarkably successful. Eco's novel was in many ways the marketing man's dream product, catering for a range of readers from the semiotician, medievalist or post-modernist theorist to the seeker for escapist entertainment. Calvino's was more overtly intellectual, appealing mostly to readers who enjoyed games with fiction and had some idea of literary theory. Though publishers in Italy and abroad hoped that the other writers they saw emerging would deliver similar products to that of Eco, it was Calvino who signaled the way forward. Taken overall the fiction of the 1980s and 90s, whether by women or men, that has been generally esteemed by trained readers and critics, has continued to demand fairly high levels of sophistication, not only stylistically but also intellectually — witness most of the women writers mentioned above, or figures such as Daniele Del Giudice, Antonio Tabucchi and Francesco Biamonti — with very often a concern with pre-war or pre-modern Italy giving an elegiac tone to the writing, whatever its indirect implications for the present. Even authors like Andrea De Carlo and Francesca Duranti, whose novels are stylistically straightforward, demand postmodern awareness, whilst Gesualdo Bufalino, who shot to fame at the age of sixty with his first novel, *Diceria dell'untore* (1981), presupposes both intellectual agility and the ability to appreciate highly wrought baroque writing.

At the same time the language of literature has become much less uniform than it was, in part at least reflecting the diversity and fluidity of language-use in the country. Dialect has increasingly given way to Italian as the normal means of spoken communication for people of all classes, whilst Italian itself has diversified regionally and become much less rigid than it was even in the 1960s. But high literature has rarely exploited linguistic diversity for purely mimetic purposes. Taking their cue from Carlo Emilio Gadda's two most famous novels, *Quer pasticciaccio brutto de via Merulana* (1957) and *La cognizione del dolore* (1963), authors with literary pretensions have preferred to use different registers of Italian and different forms of dialect for expressive or expressionist purposes within already complex literary textures. Dialect-literature itself has undergone a curious evolution. For younger writers, as for many of their readers, writing in dialect implies evocation of lost childhood and of a peasant culture which has largely vanished in the space of a few decades. One striking development in the 1980s was the emergence of a new highly literary poetry in dialect, especially in the North-East; poets such as Franca Grisoni, Ernesto Calzavara and Franco Scataglini use dialect almost as a private language, often shaping it in individual ways and endowing their writing with a complexity of thought and feeling which makes no concessions to the uninitiated. In this perspective a figure such as Franco Loi, who even in 1980s and 90s pressed on with a revolutionary populist agenda in poetry in Milanese dialect, is an isolated anomaly, though as a poet one of the most interesting and important of his time.

Traditional high literature, whether in Italian or in dialect, may have the support of traditional readers and of the literary establishment, but it is now having to compete with new forms of writing. Since at least the early 1980s there have been vastly more readers of literature of some kind than there were even in 1960; obvious signs are that illiteracy has all but vanished, the proportion of young people in tertiary education has massively increased — 40% of school-leavers entered university in 1992, even if a higher proportion did not complete their degrees[22] — and the total number of books published tripled between 1967 and 1996.[23] The new readers are middle-class in the sense that society as a whole in Italy, as in the rest of the developed world, takes middle-class behavior and attitudes as the norm, though their educational and cultural experience is quite different from that of the traditional *bourgeoisie*. These readers want a literature which is easily approached, and which offers story as much as style. Foreign fiction partly satisfies this need. Novelists such as A.J. Cronin, who was much more widely read in Italy than in England, pointed the way in the 1950s and 60s. He has been succeeded by authors as diverse as Stephen King, Daniel Pennac and Ian McEwan. It is in this context that the success of Susanna Tamaro, which horrified sophisticated critics and readers alike, can be largely accounted for: a vast number of Italians plainly liked the simplicity of the writing in *Va dove ti porta il cuore*, and were drawn to its engaging story, its aura of moral and religious seriousness and its preference for feeling over doctrine. At the same time they were not disturbed by the residues it contained of the more obviously "experimental" writing of her previous novels.

Tamaro's novel is the most striking indication of the deeper changes which were in course throughout the 1990s, and are almost certainly set to continue. Forms of fiction have had commercial success within certain markets (the student readership being obviously the largest) which do not easily conform to stereotypical categories such as "popular" or "high" or "serious" literature. Indeed, whilst a hierarchical model is still applicable to some degree to Italian literature in view of high culture's deeply rooted and deeply institutionalized sense of the literary, the diversity of actual production and reading habits suggests that sociologically a model based on difference would be more accurate, in a way that it was not in the 1960s: the same reader might now read a highly literary novel in certain circumstances but what is felt to be a less demanding work in order to relax. Some 1990s writers found their particular readerships through simplifying certain forms of modernism; Alessandro Baricco, for instance, with the minimalism of *Seta* (1996) and other novels, or Stefano Benni, with his satirical, sometimes threatening fantasies. The writer who has had most commercial success since the late 1990s is Andrea Camilleri, whose detective and historical novels of Sicily combine skill in plot and dialogue with the kind of mixture of Italian and dialect which in Gadda was notoriously difficult, but in Camilleri is colorful entertainment. At the moment all three writers, like Tamaro, are outside the established literary pale, but the boundaries are becoming increasingly porous and uncertain, particularly as regards the detective novel.

In this kind of border area between the recognizably literary and the recognizably non-literary, various writers have emerged who use "lower" or mixed registers of writing to confront contemporary issues, and to represent one segment or another of contemporary society, usually the urban young. Taking to heart the example of Pier Vincenzo Tondelli in his 1980s novels, they have opted for representations of street-wise slang and attitudes, often incorporating the narrative pace, cross-cutting and ellipses of TV and film-drama. This new departure is most evident in the earlier work of the Tarantino-influenced Niccolò Ammaniti and other novelists such as Enrico Brizzi and Silvia Ballestra. But, with one of those contradictory twists that seem to characterize modern Italian literature, the results do not seem to have had more than niche appeal, and may well be more rapidly recuperated into literature in the narrower sense than the commercially more successful narrative mentioned in the preceding paragraph.

Much more quiet but socially more significant has been the appearance for the first time ever of a literature in Italian by non-native speakers. Italy's large immigrant population[24] is a media fixation but is still a marginal subject in novels by Italians, though it is at least touched on by, for example, Camilleri, Maraini and Biamonti. Since the early 1990s a number of autobiographical narratives or novels by African immigrants have appeared, such as the Senegalese Pap Khouma's *Io, venditore di elefanti* (1990) and the North African Mohsen Melliti's *I bambini delle rose* (1995). Published by small presses, the books have not been widely read and have been judged modest achievements in literary terms, though the presence of the well-known Maghrebin writer Tahar Ben Jalloun in Rome, and the readily available translations of his French novels and stories, may be creating a climate of opportunity which could see interesting results in the next few years.[25] It is an open question whether the immigrants from Eastern Europe, who are routinely associated with violent crime and prostitution in the press, can be treated with greater understanding in literature and themselves find literary voices in Italian.

At the opposite extreme to the fluid situation in contemporary fiction, a drive towards monumentalization of the acknowledged literary masters of the 20th century has gathered force during the 1990s. As in other countries, the burgeoning of academic interest in modern literature since the 1960s has led to a plethora of critical studies, whose chronological limits now extend up to the present day. The demise of the political agenda which vitalized critical discussion until the 1980s, plus a largely pacific assimilation of once controversial critical methodologies, has left the way open for a subtle but fundamentally uncontroversial approach to become the norm, and for the philological study of literary texts, at which Italian scholarship has always excelled, to be applied extensively to 20th-century literature. Two major editions of Montale, taking account of variants and original typescripts or manuscripts, were published not long before he died by eminent scholars.[26] The works of other authors who died in the last twenty years such as Pratolini, Calvino and Caproni, not to mention the still living Zanzotto, have subsequently appeared in Mondadori's prestigious Meridiani series, whilst Gadda has appeared in the Garzanti equivalent.

Part of this monumentalization is an almost reverential attitude towards the literary greats. When it has existed at all, biography, which in English-speaking countries has felt free to discuss the intimate details of modern writers' lives as well as their political vagaries, has shown a remarkable discretion. Those collections of letters which have been published are rarely revealing, and much correspondence and other papers remain unpublished and often unavailable for consultation. In that respect an important (and not merely scandalous) dimension of the relationship between literature and social experience in 20th-century Italy, both before and after the war, remains largely a matter for speculation. The reasons for such an approach are ultimately grounded in counter-reformation ideas of decorum. Though the need for circumspection with regard to the more recent past is also a factor, Italian literary culture is actually being true to its traditions. The effect of monumentalization is to put 20th-century authors in the same elevated and remote category as literature of the past. And in many instances perhaps rightly: the issues that concerned Calvino, not just Montale or Pratolini, have lost their urgency in the Italy of 2000, though that does not mean their writings have lost their importance.

NOTES

1. I use the phrase "literary culture" to mean practices of literary production and reception, centered upon creative writing (mainly fiction and poetry,) but including criticism, reviewing, biography, literary history and overlapping with philosophy, history, psychology and the social sciences.

2. E.g. in "Mandato degli scrittori e fine dell'antifascismo" (1964-5), in *Verifica dei poteri* (Il Saggiatore: Milan 1965).

3. Unlike its English equivalent, "men of letters," the term is only now assuming the air of referring to an antiquated social category.

4. In 1973 out of a population of 49,330,000 there were apparently 7,770,000 readers of novels and other forms of narrative and 2,360,000 readers of more technical and specialized forms off writing (figures in *Aspetti delle letture in Italia. Quaderni di vita italiana, 9*, (Istituto Poligrafico dello Stato: Rome 1975, p. 17).

5. According to the figures given in *Aspetti delle letture*, p. 73, the numbers of university students in course in 1948-9 were 90,940; in 1956-7 145,370; in 1964-5 259,338; and in 1972-3 657,620.

6. See M. Caesar and P. Hainsworth (eds), *Writers and Society in Contemporary Italy* (Berg Publishers: Leamington Spa 1984), pp. 18-21.

7. In the prose-poem "Visita a Fadin" in *La bufera e altro* (1956).

8. Vittorini's argument is summed up in the extracts in his *Diario in pubblico* (1957) (2nd ed. Bompiani: Milan 1976, pp. 294-305).

9. Carlo Muscetta, "Metello e la crisi del neorealismo" (1956), now in *Realismo, neorealismo, contrarealismo* (Garzanti: Milan, 1976), pp. 106-160.

10. Especially in *Scrittori e popolo* (Samonà e Savelli: Rome 1965).

11. See Stephen Gundle "From Neo-Realism to *Luci rosse*: cinema, politics, and society" in Zygmunt Barański and Robert Lumley (eds.), *Culture and Conflict in Post-War Italy* (Macmillan: Basingstoke 1990), pp. 195-224.

12. Paul Ginsborg, *A History of Contemporary Italy. Society and Politics 1943-1988* (Penguin: Harmondsworth 1990), p. 433.

13. The documentation is presented and discussed in Dario Biocca and Mauro Canali, *L'informatore: Silone, i comunisti e la polizia* (Luni Editrice: Rome 2000).

14. Vittorini's essay "Industria e letteratura" introduced *Menabò* 4 (1961), the whole of which was dedicated to the problem.

15. Montale's Nobel prize speech of 1975 was entitled "È ancora possibile la poesia?" (later appearing as the introductory essay in Eûgenio Montale, *Sulla poesia*, ed. Giorgio Zampa (Mondadori; Milan 1976), pp. 5-14. Cf. Zanzotto's "Poesia?" in *Il verri* 6th series, n. 1, pp. 110-113.

16. Poetry sales over the longer term are nonetheless surprising. School and university syllabuses are responsible for the 5.1 million sales of Sapegno's edition of the *Divina commedia* from 1955 to 1996, but the same cannot be true of some of Mondadori's best selling modern poets up to 1996 — Montale (424,214 copies of his various collections), Ungaretti's *Vita di un uomo* (74,378 in the Meridiani series), and Trilussa (485,400 copies of his various collections). (Source: *Panorama*, 1 February 1996, pp. 86-7.)

17. The first scholastic anthology, which subsequently went through various editions, was Giacinto Spagnoletti, *Poeti del Novecento* (Mondadori: Milan 1952).

18. The canonical collection of essays is Pier Vincenzo Mengaldo *La tradizione del Novecento* (Feltrinelli: Milan 1975), the first in what so far are three collections with that title.

19. The reasons for the unprecedented success of *Il gattopardo* are discussed by Alberto Cadioli, *L'industria del romanzo* (Editori Riuniti: Rome 1981), pp. 66-85. Sales eventually topped 2 million.

20. See, for instance, the discussions of Francesco Leonetti and Paolo Volponi in their joint *Il leone e la volpe* (Einaudi: Turin 1995).

21. *Panorama* (7 April 1995, pp, 72-74), in an article on Tamaro written when sales of her novel had still a long way to go, gave the figures as: *Il gattopardo*, over 2 million; *Il nome della rosa*, 2.2 million; *Lettera a un bambino mai nato*, 1.15 million; *Varcare la soglia della speranza*, 1,024,224; *Io speriamo che me la cavo*, 1,015,002; *Va dove ti porta il cuore*, 1.5 million (which by May 1996 had risen to 2.3 million). The list also included Calvino's *Marcovaldo* (1963), which had sold 1.5 million but over an extended period of time.

22. ISTAT, *Rapporto sull'Italia. Edizione 1999* (Il Mulino: Bologna 1999), p. 73.

23. 15,119 books were published in 1967 (Cadioli, p. 160) and 51,134 in 1996 (*Rapporto sull Italia*, p. 192).

24. In 1999 just over 1 million immigrants, the majority from Africa and Eastern Europe, had residence permits, according to figures in *Rapporto sull Italia*,

p. 132. There are also, of course, an unknown number of illegal immigrants.

25. I am indebted to Jennifer Burns, "Recent immigrant writing in Italian: A fragile enterprise," *The Italianist* 18 (1998), pp. 213-244.

26. Eugenio Montale, *L'opera in versi*, edited by Rosana Bettarini and Gianfranco Contini (Einaudi: Turin, 1980) and Eugenio Montale, *Tutte le poesie* edited by Giorgia Zampa (Mondadori: Milan 1984).

CHARLES KLOPP

Rallying Points: Literary and Cultural Journals, 1945 to the Present

The story that will be told in this article can be — indeed has been — told in a number of different ways.[1] A survey like this one of Italian intellectual and cultural journals during the last half-century cannot avoid being both selective and partisan. Not only is it impossible to mention all of the serious so-called little magazines that appeared in Italy during the period surveyed, it is also difficult to avoid choosing what will be discussed according to one's individual notions of what is important and what is not. In the pages that follow, I have restricted my discussion to those publications I believe have served as rallying points for Italian intellectuals in this period — true points of reference for the thought of the era.

In preparing this survey, however, certain omissions have been unavoidable. Despite the daily presence in Italy's newspapers of a literary and cultural "third page," plus a weekly supplement dealing with literary and cultural matters, it has not been possible to consider the intellectual debates of the period as they were reflected in the daily press. Nor will I discuss the large-circulation weeklies that in recent times have come to dominate representations of culture for a mass audience in Italy. Even though the quality of the thought and the writing — whether book reviews, essays, or other reportage — in Italian newspapers and large circulation magazines is generally very high (partly because the authors of this kind of work are often the same people whose articles appear in the little magazines), in this survey I will have to pass over material of this sort in silence. The same is true for commentary that appears in such literary or philological journals as *Lingua nostra, Studi sul Boccaccio, Studi danteschi, Italica,* and the like. Although these publications too reflect current thinking on cultural and intellectual matters, they are directed toward a more sectarian, academic audience than that envisaged by the more broadly aimed journals to be considered here. The analysis that follows, then, will outline the accomplishments of a selected group of publications that played the greatest and most original roles in the cultural debates of the last fifty years, journals that caused and were the sites of important cultural commentary, generators as well as disseminators of ideology.

One of the most important characteristics of Italian life since at least the Renaissance is the fervid romance between literature on the one hand and political activism on the other. One reason for this interest in politics on the part of writers and other creative people is that "Italy" existed as an intellectual category long before it became an actual political state. Beginning in 1947, moreover, with the promulgation of the ideas worked out in a Fascist prison by the Communist thinker and activist Antonio Gramsci — especially his thoughts on the role played by intellectuals in modern society and his notion of the "organic intellectual" — the relationship between culture and politics became an even more important one for Italians. Debates on the proper role of intellectual leadership in Italy, however, have a tradition that stretches back at least as far as the Enlightenment when such journals as *Il caffè* and *La frusta letteraria* served as early rallying points for civic minded thinkers and reformers. During the Risorgimento movement for national liberation during the first half of the nineteenth century, such periodicals as *Il conciliatore* again set out programs for reform that were often both literary and political. The "militant" or "committed" man or woman of letters so prominent in Italy during the twentieth century is therefore hardly a newcomer on the intellectual scene. This vital continuity between earlier reformers and those of the century that has just concluded has been underlined by the very titles of a number of journals published during this period. *Il Baretti, Il Verri,* and *Il Politecnico,* for example, are all twentieth-century publications that through their titles deliberately hark back to earlier efforts at reform.

The goal, in a sense, of all Italian literary and cultural activists of the sort I have been discussing, whether during the Enlightenment, the Risorgimento, or the 1950s, '60s, '70s, '80s, and '90s, has always been the same. All these activists were attempting to reinvigorate a stale or stalled intellectual life with new ideas and points of view (usually through the fiction, poetry, and essays of a newer, younger, and as yet untested generation of writers). These cultural Young Turks in Italy were especially energetic in the first decades of the twentieth century. Of the many journals that appeared on the scene in this period, perhaps the most important historically and critically was *La Critica*, edited beginning in 1903 by the historian, philosopher, and literary critic Benedetto Croce. In *La Critica*, as well as in his books and other writings, Croce put forward the ideas that made him a dominant presence in Italian thought for most of the first half of the century. *La Critica*, however, was also sharply sectarian and so neutralist (as distinct from non-interventionist) in regard to Italy's position on the hostilities of World War I, that the journal has been criticized for behaving "as if the war did not exist."[2] Its editor's aloofness from political events in their more contingent forms was not only deplored by many of Croce's contemporaries, such detachment was found abhorrent by most other journals of the period — and by those of later years as well. *Leonardo*, for example, which was founded the same year as *La Critica* and published until 1905, took an aggressive approach to intellectual life that contrasted sharply with Croce's more Olympian attitude. This short-lived venture edited by Giovanni Papini and Giuseppe Prezzolini was determined to prove that ideas had consequences and that those espoused in its pages could serve as a guide for understanding and affecting the confusing political events swirling about *Leonardo's* readers. A similarly insistent moral earnestness characterized what was perhaps the best known and later most respected journal of the period, *La Voce* (1908-1914). It too was edited by Papini and Prezzolini, but now with a plethora of additional, independent minded and ideologically heterogeneous contributors who included some of the best minds of the time. *La Voce* was brought down by the war and its own indecisiveness as to whether it wanted to be a militantly political or a primarily literary venture. But while it lasted, it provided what was perhaps the most determined and intelligent commentary on Italian political and cultural affairs of the day.

Seen at least from today's perspective, other reviews of the period seem to fall into one or the other of two camps. The nationalist publications like *Hermes* (1904-1906) and *Il Regno* (1903-1906) that flourished in the years before the advent of Fascism in 1924 can in hindsight be viewed as "proto-Fascist" for their strident parochialism. Others, like Gaetano Salvemini's *Unità* (1911-1920)[3] and Piero Gobetti's *Ordine nuovo* (1919-1925), by contrast, today appear beacons of inspiration for the later anti-Fascism that many of those who wrote for their pages were to embrace. A less overtly political publication was *La Ronda* (1919-1923), whose call for a return to order had more to do with literature than with politics, no matter how ominous that appeal might appear during a period of often brutal clamping down on political disorder. During the darker years of

Fascism and the checks it imposed on publications of all sorts, freewheeling public debate of the kind carried on earlier by journals from both the right and the left was effectively stifled. Opposition to the regime and its values was carried forward, however, in more clandestine form by such journals as *Il Baretti* (1924-1928), which was also edited by Gobetti, and, especially, *Solaria* (1926-1934), founded by Alberto Carocci. Although a studiedly literary and apparently apolitical publication, *Solaria* can be considered tendentially anti-Fascist — if only because so many of its contributors went on to become opponents of the regime, many of them serving in the armed Resistance of the 1940s. One critic, in fact, has categorized *Solaria's* position (or positions) as lining up in "sharp opposition in regard to the official culture imposed by the Fascist regime."[4] A publication of eclectic and Europeanist outlook, *Solaria* was one of the first to recognize the importance of the writers Svevo and Tozzi, once consigned to the peripheries of Italian letters but now considered among the founding fathers of the twentieth-century Italian novel.

One sign of the confusion and lack of ideological coherence of the later years of the Fascist period is that a government-supported publication like *Primato*, which was founded by Giuseppe Bottai and published from March 1940 until July 1943, could offer hospitality in its pages to so many young writers and intellectuals who would later fight in the Resistance I have just mentioned. These contributors to a publishing venture whose intent was the defensively nationalistic one of fostering an Italy "tutor and guardian of a [certain] civilization and culture" and thus the locus of "spiritual primacy," included a number of individuals who would later become pillars of the Communist and Socialist establishment, including Mario Alicata, Gaetano Della Volpe, Renato Guttuso, Carlo Muscetta, Cesare Pavese, and Vasco Pratolini.

The end of the war and of Fascism in 1945 roughly coincided with the end of *La Critica*, which had ceased publication the previous year.[5] The post-war period was a time of rebuilding for Italy — and not only of its ruined economic infrastructure. For intellectuals, now free from censorship and in touch once again with what was happening in the rest of Europe, it was a period of almost euphoric hope for dramatic renewal in all aspects of Italian life. While a significant number of the journals from the pre-Fascist era — not to speak of those from the two decades of Fascism — had been anti-socialist, it was now the turn for the socialists and Marxists to take the stage, and the little magazines of this era began to speak with a new voice. In this regard, it must be remembered that, for all of its long history in European thought, Marxism was as yet not very well known in Italy. While some intellectuals were familiar with the main tenets of this materialist school of thought,

Italians of the post-censorship era had a certain amount of catching up to do. A principal goal of many of the journals that flourished in the years right after the war was to help with this "aggiornamento."

The new society, however, whose outlines were being sketched so vigorously in this period, did not look the same to all the Italians doing the sketching.[6] There were those, for example, who wanted to return to the liberal society that had existed before 1924. Other more radical thinkers were in favor of revolutionary changes that would lead to a completely different country similar in at least its economic organization to those being erected at war's end elsewhere. A third group was in favor of the creation of a new society that would be neither that of pre-Fascist Italy nor a socialist state of the kinds being proposed by thinkers further to the political left.

Much of the debate on these issues was carried forward by journals associated with the Italian Communist Party. The discussion, as already noted, was energized beginning in 1947 by the publication of the prison writings of Antonio Gramsci, especially his *Prison Notebooks*. One of the most prominent of these leftist journals — *Rinascita*, which began publication in 1944, even before the end of hostilities, and continued to appear until 1991 — was founded and edited by Palmiro Togliatti. Togliatti, who was also one of the first editors of Gramsci's writings, was General Secretary of the Italian Communist Party at the time. In the late 1940s and early 1950s, before de-Stalinization and the other changes that were to take place in the Communist movement later, *Rinascita's* position on the relations between art and politics was unequivocal. "We are unable," Togliatti wrote in its pages in 1944, "to erect hypocritical and artificial barriers between the different activities — economic, political, or intellectual — of a nation. We do not and we cannot separate ideas from facts, the progress of thought from the development of relations among actual forces, politics from economics, culture from politics, individuals from society, art from real life. Within this unified and realistic conception of the world as a whole lies our strength, the strength of Marxist doctrine."[7] For Togliatti and *Rinascita*, then, art and politics were indissolubly joined. A Marxist writer had an obligation to adjust his or her creative expressions to the greater goals of the revolution. Over the years, *Rinascita* continued to expound the positions of the PCI on a variety of social and other issues. It was in its pages, for example, that the Party's views on the "Italian road to socialism" — a strategy for attaining the socialist state independently of the programs of such other Communist parties as that of the Soviet Union — were presented to its readership.

Another journal close to the Italian Communist Party in these years was *Il contemporaneo*, founded in 1945 by the novelist Romano Bilenchi and the historians and social critics Carlo Salinari, and Antonello Trombadori. *Il contemporaneo* began as a weekly, though after 1965 it appeared as a monthly supplement to *Rinascita*. A less highbrow publication than the sometimes austere *Rinascita*, *Il contemporaneo* played an important role in such debates as that on neorealism in the 1950s. In regard to the fiction being produced at the time, its editors held that, after a period of chronicling such recent events as the war and Resistance, it was time for novelists to abandon neorealism and move forward to historical interpretations of those events in a shift of emphasis from "chronicle" to "history." The debate concerning fiction as chronicle and fiction as history and on neorealism in general was to have important ramifications for the history of the novel in Italy throughout the 1950s and beyond.

A third journal that spoke for the left during this period was *Società* (1945-1961). In the beginning a Marxist but not a Communist publication, *Società's* contributors, in its early years, included a number of professors and academicians, among them such philosophers and historians as Antonio Banfi, Delio Cantimori, and Ludovico Geymonat. Later, it drew contributors more exclusively from the Party or those whose views were very close to it. Like other leftist writers of the period, those who wrote for *Società* were striving to construct a new, materialist culture sharply distinct from that envisaged by the idealist and liberal anti-Marxist Croce. Throughout its long run, *Società* maintained a high intellectual and scholarly level; in 1963, it was succeeded by *Critica marxista*.

The most famous and influential, probably, of all of the journals of the immediately post-war period was *Il Politecnico*, published in Turin between 1945 and 1947 by the novelist, polemicist, and essayist Elio Vittorini. Even before the end of Fascism, Vittorini had managed to publish what might be called a crypto-anti-Fascist novel in his *Conversazione in Sicilia*, which in 1938-39 was published in *Letteratura*.[8] With Fascism now cashiered and the war over, Vittorini positioned *Il Politecnico* at the center of the most vigorous debates on literature and culture of the period. The journal's name was a deliberate throwback to Carlo Cattaneo's *Il politecnico* of 1839-1865, a venture that was part of this earlier thinker's project to promulgate ideas of scientific and technical advancement to readers in Risorgimento Italy. Vittorini's choice of this name underlines his journal's commitment to interdisciplinarity and its openness to discourses other than that of literary criticism. *Il Politecnico* was not to be an exclusively literary publication but one that instead was willing to engage with a number of different discourses including those of politics, history, economics, and philosophy. Through his journal Vittorini was attempting to create a new kind of culture designed not to console those suffering — as such earlier cultures as that of a certain sort of Catholicism had perhaps done — but to liberate the sufferers and perhaps even eradicate the causes of their pain. Working with Vittorini on this enterprise were such other intellectuals as the poet and essayist Franco Fortini, who would also contribute to several other journals of the period, and Piero Calamandrei, who later founded *Il Ponte*. Other contributors to *Il Politecnico* included such narrative writers as Massimo Bontempelli and Italo Calvino and such once hermetic but now increasingly politically committed poets as Alfonso Gatto and Vittorio Sereni. The journal also published a number of non-Italian writers, among them Sartre, De Beauvoir, Lukàcs, Brecht, Michaux, and Pasternak. Its frequent special issues included numbers devoted to discussion of Hemingway's *For Whom the Bell Tolls*, of Dostoyevski, and of Kafka, plus a first publication of some of Gramsci's prison letters and of Lukàcs's theoretical criticism. In accordance with the Marxist dictum that the intellectual's task is not just to analyze the world but to change it, *Il Politecnico*'s goal was to create a new kind of society made up of new men and women. In order to achieve this goal, the journal reached out in its articles and choice of contributors to intellectuals who included Catholics or even Croceans as well as Marxists. Vittorini, who believed that "being concerned with bread and work is also a way of showing one's concern for the soul," did not find this strategy incoherent or contradictory.

Such an approach, however, was anathema to Togliatti. In the intellectual history of the period, *Il Politecnico* is perhaps most famous for the debate carried on in its pages and those of *Rinascita* between Vittorini on the one hand and Togliatti and Mario Alicata on the other.[9] In this debate Togliatti and Alicata accused Vittorini of believing that the revolution could be accomplished by merely disseminating information. This was wrong, they felt, because the logic of journalism demanded that priority in publishing be given to what was new or novel rather than to supporting what at the moment was the best strategy for political success. Vittorini's response to these critics was that it was important for leftist writers to maintain their artistic autonomy and in this way do significantly more than "tootle the flute for revolution." In Vittorini's view, the artist is a visionary able not only to conceive what line should be taken on immediate political issues but also to define the greater goals that lie beyond a specific struggle. "We know," he wrote in response to *Rinascita*, "what has happened to politics and culture in every great revolution. We know that poetry has always become Arcadian [by this Vittorini means devoid of contact with actual social reality]. We know that culture has always become the maidservant of politics. And we accept in advance the possibility that the same thing will happen to our revolution."[10] The two positions, that of Alicata and Togliatti and that of Vittorini and others who thought the way he did, were thus in the end irreconcilable. After *Il Politecnico* ceased publication in 1947, Vittorini went to work for the Einaudi publishing house, where he was in charge of the "I gettoni" fiction series in which a number of writers who would be crucial components of post-war literary culture were published for the first time. He also left the Communist Party.

Officina, whose run in Bologna and then Milan lasted from 1955 to 1959, was edited at first by Francesco Leonetti, Roberto Roversi, and Pier Paolo Pasolini. Later, Angelo Romanò, Gianni Scalia, and Franco Fortini joined its staff. The years when *Officina* was published were those of the solidification of the Christian Democrat hegemony in Italy, this on the heels of their 1948 victory at the polls marking the end of the post-war coalition that had included left-wing parties in the government. *Officina*, then, dates from the beginnings of the Cold War. Its title means "workshop" or "factory," and was chosen to affirm the solidarity felt by its editors with Italian blue-collar workers who shared the political leanings if not necessarily the cultural tastes of its editors and contributors. Initially, *Officina* had an extremely small press run, with as few as 600 copies pulled of its earliest numbers. This is an indication not so much of its editors' modesty as of the restricted nature of the journal's elitist audience. In poetry, *Officina* was associated with "neo-experimentalism," that is, the fusion of the neo-realistic commitment that had dominated the prose fiction of the preceding period with the hermetic traditions of the more distant past. The point of this blending was to create a new kind of poetry that was realistic, even banal, in its language while conserving the emotional and intellectual complexities of the sometimes obscure poetic works of the 1930s. The verse that appeared in the journal (Pasolini's *Le ceneri di Gramsci*, for example, or any number of works by Fortini) was written in a neutral, broadly accessible Italian that was experimental more in terms of language than of content. This simpler language, however, as Pasolini put it, was not to be understood as a passive description of an already-known entity but should be thought of instead as a means of coming to know a refractory reality brought into existence by the poem's own gnoseological effort. Subtitled "a magazine of poetry," *Officina* published verse by such distinguished members of what would later become the literary establishment as Attilio Bertolucci, Giorgio Caproni, Luciano Erba, Mario Luzi, Elio Pagliarani, Sandro Penna, Clemente Rebora, Edoardo Sanguineti, Camillo Sbarbaro, and Giuseppe Ungaretti. It also found space in its pages for prose by such novelists of the period as Giorgio Bassani, Carlo Emilio Gadda, and Paolo Volponi. *Officina* published essays, too, some of which proposed reevaluations of the poetic tradition of both the nineteenth and the twentieth centuries. The poet, novelist, essayist, and eventually filmmaker Pier Paolo Pasolini, who would become one of the most important players on the Italian cultural scene until his premature and violent death in 1975, wrote one such essay on the poetry of Giovanni Pascoli. Appearing during years marked by de-Stalinization and the invasion of Hungary by Soviet troops — events that led to a tremendous crisis for Italian intellectuals on the left — *Officina* can be taken to mark the transition between the politically committed neo-realist narrators of the 1950s and the more freely experimental "neo-avanguardia" of the 1960s.[11]

When Vittorini returned to journal publishing in 1959, it was with a new magazine in a new context. *Il Menabò* (1959-1967), at the same time, was in many ways a return to some of the concerns of *Il Politecnico* in that it espoused the same broad outlook and interest in general social issues characteristic of Vittorini's earlier venture. Ably assisted by co-editor Italo Calvino and with a group of contributors that included Pasolini and Fortini, Vittorini brought out ten monographic issues of this journal. "Menabò" means "the dummy" or "the layout" in typographical parlance, and the format of the new magazine was designed to emphasize its divergence from earlier publishing enterprises. The watchword for the discourse put forward by the new journal was "rational tension." In addition to providing them with provocative and well-written fiction and poetry, then, *Il Menabò* encouraged its readers to consider the larger social context in which this creative writing was being produced. The poetry and fiction — including, over the magazine's run, several quite distinguished short novels — were thus complemented by essays tying this writing to such broader cultural issues as the use of dialect for expressive purposes, the nature of war fiction in Italy, and literature and the work-place, especially — in these years of burgeoning industrial activity in Italy — the factory. Among the topics debated in its pages was that of the deleterious effects of neocapitalism and the alienation it was creating for workers and consumers alike in these years of the "miracolo italiano." A memorable article on this topic is Fortini's "Astuti come colombe" in which this poet and social commentator counsels a new use of language as a weapon turned against the nascent Italian capitalism with a human face.

Other writers, in addition to Fortini and Calvino (Calvino's essays on "Il mare dell'oggettività" and "La sfida al laberinto" were both written for special issues of *Il Menabò*), who contributed to Vittorini's journal included the young Umberto Eco. Another contribution of historical importance that first appeared in the pages of *Il Menabò* was Edoardo Sanguineti's *Capriccio italiano*, a novel that has become a defining example of the experimental fiction of the "neoavanguardia."

Il Menabò also had an international side, and entire issues of the journal were devoted to contributions by French and German writers of the period. Its final number, in 1967, was a memorial issue for Vittorini who had died that year at the age of fifty-eight. The journal, then, came to an end just a few months before 1968 and the beginnings of the student movement that created such immense changes in political and intellectual life throughout Italy and elsewhere.

Another publication of a slightly different sort that was of importance in the 1950s was *Botteghe oscure*, which was published in Rome from 1948 to 1960 under the patronage of Marguerite Caetani, an American-born Roman princess. Its editor was the novelist and man-of-letters Giorgio Bassani. *Botteghe oscure* (named for the street where the magazine's editorial office was located and which, by coincidence, is also the location of the headquarters of the Italian Communist Party) published poetry and fiction not only in Italian but also in English, French, German, and Spanish. Unlike some other journals of the period, *Botteghe oscure* was not only unselfconsciously international, it was also remarkably non-sectarian, offering hospitality in its pages to writers of very disparate ideological views. By the time the magazine ceased publishing in 1960, it could boast of having featured writers from more than thirty countries throughout the world. Unlike all the other journals mentioned in this survey, *Botteghe oscure* published only fiction, poetry, and translations, not essays. Its participation in the cultural debates of the times was thus more by implication than through the explicit polemical positions of its writers. It was also unusual in that it paid its contributors.

Perhaps because of its non-sectarian orientation, the Caetani/Bassani enterprise attracted writers of extremely high quality. Among American authors, *Botteghe oscure* published work by such luminaries on the later literary scene as Truman Capote, e.e. cummings, Robert Duncan, Archibald MacLeish, Carson McCullers, James Merrill, George Steiner, Wallace Stevens, and William Carlos Williams. Italian contributors included Anna Banti, Giorgio Bassani, Attilio Bertolucci, Italo Calvino, Giorgio Caproni, Carlo Cassola, Luciano Erba, Franco Fortini, Carlo Emilio Gadda, Eugenio Montale (whose "L'anguilla" was the leading text in the journal's first number in 1948), Elsa Morante, Alberto Moravia, Pier Paolo Pasolini, Sandro Penna, Vasco Pratolini, Rocco Scotellaro, Mario Tobino, and Paolo Volponi among many other. The French authors ranged from Artaud to Valéry, and there were contributions by writers in Spanish and in German as well. As is evident from the names on this list, the writers published by *Botteghe oscure* were those whose work came to define European and American modernism in the second half of the twentieth century.

With *Il Verri* we return to a more familiar and more exclusively Italian enterprise. This journal was founded in 1956 by Luciano Anceschi, a professor of aesthetics at the University of Bologna. It continued to be published until Anceschi's death in May of 1995. *Il Verri* was devoted especially to poetry and to avant-garde poetry in particular, though fiction and essays on a very wide range of topics appeared in its pages as well. In both his professional and his journalistic work, Anceschi was influenced by the phenomenology of Husserl and of Antonio Banfi; *Il Verri* is usually credited with helping promulgate this school of philosophical investigation in Italy. But Anceschi's was also an eclectic journal whose special numbers explored such controversial topics as linguistic structuralism, psychoanalysis, the new music, and rereadings of Nietzsche. Its contributors and editors included members of the neo-avant-garde Gruppo 63 (so called because the group was founded at a meeting in Palermo in 1963) plus many of Anceschi's colleagues from the University of Bologna. Anceschi himself was extremely restless intellectually, intensely curious about what was happening in the realm of ideas throughout the world and reluctant, therefore, to remain within the limits of the old formulas. For this reason, he was especially attentive to new ideas, projects, and texts, and the magazine he published was an unusually lively and unpredictable one.

Quindici (Rome, 1967-1969) is another journal associated with the Gruppo 63 and is often considered a kind of spinoff from *Il Verri*. *Quindici's* editors were Alfredo Giuliani and Nanni Balestrini, both of them poets as well as critics. Its contributors numbered more than the fifteen evoked in its title. They included such well-known Italian writers as Alberto Arbasino, Renato Barilli, Guido Davico Bonino, Umberto Eco, Angelo Guglielmi, Giorgio Manganelli, Elio Pagliarani, Antonio Porta, and Edoardo Sanguineti — the big names of experimental poetry and fiction of the period. An iconoclastic group determined to introduce a sense of disorder and doubt onto what they thought was the excessively staid literary scene of the period, the group's intellectual adversaries included such more established writers as Moravia and Pasolini, the philologist Gianfranco Contini, and the academic critics Maria Corti, Dante Isella, and Cesare Segre, whose own rallying point was the more conservative *Strumenti critici*. *Quindici* conceived the material it presented as an alternative to the information being disseminated by the universities, television, and political parties. This, it is evident, was a quite different tack from that taken earlier by Vittorini in *Il politecnico*, since Vittorini, at least at the beginning, tried to work together with representatives of the leftist parties, even if this meant nothing more than disagreeing with them in public. While one critic has described the writers for *Quindici* as members of an "avanguardia disimpegnata" who assumed "a kind of neutrality in regard to the real,"[12] the journal supported the student protests of the era and opposed the war in Viet Nam, while supporting the Cuban Revolution and the Black Power movement in the United States. Some have suggested, in fact, that this attempted conjugation of avant-garde poetry and revolutionary politics is what led to the journal's demise. But the extreme heterogeneity of its principal contributors' political and aesthetic views was also a major factor contributing to its coming to an end, just as it had been for a number of its predecessors as far back as *La Voce*.

Marcatré, which was founded in Genoa, ran from 1963 to 1971, that is, just a little longer than *Quindici*, with which it is often associated. A multidisciplinary enterprise that carried articles on art, architecture, and music as well as literature, *Marcatré's* contributors included Gillo Dorfles, Umberto Eco, and Edoardo Sanguineti. It too was interested in the unconventional or confrontational in cultural matters and published articles on such topics as pop music, outsider art, the Beat Generation, and the underground cinema.

The late 1960s and the entire decade of the 1970s saw an immense proliferation of journals, broadsheets, manifestos, and other publications, most of them short-lived and most of them emanating from student groups in or outside the university.[13] These were often mimeographed or otherwise simply produced and have been characterized as "anti-publications" — a questioning of the political and cultural power structures of the country in both their content and their physical format. Often these journals were not sold but distributed free. Their content tended more to the political than to the broadly cultural and was typically concerned with strategies of struggle for the immediate future on the part of workers and students.

Quaderni rossi, which has been called "the theoretical matrix of the new Left,"[14] was founded in 1961 by Raniero Panzieri. It lasted until 1965. Published in Turin, its principal point of reference was the FIAT factory in that city, the working conditions in that factory, and the nature of neocapitalism more generally. For these reasons, it could be said that *Quaderni rossi* carried forward at least some aspects of the debate begun earlier by *Officina* and *Il Menabò*. This time, however, discussion was joined with infinitely greater, and more revolutionary, political fervor by contributors who proclaimed that their positions were now more in line with those of the Communist Party of China than they were with the political and cultural views of the Italian PCI. Unlike the political and cultural journals of the 1950s and 1960s but consonant with the collectivist convictions of the era, *Quaderni rossi* was determined to voice its ideas though collective utterances rather than by individual and possibly contrasting voices. An important aspect of its political project was to involve the workers in the struggle for greater personal and class freedoms. The similarly named *Quaderni piacentini* ("Notebooks from Piacenza," rather than "Red Notebooks") began in 1962, one year later than *Quaderni rossi*, and continued until 1985. It was edited by Giorgio Bellocchio, Grazia Cherchi, and Goffredo Fofi. *Quaderni piacentini's* contributing editors included, Alberto Asor Rosa, Cesare Cases, Franco Fortini, Gianni Scalia, and Sergio Solmi. Guido Viale, leader of the Student Movement in Turin, also contributed to its pages. This journal, too, whose perspective was anti-Stalinist and iconoclastic, dealt with such topics as imperialism, the student culture, and the street terrorism of the 1970s. Written by dissenting Marxists rather than disciplined Party members, *Quaderni piacentini* was concerned with unmasking the scandals of the day in whatever areas they occurred, including those under the purview of the PCI. It had harsh words for what it considered the irresponsible and self-serving positions of Italian intellectuals and establishment activists.

Other journals of this tumultuous period of political and cultural upheaval include *Classe operaia* ("The Working Class"), edited by Mario Tronti from 1964-1967, *Contropiano* ("Alternate Plan"), edited by Alberto Asor Rosa and Massimo Cacciari from 1968 to 1971, and *Che fare* ("What Should be Done"), issued irregularly from 1967 to 1975. Among these activist journals *Lotta continua* or "Constant Struggle," stands out. This is in part because of the incisive analyses of current events it often contained — including that of the death of the anarchist Pino Pinelli while in police custody in 1969 — and in part because "Lotta continua" was an important extra-parliamentary political organization as well as a new left publication.[15] Beginning as a weekly, *Lotta continua* became a daily paper in 1972 and continued as such until 1982.

A somewhat less strident but not for that less serious journal from the end of this time period is *Alfabeta*, which was published from 1979 to 1988 by writers and critics drawn for the most part from university circles. Aimed at a "post 1968 generation," it devoted a good deal of attention to comments and debate on terrorism, a burning issue for intellectuals of all stripes in this period. Unlike the journals from the new left that had preceded it, *Alfabeta* did not attempt to speak with a collective voice but turned over its pages to what were often contradictory views by both well-known intellectuals and such newer figures on the Italian scene as Romano Luporini, Toni Negri, and Gianni Vattimo. Topics debated by this magazine included the crisis of reason, the culture of extremism, what constitutes the postmodern, and what sense literature can have in a time of political extremisms.

In addition to these mostly short-lived and vociferous publications of the hot years of the 1960s and 1970s, there were a number of other journals from the period and even earlier that continue to be published today, even if they were not always in the thick of the discussions that have been sketched in the pages above. One of the most venerable of such publications is the *Nuova Antologia*, founded in 1866 by Francesco Protonotari and Bettino Ricasoli. During Fascism *Nuova Antologia* stuck resolutely to the middle of the road, careful not to offend the regime. For this reason it has not been especially well regarded by the anti-Fascist post-war establishment. It should be remembered, however, that at the beginning of its publishing history, *Nuova Antologia* offered hospitality in its pages to such writers as Antonio Fogazzaro, Guido Gozzano, Luigi Pirandello, and Giovanni Verga, all of whom are now considered major writers in the history of Italian literature and in this way helped define the nature of Italian culture today.

In this survey, little has been said about the Catholic journals, many of which are also still with us today. The most important of these, perhaps, is *Civiltà Cattolica*, founded in 1855 by Jesuit priests and active in the debates of the 1950s on the importance of the individual and the dignity of human life. This discussion had a special impact on those Catholics who had been led by their religious views to oppose Fascism by means that, for some, included fighting in the Resistance. Other prominent Catholic journals include *Vita e pensiero*, which has been published since 1914, and *Cronache sociali*, which lasted for only a few years between 1947 and 1951. The latter publication was committed to the examination of social problems in the light of Catholic belief. It was associated with the leftist Catholic Giuseppe Dossetti and other members of the Democrazia Cristiana including Giorgio La Pira (mayor of Florence several times during the period 1951-1965), and the DC ministers and Prime Ministers Amintore Fanfani and Aldo Moro.

Several secular, more middle-of-the road journals that were founded after the war have stood the test of time better than the radical publications from the 70s that I have been reviewing above. *Nuovi Argomenti*, which was founded 1953 by Alberto Carocci (who much earlier had been the editor of *Solaria*) and the novelist and social commentator Alberto Moravia, has presented discussion of such issues as the working conditions of Italian miners in the early 1950s (with reportage by Carlo Cassola and Luciano Bianciardi), the anti-colonialist uprising in Algeria, and the war in Viet Nam. Especially effective were the polls this journal sponsored that solicited the opinions of intellectuals and other public figures on political and cultural matters of the times, responses that today constitute a valuable record of what was thought about such matters in the first decades after the war. *Nuovi Argomenti* publishes poetry and fiction and has been especially hospitable, over the years, to the work of new writers.

Il Ponte, founded in 1945 by Piero Calamandrei and still being published today, is another journal that belongs to this group. Many of its earliest contributors were drawn from university circles or the Action Party, a leftist and progressive secular anti-Fascist movement active during the Resistance and then just after the war. For many of those who contributed to *Il Ponte*, politics was viewed not so much as a means of attaining power as an opportunity to spur moral regeneration in the best spirit of the Resistance. Critical of the centrist governments during the first years of the Italian republic, *Il Ponte* considered itself a "third force" that was neither communist nor anti-Communist in the often knee-jerk style of the governmental forces of the period. But it was firmly opposed to the war in Viet Nam and to the Greece of the colonels. Among its special numbers was one devoted to Eugenio Montale when he won the Nobel Prize for Literature in 1975 and another, in 1980, discussing the significance of the life and thought of Leon Trotsky.

Il Mulino began publishing in Bologna in 1951. A "mill" rather than a "bridge," its project was to sift what was most valuable from all three of the dominant cultures of the period: secular liberalism, materialist Marxism, and Catholicism. Viewing itself as a mediating force much like *Il Ponte*, *Il Mulino* too has encouraged debates and the exchange of opinions among individuals from different intellectual backgrounds and points of view. *Belfagor* was founded in 1948 by Luigi Russo, at that time one of the few remaining disciples of the thought of Benedetto Croce. A publication of considerable intellectual and scholarly rigor, *Belfagor* has published an impressive body of work of historical, philosophical, and philological interest. Its contributors have included prestigious academics in the fields of literature, philosophy, and historical studies. In the best secular leftist tradition, the magazine has always been opposed to dogmatism and political opportunism. Another venerable publication of this non-aligned sort is *Nord e Sud*, which began publication in 1954 with a focus on the problems and the development (or lack thereof) of the South of Italy. Its work can be considered a continuation of the struggle for betterment in this region begun by Salvemini many years earlier with the first *Unità*.

Other journals of general cultural interest still coming out today include *Paragone*, founded in Bologna in 1950 by the art critic Roberto Longhi. *Paragone* alternates issues that deal with art with others devoted to literature. Its literary version, *Paragone letteratura*, presents poetry, fiction, and essays by many of the most interesting of the current generation of Italian and foreign men and women of letters including the critics Gianfranco Contini, Guido Fink, and Jean Starobinski. *Aut-Aut*, which was founded in 1951 by Enzo Paci, is a journal devoted to phenomenology that has broadened its focus to embrace not only philosophy and literature but also such related topics as architecture, sociology, and twelve-tone music. Other subjects that have been treated in its pages include the relation between Marxism and structuralism and, in later years, the thought of Louis Althusser, Michel Foucault, and Jacques Lacan. It has also published work by such literary figures as Luciano Anceschi, Carlo Bo, and Giacomo Debenedetti. *Strumenti critici*, which was founded in 1966 and edited by Maria Corti, Dante Isella, and Cesare Segre, has already been mentioned here for the fire it drew from certain members of the Gruppo 63. Respected both in Italy and abroad for the high intellectual and scholarly quality of its critical essays, *Strumenti critici* was associated, especially in its early years, with structuralism and has drawn most of its contributors from the academic establishment. It is another publication especially sensitive to critical work generated outside of Italy.

Along with these long-lived journals that are still contributing to the cultural scene in Italy, there are also a number of newer publications. Among them, several are devoted to women's issues. One of the most interesting is *Via Dogana*, named after the street where the Women's Bookstore of Milan is located. Its project, in the words of a recent commentator, is "to create a new symbolic order based on women's love of freedom in all spheres of thought and action."[16] Many of *Via Dogana*'s activities are carried on through letters from and debates with its readers, a part of the journal's strategy to create a different kind of intellectual discourse that is congenial with its militant and, for the most part, sexually homogeneous if often dissenting readership.

Another review of importance that is still being published is *Micromega*, founded in 1986 by Lucio Caracciolo, Giorgio Ruffolo e Paolo Flores D'Arcais. Its contributors have included the philosopher (and current mayor of Venice) Massimo Cacciari and the feminist activist Miriam Mafia. Two other current journals specializing mostly in essays and reviews rather than fiction and poetry are *L'indice*, founded in 1984, and *La rivista dei libri*, a joint venture with the *New York Review of Books* that began publishing in 1991.[17]

A fitting conclusion to this survey might be a note on a journal published not in Italy but in Flushing, New York. *Differentia*, which appeared from 1986 to 1999, is a venture whose very existence indicates how much the dissemination of Italian culture at century's end has begun to take place outside as well as inside Italy. Published entirely in English, *Differentia* was founded and edited by Peter Caravetta. Its stated aim was to "expand and intensify the dialogue between Anglo-American and Italian cultures" through the "diffusion in English of contemporary Italian thought, primarily in the area traditionally called philosophy and with particular emphasis on the history of ideas, social criticism, and literary studies." To this end *Differentia* published poetry, art, photography, and fiction as well as essays and reviews. The journal's Italian contributors (often in English translations of work that had already appeared elsewhere) included Giorgio Agamben, Alessandro del Lago, Umberto Eco, Aldo Garbani, Mario Perniola, and Gianni Vattimo. Special numbers of the journal were devoted to such topics as "The Place of the Subject," "Interferences," "Humanism-Modernity-Postmodernity," and "Italian American Culture," this last guest edited by Ron Scapp and Anthony J. Tamburri.

What can be said, finally, about the Italian little magazines of the second half of the twentieth century that have been cursorily reviewed here? Over the long run, many of them, surely, must be considered "ephemera," that is "printed matter . . . meant to be of use for only a short time, but preserved by collectors,"[18] the collectors in this case being the literary historians of the period. Paradoxically, however, these mayfly-like journals have often proved of greater historical importance than other publications like *Nuova Antologia* or *Civiltà cattolica* that have long been mainstays on the Italian cultural scene. It might be concluded that journals of this short-lived sort disappeared from the scene because the passionate ideas their editors and contributors espoused proved too combustible to hold such publishing enterprises together for very long. After the perceived emergency the journals had been founded to address had either dissolved or mutated into something else, the publications usually disappeared or merged with newer ventures. While it was the clash between different positions that made the debates sponsored by these magazines so lively while publication lasted, it helped to assure a longer life for such journals if the debates were carried on with their readers or other journals and not among members of the editorial board. For this reason such publications as *Il Verri* or *Belfagor* or *La Critica* that were managed by a single, often strong-minded, individual had a better chance of surviving than those edited by a board of heterogeneous personalities. But, as has been the case for Italian governments from the First Republic onward, while alignments changed, the personalities involved in those alignments responded to changes in the larger cultural scene by moving with sometimes startling aplomb from one assignment — in this case from one publishing venture — to another. Examples of peripatetic social commentators of this sort who contributed to a large number of journals of the period include Fortini, Pasolini, Eco, Sanguineti, and many others.

One important constant in all of the debates joined by those who wrote for these journals is their concern as intellectuals for the working class, a concern perhaps more typical of Italian intellectual life than of that elsewhere in Europe. But in this regard it must be remembered that the journals for which these intellectuals wrote were not publications that workers could make much sense of. This is especially true for the New Left publications of the 1960s and 1970s, which often were written in a forbidding and sometimes barely comprehensible jargon. There is, therefore, a certain narcissism about the debates that appeared in their pages. Despite what were sometimes their best efforts, the authors of the articles that appeared in these journals were talking about themselves to readers very much like them. This is not to say, however, that the implications of these debates were without importance for other sectors of Italian life. They had a significant influence on the thought of the period for the cultural, media, and, above all, the educational establishments of the country.

At this point, one might ask what the future might hold for intellectual and cultural debates of the sort described in these pages. In an Italy now very much part of the "global village," on-line communication is complementing if not supplanting more traditional means of intellectual discourse. Web-sites are in place at this writing, for example, that can be consulted by admirers of the writings of such novelists as Gesualdo Bufalino, Andrea Camilleri, and Leonardo Sciascia. *Via Dogana* is also on line, as are most of the country's dailies and the important weeklies. Some of these sites, moreover, are interactive, which means that those interested in the cultural and literary debates they sponsor are invited not just to observe passively but to join actively into the discussion. It is also possible to follow on-line such cultural events as the annual "Fiera del libro" book fair, and to respond to a variety of literary and cultural polls on a number of controversial topics. As the new millennium opens, these on-line opportunities are clearly becoming additional rallying points for those interested in following and, increasingly, in joining in the literary and cultural debates that used to take place more exclusively in the pages of the printed media.

NOTES

1. Comprehensive surveys of literary and cultural journals in Italy during the twentieth century include Giorgio Luti, ed., *Critici, movimenti e riviste del '900 letterario italiano*, Rome, La Nuova Italia Scientifica, 1986; Elisabetta Mondello, *Gli anni delle riviste. Le riviste letterarie dal 1945 agli anni ottanta*, Lecce, Milella, 1985; Renato Bertacchini, *Le riviste del novecento. Introduzione e guida allo studio dei periodici italiani*, Florence, Le Monnier, 1981; Augusto Simonini, *Cent'anni di riviste. La vittoria della critica sulla letteratura*, Bologna, Calderini, 1993; F. Saverio Festa, *Potere e intellettuali nelle riviste del novecento*, Urbino, Quattrolibi, 1984. See also Luigi Fontanella and Luca Somigli, eds., *The Literary Journal as a Cultural Witness 1943-1993. Fifty Years of Italian and Italian American Reviews*, Stony Brook, New York, Forum Italicum, 1996; Caterina Verbaro, "Il dibattito letterario.

Idee, poetiche, movimenti, gruppi letterari a confronto dal secondo dopoguerra ai primi anni Settanta" in Giorgio Luti, ed, *Il novecento*, Padua, Vallardi, vol, II, 1993, 1311-1361; Giuseppe Leonelli, "Politica e cultura. La letteratura tra impegno e sperimentazione," in Enrico Malato, ed., *Storia della letteratura italiana*, vol. IX, *Il novecento*, Rome, Salerno, 2000, 689-727; and Giuliano Manacorda, *Letteratura italiana d'oggi (1965-1985)*, Rome, Editori Riuniti, 1987. I would like also to express my gratitude to Beau David Case of the Ohio State University Libraries for helping me procure the necessary materials for this paper and for doing so at what was often the last minute as well as beyond the call of his usual duties.

2. Luti, *Critici*, p. 172.

3. This weekly publication later lent its name to the Communist Party daily that has continued publication even after the collapse of the PCI in 1991.

4. Luti, *Critici*, p. 242.

5. *Quaderni della Critica* continued, however, until 1951. Croce died in 1952.

6. See Norberto Bobbio, *Ideological Profile of Twentieth-Century Italy*, Princeton, Princeton University Press, 1995, pp. 143-156.

7. Quoted in Giuliano Manacorda, *Storia della letteratura italiana contemporanea (1940-1965)*, Rome, Editori Riuniti, p. 5.

8. Founded in 1937 by Alessandro Bonsanti, who had broken away from the editorial board of *Solaria*, this journal continued publishing until 1947, resuming after the war with three new series that lasted until 1971.

9. A recent appraisal of this debate and its significance is that by Robert S. Dombroski, "Vittorini's *Il Politecnico*," in Fontanella and Somigli, pp. 13-18.

10. Quoted in Salvatore Guglielmino, *Guida al novecento. Profilo letterario e antologia*. Milan, Principato, 1971, II, p. 522.

11. Simonini, p. 161.

12. Verbaro, p. 1338.

13. For a review of them, see Attilio Mangano and Antonio Schina, *Le culture del Sessantotto. Gli anni settanta le riviste il movimento*. Pistoia, Centro di Documentazione, 1998.

14. Quoted in Bobbio, p. 186.

15. Two recent books dealing with the history of Lotta Continua are Aldo Cazzullo, *I ragazzi che volevano fare la rivoluzione. 1968-1978. Storia di Lotta continua*, Milan, Mondadori, 1998, and Luigi Bobbio, *Storia di Lotta Continua*, Milan, Feltrinelli, 1988.

16. Rebecca West, "*Via Dogana*: A Journal By and For Women," in Fontanella and Somigli, 149-190, p. 150.

17. For information on other reviews of the 1980s, see Manacorda, pp. 341-360.

18. *Webster's New World Dictionary*, New York, Prentice Hall, 1993, p. 455.

JOHN PICCHIONE

Major Trends in Italian Poetry: From the Post-War Years to the Present

In the last fifty years, Italian poetry, with its diverse directions, movements, and currents, has shown a persistent restlessness and a creative tension that has constantly produced a climate of renewal and innovation. Even though in the years following World War II, echoes of the Hermetic movement were still audible in the style of a number of poets, the emerging new trend was characterized by the shift toward a realistic mode of writing motivated by historical and social issues. The Hermetic position (extremely influential and dominant from the thirties to the early forties) of a poetic language as pure and spiritual intuition, composed of sudden illuminations and revelations of truth, was being replaced by a poetry devoted to capturing the atrocities of war and the break down of society. This new trend rejected the Hermetic concept of writing as an ontological medium in behalf of a poetry of the here and the now, in the attempt to make sense of the events that had so deeply traumatized the human psyche. If Hermeticism reveals religious and metaphysical underpinnings which fostered a closed and abstract language full of obscure and allusive analogies, the poetry of the immediate post-war period adheres both to history and to a language open to everyday usage.

The Catholic wing of the Hermetic movement, represented by such poets as Carlo Betocchi, Piero Bigongiari, and Mario Luzi, continued to show a religious thrust also in the years following the war. Poetry, in its fundamental function, is envisaged as a point of contact with metahistorical realities. (For Luzi, however, it is important to point out that the transcendental dimension of history, tied to the presence of the divine, is continuously scrutinized in private and social events; e.g. *Quaderno gotico, Primizie del deserto*. The secular wing of the movement, with poets like Alfonso Gatto and Vittorio Sereni, was open to historical realities and a preoccupation with civil issues. Sereni's poetry in particular moves from the experience of the war to the alienating human condition brought about by the process of urbanization and industrialization in the fifties and the sixties (see *Diario d'Algeria* and *Gli strumenti umani*.

Hermeticism reached a crisis also with a poet like Salvatore Quasimodo (Nobel prize for literature in 1959), for whom, in the thirties and early forties, it had been the main source of inspiration. After World War II, Quasimodo openly rejected Hermetic tendencies and embraced, with great popular success, a realistic vein centered around the themes of war, death, and human suffering (*Giorno dopo giorno, La vita non è sogno, Il falso e vero verde*).

More faithful to the lyrical tradition remains the poetry of Giuseppe Ungaretti, whose *Sentimento del tempo* (1933) had been a central point of reference for the Hermetic movement. Also Ungaretti, however, in collections such as *La terra promessa* and *Il taccuino del vecchio* pursues a form of neo-baroque stylistic adventure that searches for new formal solutions.

Radical stylistic shifts and innovative thematic nuclei are easily uncovered in the post-war production of, arguably, Italy's most representative twentieth-century poet, Eugenio Montale. More than any other poet of his generation, Montale is fully open to new formal experimentation and to the cultural changes that occurred in the decades following the war (he received the Nobel prize for literature in 1975 and died in 1981). Montale's first collections (*Ossi di seppia*, 1925, *Le occasioni*, 1939) is underscored by a metaphysical gaze that stoically penetrates into the limitations of human existence uncovering a senseless world devoid of any essence or transparency. The only form of resistance against the negativity of the human condition is represented by the ethical force of a secular culture — and of poetry as its voice — allegorically portrayed as a Dantesque female figure of deliverance.

These and other utopian expressions of redemption and salvation come to an end in his first post-war collection, *La bufera e altro* (1956), which addresses the historical and cultural collapse brought about by Nazism and its horrors. This overpowering historical "storm" (*bufera*) destroys any hope of overcoming the negativity of life. Although the affirmation of life lingers through the presence of eros, as a primeval drive of attachment to life, and other expressions of possible regeneration, poetry and culture are forced to declare their defeat and impotence in front of the darkness of history and the triumph of evil.

Montale's silence as a poet for over a decade can be interpreted as a consequence of this outlook. When in the seventies he publishes *Satura, Diario del '71 e '72, Quaderni di quattro anni*, the transformations are profound and significant. What emerges is an absurdist vision of everyday life portrayed through a diaristic, aphoristic, or epigrammatic style that adopts the modes of sarcasm and parody. Montale's "stile alto" of the preceding collections now dissolves, favoring the colloquial and prosaic language aimed at transcribing the elusive and insignificant moments of everyday existence. Faced by the bleak cultural prospect of the consumer society of the post-war period, Montale's poetry seems to reaffirm with a caustic sense of irony and self-irony the senselessness of a universe in which the human presence is accidental and superfluous.

Even the poetry of Sandro Penna, Attilio Bertolucci, and Giorgio Caproni had contacts with the Hermetic movement. However, although these poets have retained some of the Hermetic lyrical compression, they moved toward a linear and narrative style, with Umberto Saba as the prime literary antecedent. Classified by Pasolini under the current of "antinovecentismo," to distinguish them from the intuitive, symbolic procedures of the Hermetic movement, these poets display a form of impressionistic realism aimed at capturing the happenings of everyday life. Penna brings into poetry a delicate sensuality and a sense of exclusion from the social for being gay — indeed, a daring topic for the 1950s (e.g. *Appunti* and *Una strana gioia di vivere*).

The distinct poetic line which emerged as a forceful reaction to Hermeticism was made up of poets who adopted an ideologically oriented realism as the way for poetry to regain a social and political voice. These poets owed their intellectual formation to Marxist ideology, to Antonio Gramsci in particular, even though they never ceased to come into conflict with the Communist party itself. This trend was to be identified with the journal *Officina* (1955-1959). Pier-Paolo Pasolini, Roberto Roversi, and Franco Fortini played major roles in the life of this journal, but Pasolini was undoubtedly its driving force. His ideological nonconformity and his passionate engagement in political and social debate, often embracing self-contradicting positions, made him one of the dominant literary personalities of the post-war period. However, if we put aside Pasolini's overall cultural impact through his filmic and journalistic activities, we can see that his poetry is not as innovative as one might expect. His use of a common language, tied to elements of slang and dialect, can be traced back to Cesare Pavese's *Lavorare stanca*, (1936, second edition 1943) and to the general stylistic modes set by *neo-*

realism in its filmic and narrative expressions.

Pasolini is dramatically aware of the leveling linguistic and cultural effects of late capitalism — as expressed by the emerging consumer society of the mid-fifties and early sixties — and he reacts by mythologizing the lumpen proletariat of the popular Roman neighborhoods, as he had already done in earlier years with the peasant class of his native Friuli. For Pasolini, the marginalized condition of these classes represented the final and only opposition to the bourgeois homogenization of the world. The authentic and vital drives of these classes constituted a form of resistance to a decaying and alienating process of embourgeoisement of the entire society. Undoubtedly, Pasolini had a lucid perception of the links between the personal, the social and the political, but his autobiographical confessionalism often echoes the lamenting strains of the lyrical tradition, or of the "Crepuscular" poets of the turn of the century, without any dosage of their counteracting irony. Nevertheless, in collections such as *Le ceneri di Gramsci* and *La religione del mio tempo*, Pasolini's merit was that of connecting poetry with such issues as the cultural margins, the body, consumer society and the death of eros, oppression by the church as an institution and the dangers of progress as conceived by late capitalism. Through these and other topics, Pasolini anticipated pivotal questions that were to animate the cultural debate for years to come.

Several poets, including Luciano Erba (*Il male minore*), Nelo Risi (*Pensieri elementari*), and Giovanni Giudici (*La vita in versi*) reveal a tendency different from the ideologically oriented realists. They too, like the realists, conceive poetry as an instrument of social awareness and revolt. However, in their emphasis on irony and anti-rhetorical style, they also demystify the role of the poet and poetry itself, making impossible the construction of any myth or of any utopian project. These poets adopt a subdued and prosaic language, but one seasoned with strong doses of irony that often becomes sarcasm or biting satire directed at the superficiality and hypocrisies of contemporary life. Identity and subjectivity are constantly questioned, making it impossible for the figure of the poet to claim any privileged position within the alienated existence of mass culture. Although this poetry can be seen as an expression of a religious and ideological crisis, it never surrenders to any form of nihilistic resignation. Irony and social critique become instruments of strength and courage.

The publication of *I Novissimi* in 1961, including the work of Elio Pagliarani, Edoardo Sanguineti, Nanni Balestrini, Antonio Porta, Alfredo Giuliani, and edited by the latter, marks a turning point of Italian literary history in the latter half of the twentieth century. This provocative and revolutionary anthology was to open the way to the formation of the

Gruppo 63, a movement which was soon identified as the new Italian avant garde. In general terms, the five poets reject the normal linguistic code because of its reification and commercialization, and because of the conservative ideological implications it conveyed. The alternative language was to be that of ambiguity, estrangement, and disorder. The Novissimi showed aversion for symmetry and constructed texts dominated by rhythmic dissonances, temporal discontinuities, semantic distortions and syntactic dislocations that reveal the refusal of the sublime and of traditional and hackneyed principles of literature.

The blasphemous and subversive writing of the Novissimi, with its programmatic laceration and fragmentation of language, was a poetic project aimed at thwarting the reader's habitual horizon of expectations and engendering a crisis in the standard and worn out interpretative grammars of reality. As the locus of a defying and anarchic linguistic construct, poetry is conceived as a "schizomorphous vision." What matters is not what poetry says: it is the perturbing effects on the reader caused by the formal ruptures that constitute new messages, new ways of establishing contact.

In Giuliani's case, poetry is totally guided by the desire to explore the inner movements of language. However, paradoxically, he soon realizes that the proliferation of images without beginning or end, the vertiginous verbal adventure, is a constant reminder of the impossibility of arresting the flux, of finding reassuring linguistic crystallization. Language's vitality coincides with its own annihilation. The continuous movement from one image to another cannot but effect the dissolution of any possible unity. Poetry is torn between presence and absence, voice and silence, between the search for an authentic reality free from a priori schemes of perception and the insurmountable mediation of language. There is no access to direct, primordial awareness. There seems to be no escape from the prison house of language.

Giuliani aims at reducing the linguistic sign to pure movement, to action, gestural invention — not the arbitrary entity that replaces or represents as a double, as a mirror, objective reality (see for example *Povera Juliet* and *Chi l'avrebbe detto*). The aesthetic matrix of this operation includes the theatre of Artaud, the Living Theatre, Dadaistic experiments, Cage's music. Closed in its verbal space, poetry reveals for Giuliani a dualistic movement: the orgiastic vigor of the linguistic sign and the solitary void of its narcissistic nature. In a psychotic delirium, his characters, as half human creatures, move in a surreal labyrinth populated by tailed howling embryos, fizzy corpses, and worms with swollen feet. In this world dumped with excrement only meaningless rituals and onanistic acts are performed: nature no longer exists (the corporeal and the primordial are presented in the form of a tragic impossibility to ground ourselves in nature).

Another central figureof Gruppo 63 is undoubtedly Edoardo Sanguineti. At the base of Sanguineti's poetics lies the postulate that literature is in its essence a metalinguistic production of ideologies. He argues that a writer's form of language is his ideology and that poetry "is not in the service of the revolution, but *is* the revolution at the level of words"(*Ideologia e linguaggio*,133). Influenced by the thought of the Frankfurt School (by Adorno in particular), Sanguineti aims at bringing to its limits the experimentation initiated by the historical avant garde. In his case, the project of formal disorder expresses the denunciation of the false harmonies and reconciling modes of bourgeois writing, the function of which is to conceal alienation and social contradictions.

The linguistic disorder manifests itself in Sanguineti's poetry as a pathological language, as an objective representation of social alienation relived from the inside, on the page. Sanguineti's first collection, *Laborintus* (written in 1954) represents the most radical break of that period from the tradition of Hermetic and Neo-realistic literary models. It portrays the descent into a historical hell, into the stinking swamp of capitalist alienation in which one's conscience is lost in the falsity of bourgeois ideologies. Through a Dantean journey into the psychological and social chaos of contemporary reality, Sanguineti transcribes a delirious "mental collapse" with the intent of resolving the "complicatio" into a liberating, therapeutic process. What makes *Laborintus* a modern epic of the alienated and neurotic state of mind is the fact that such a condition is represented by form itself, an abnormal, dismembered, quasi aphasic language often made up of shredded words or clusters of solitary phonemes.

Sanguineti's collections (*Erotopaegnia, Wirrwarr*) are mostly constructed as plurilinguistic, asyntactic, and anarchic montages which recall Pound's *Cantos*. One of Sanguineti's objectives was that of bridging the gap between the traditional and exhausted language of Italian poetry and the innovative expressions reached in the other arts. The atonality and dissonances of his texts are a poetic equivalent of the disharmonizing elements present in dodecaphonic music or action painting. In other collections such as *Stracciafoglio*, poetry becomes a medium of derision and self derision, a language of destruction and self destruction. Sanguineti is inevitably confronted with an insurmountable paradox: as a bourgeois superstructure, poetry must be sabotage, but the task of sabotage is assigned to poetry itself.

Also Antonio Porta reaches radical moments of experimentation. In the early 60s he advances a conception of poetry as a discourse reduced to zero: the reduction of language to zero as negation of present reality and as tension awaiting new and liberating conditions of existence. A case in point is the experiment entitled *Zero*, in which the verbal signs, freed from syntactic constrictions and rhythmic recurrences, bring to life a montage of disconnected perceptions, a disquieting and crumbling world. This experiment aims at destroying the pseudo-rational order of daily communication and creates a poetic language that is comparable to the magmatic effects reached by Abstract Expressionism.

Porta's initial experiments (*La palpebra rovesciata*, 1960, *Aprire*,1964, *I rapporti*, 1966) feature a visual approach to reality and the reduction of the "I," a phenomenological bracketing of one's subjectivity. Porta constructs an apparently impassive montage of traumatic external events which present hallucinating and schizoid characters, nightmarish and sadomasochistic encounters verging on the absurd and the surreal. Reminiscent of Beckett's representations or of the deforming Expressionism practiced by painters such as Beckmann and Bacon, Porta's texts are marked by a fragmented narration that produces a state of suffocating alienation, a tragic vision of existence inevitably dominated by cruelty, death, and social atrocities.

Pagliarani's linguistic pluralism and syntactical fractures show a clear predisposition toward open forms and experimentation. However, from the beginning of his career Pagliarani had a tendency toward the epic narrative voice, which often embraces political and ideological content in a straightforward way. This aspect connects his production (in particular *La ragazza Carla*) to the canons of realism and to the *Officina* group.

Balestrini, on the other hand, takes to the extreme the revolt of the Novissimi against conventional linguistic codes and traditional modes of writing. In a world in which capitalism has reduced language to commodity, Balestrini finds it mystifying and self-defeating to search for any form of poetry as an authentic expression of the self. His poetry instead can be defined as a series of neo-dadaist collages obtained by a cut-and-paste technique which assembles together the most disparate fragments of linguistic messages that seem to communicate the loss of all meaning. It must be said, however, that language becomes the subject of its own operation and it takes on the task of recovering new possibilities of meaning. In pursuing this reduction of the self, Balestrini is one of the first in Italy to practice a form of electronic poetry obtained with the use of a computer. The texts "Tape Mark I" and "Mark II" (*Come si agisce*), which present a devastating vision of the first atomic bomb, are generated by an IBM computer program by randomly selecting material from works by Lao-Tsu, Michihiko Hachiya, and Paul Goldwin.

Women poets who were deeply involved with the new Italian avant-garde are Amelia Rosselli, Giulia Niccolai. Rosselli, in fact, was an active participant in the formation of the Gruppo 63. Rosselli's poetry, with its semantic displacements and asyntactical structures, presents an hallucinatory exploration of the psyche often on the verge of a mental breakdown. Passions, desires, expressions of love, or emotional sufferings manifest themselves with such an explosive force that cannot support the adoption of a rational and linear discourse. In her journeys into the unconscious, Rosselli's poetry cannot depart from a linguistic transgression and a narrative fragmentation as the only way (as for instance in *Variazioni belliche* and *Serie ospedaliera*) of documenting the inevitable lacerations of the self. The results are inventive and unsettling. In contrast, Giulia Niccolai is a proponent of the poetry of nonsense, aligning herself with other poets like Milli Graffi and Toti Scialoja. With a transgressive playfulness, Niccolai searches for unusual linguistic associations and analogies. Collections such as *Greenwich* and *Russky Salad Ballads & Webster Poems*, are full of puns, etymological nuances, and multi-lingual pastiches. The intent is to liberate language from stereotypes and fossilization by reactivating its polysemic possibilities. Niccolai is able to create an ironic, absurd and whimsical poetic space that constantly seeks to provoke movements and shifts in our conventional perceptions of the world. (Another woman poet close to the Gruppo 63 is Patrizia Vicinelli; in the sixties and seventies, she was very active with experiments of sound and visual poetry.)

A poet who was influenced by the Hermetic modes at the start of his career, but was later deeply affected by the experimentation of the sixties generation, is Andrea Zanzotto. Through his poetry Zanzotto aspires to rediscover an authentic subject, a union of signification and being, existence and essence. As for Heidegger, poetry becomes an activity for listening to language and for seeking access to being through language. This poetics is mediated by Lacanian psychoanalysis, according to which the world of language creates the world of things. In Zanzotto (e.g. collections such as *La beltá, Pasque* and *Il galateo in bosco*) the manipulation and association of signifiers aim at liberating repressed material. It is the signifier that establishes the point of contact with the unconscious. Entangled in the threads of a chain constituted by free-flowing signifiers that can never come to a standstill, the self experiences the signifieds always as an absence. This is why Zanzotto's poetry is suspended between emptiness and desire for fullness, as it moves through slippage, the uncontrollable proliferation of signifiers, always more fleeting and ungraspable. This poet's search for an ultimate signification through the stratification of language leads to a state of incessant existential questioning.

Another important experimental poet of the sixties is Edoardo Cacciatore. His poetry (see for example, *La restituzione*) presents a philosophical slant through provocative linguistic montages. Obsessive alliterations and other homophonic reverberations often create hallucinatory and absurd visions that seem to relate the senselessness of our everyday experiences. However, one soon realizes that Cacciatore's poetry is guided by a cognitive tension that aspires to find an ontological message behind objects and events. However, no transcendence is ever possible and he is left with unrelated and apparently pointless actions, without the reassuring certainty of an atemporal truth. The events of our life-world are inevitably dominated by contingency and thus resistant to any form of totalized knowledge.

If the Novissimi aimed at destroying the conventional literary institutions without abandoning the linguistic medium, various other groups — although their methodologies vary widely — share the desire to overcome the limits of poetry as a strictly verbal form of communication, transforming it through iconographic and figurative compositions of numerous kinds.

The roots of the visual experimentation lie in the historical avant-gardes and in the works of previous experimental poets: Carlo Belloli, Emilio Villa, the "Noigandres" group, together with Gomringer, Max Bense, and others. At the same time, they take advantage of many new insights offered by the development of structural linguistics, information theory, and semiotics. Often classified as "visual writing," "new writing," or "verbal-visual poetry," this form of experimentation attracts a large number of groups whose work is centered around journals such as *Ana eccetera*, *Techne*, and *Lotta poetica*. It is possible, however, to distinguish three main trends: concrete, symbiotic, and technological poetry.

The concrete poetry of Arrigo Lora Totino, Mirella Bentivoglio, Adriano Spatola explores the material base of language and the graphic possibilities it can produce. This poetry communicates its own formal structure, generally establishing a homological relation between form and content. "Concrete poetry" — writes Lora Totino — "is an ideogram or a structured field of functions which relate to one another in all parts: graphic, spatial, oral, acoustic functions, as well as those pertaining to content" (Lora Totino, 45). In some cases, as in Spatola's series entitled *Zeroglifici*, the word explodes leaving behind only its own shards. Here, fragmented words, shattered syllables and phonemes are not only charged with ideological overtones but emphasize the materiality of language. This metalinguistic operation, on the one hand, de-semanticizes the verbal sign and, on the other, semanticizes it at an iconographic level. (For an overview of poets who conduct radical experiments with single words, phrases, or even isolated letters, see the anthology edited by Renato Barilli, *Viaggio al termine della parola*.)

The merging of poetic writing and visual codes is also pursued with different materials and techniques by the poets who can be grouped in the area of symbiotic writing in which various elements (phonetic, graphic, spatial, figurative, chromatic) interact, conditioning and modifying their ordinary meanings. The aim of Ugo Carrega and Vincenzo Accame is to go beyond the traditional boundaries of artistic communication, attempting a unified aesthetic act, embracing a form of "total poetry", a symbiosis of many different media.

The poets belonging to the Gruppo 70 (Lamberto Pignotti, Eugenio Miccini, Emilio Isgró, Lucia Marcucci, Luciano Ori, Michele Perfetti) make extensive use of extra-linguistic materials produced by the mass media (commercial photographs, advertisements, comic strips, photo romances and so on). Defined as technological poetry, this experimentation shifts the focus of poetry from an exclusively verbal practice toward a general art of the sign. This poetry is the result of a convergence of different codes of communication, which, by interacting, offer new possibilities of signification. The intent, however, is political and ideological. The materials of mass communication are constantly de-contextualized and de-mystified through the use of desecrating and provocative collages. It is a sort of semiological warfare against the consumerist messages of our age. The aim of the technological poet is to return to the sender — the consumer society — its own products, shattered and shredded. "Pieces of our technological world," writes Pignotti, "are taken apart, classified, reassembled, inverted: It is essential to understand the mechanisms which regulate them . . . . The result is comic-strip poetry, tabloid-poetry. Or, better said: counter comic-strip poetry, counter advertisement-poetry, counter tabloid-poetry. Forms and means of today's mass media are utilized and subverted at the same time" (*L'istruzione per l'uso*, 126). Two other poets of Gruppo 70, Miccini and Perfetti, claim that technological poetry is a "semiological transfiguration of all anthropological events of our times. It does not ignore its own civilization, it rejects it" (*Poesia e/o poesia*, 3-4).

Verbal and visual stereotypes are perceived as alienating and reified social products. Through techniques of irony, derangement and de-familiarization, these poets intend to practice an act of subversion against the commercial exploitation of the various means of communication. The intent is to unmask the rhetorical mechanisms concealed behind words and images together with their emotional and subliminal effects. Poetry becomes a political struggle which aims at developing a critical awareness capable of bringing about a cultural revolution charged with liberating effects.

The political and social unrest, which broke out in Italy and other parts of the world in 1968, had deep repercussions in the field of literature, particularly in poetry. The political commitment of the young generation of that time, its struggle for a new society, and its desire for an immediate revolution, threw literary discourse into serious crisis. An unexpected event, symptomatic of that time, was the demise of the Gruppo 63 in 1969. The breakdown of the neo-avanguardia was a strong indication of the new social realities. All energies suddenly shifted toward specific political issues. Praxis took over poiesis. Direct involvement in changing the world took the place of the literary word.

The movement of 1968, however, crumbled quickly, and the promise of a revolution soon began to vanish. What followed was a sense of profound disillusionment, a sense of void and political impotence. As a reaction, a literary model which rejects any form of ideological or political engagement begins to appear. We enter the years of the so-called "riflusso," a falling back on more traditional and conservative positions, characterized not only by the disintegration of a social project (with the consequent escape into the domain of the personal and the private) but also by the rejection of radical formal and stylistic innovations.

The publication of the anthology *Il pubblico della poesia* (edited by Alfonso Berardinelli and Franco Cordelli in 1975) confirms this new reality. In his introduction, Berardinelli maintains that "[it] is very difficult today to give life to ideological and literary projects and to sustain them" (15). And concerning the search for a new poetic language, he concludes, without hesitation, that "nothing clamorous can be detected concerning innovation, shock and openings toward a new horizon of poetic research" (21).

The works produced by the young poets, as another anthology, *La parola innamorata* (edited by Giancarlo Pontiggia and Enzo Di Mauro in 1978), would reveal a few years later, often present a mode of writing which closely recalls that of the symbolist movement. Orphic and visionary, oracular and cosmogonic, this poetry welcomes the collapse of rationality and ideology and grants privilege to the dimension of myth. As we witness a pervasive disintegration of all paradigms of reason, many young poets begin to embrace various forms of mysticism. Generally their mysticism takes the form of a search for an original, timeless vitality, the yearning for a return to a natural state of things, or the recovering of a primeval form of spontaneity. Rejecting a critical perspective on historical issues and, at the same time, a critical language capable of arousing tension, their poetry advocates a seductive poetic word, a word essentially in love only with itself. Devoid of a political and historical function, poetry is defined by the editors as "superfluous grace," "futile and irresponsible play," "a form of lightness," "an absolute vacuum" (18, 19). The anthology includes texts produced by the editors and by poets such as Giuseppe Conte, Maurizio Cucchi, Milo

De Angelis, Valerio Magrelli, and Cesare Viviani.

This poetry emerges in a cultural and intellectual context characterized by a strong interest in Nietzschean and Heideggerian philosophy, Lacanian psychoanalysis, and the explosion of Deconstruction. In these perspectives, there is no ground for truth, for the "self" or for a collective sociopolitical project. All seems to signal the collapse of a unitary, ultimate meaning in history and the impossibility of referentiality. In this general tendency, every form of writing is placed within the domain of rhetoric. Poetry cannot escape such a destiny and is forced to abandon all epistemological claims. As Pontiggia and Di Mauro maintain, poetry "does not have any revelations, it does not have any truth to exhibit." And they quickly add: "is there anything at all behind a mask that is not another mask?" (15)

The concept of a subject, of a unitary "self," is dissolved by many of these young poets (the subject is groundless in so far as it results from linguistic and symbolic structures which transcend it). In an influential statement of poetics, Viviani (a poet who, in many respects, is rather different from the rest of the group) affirms that "the subject ... has begun to dismantle its defences, to come out from preconstituted and egocentric certainties ... the hidden thrusts of desire and many other impulses emerge, reality is multiplied, the subject is de-centred" (11-12). Indeed, the de-centred subject often becomes a non-locus, a purely linguistic or symbolic construction. As a result, the origin of signification does not reside in an individual consciousness but is motivated only by the endless play of the signifiers. Or, as in the case of Cucchi, the subject's inability to place the events in an order or perspective gives rise to a dispersion which reveals a neo-crepuscular vein.

Liberated from the control of the subject, to which traditionally was assigned the function of guiding and grounding a discourse, language does no longer perform a mimetic operation, it ceases to be employed as an instrumental medium and becomes a labyrinth in which all directions are lost as the signifiers trigger an infinite dissemination of signification. This is clearly evidenced in Viviani's collections *Ostrabismo cara* and *Piumana* where we witness the return of repressed linguistic acts — slips of the tongue, anomalous inversions and permutations of phonemes, continuous displacements of meaning — which all contribute to create a sort of oneiric writing.

It is not only psychoanalysis to function as a stimulus for these poetics. They also reveal affinities with Michel Foucault's research on the relation between power and subject, authority and the practices of social interdiction of discourses. In fact, the distancing from the centrality of the subject is interpretable as a possibility of bracketing the dominant models of western civilization. This process, in turn, should enable the repressed and the marginalized to come to surface (i.e. the bodily and instinctual urges, the otherness, the spontaneous desires). From this perspective, a decisive catalyst is represented by the encounter of the young poets with Nietzsche's thought which undergoes, particularly in the 1970s and 80s, a significant reevaluation. The young poets, on the one hand, are attracted by Nietzsche's unmasking and de-empowerment of the subject, together with his aversion toward civilization and social constrictions and, on the other, they are seduced by his Dionysian dimension — the lightness and elation of being, the drives of the vital instincts, the free flow of nature's forces. It must be pointed out, however, that the new poetics inevitably reveal an image of Nietzsche cleansed of the iconoclastic fury and the destructive force of his thought, preferring to explore the territories of myth and orphism.

A case in point is represented by Giuseppe Conte's poetry and poetics. For Conte, poetic language must take on the function of bringing us closer to the "primitive force of chaos through the abolition and the deviant use of the process of repression in which culture and 'civilization' are grounded" (*Le istituzioni*, 56). Conte is against the foundations of the Hebrew, Platonic, and Christian thought, responsible, according to him, for the destruction of human rapport with the body, eros, and nature. In a Nietzschean mode he longs for the return to a primeval energy of existence and to a Dionysian form of vitalism. Poetry must transform itself into a force capable of restoring, in Conte's words, "the desire to break the knots of civilization and to reestablish the inebriation of life-energy, of bodies' diffused love, of dreams about the continuous rebirth of oneself" ("La forma del fuoco," 32). In the context of this poetics, poetry is transformed into a form of dance, a ritual capable of reactivating the fire of Eros and allowing us to hear the distant echoes of ancient mysteries. All possibilities of a rational re-encounter with the world have forever collapsed. Any project guided by rationality or ideology is considered an expression of a "lager" or a "gulag." As a result, poetry must become the space where the sacred and the savage, the divine and the original can reappear.

As a consequence of the failure to establish a social Eden — the shattered hopes of the 1968 revolts is the most revealing aspect of this situation — poetry attempts the conquest of a private Eden identifying it with nature, the universe, and love. Presuming that reason is now a total wreck, these poets embrace a mystical vitalism, the myth of the origin and the idea of savage spontaneity. Myth dissolves history and denies the concept of consciousness as a historical process (history is reduced to groundless tropes, figures without real events). In the introduction to the aforesaid anthology, Giancarlo Pontiggia and Enzo Di Mauro, as two Rimbaudean neo-seers, cry out: "Take history away from me, otherwise how can I begin anew?" (15)

One of the other major poetic trends of the seventies is represented by feminist poetry. The anthology *La poesia femminista italiana*, edited by Laura Di Nola in 1978, offers a significant point of reference. This poetry, centered around the themes prominent in feminism, expresses an urgency to give a poetic voice to women. It articulates discontent with a pervasively patriarchal civilization in which a woman needs to liberate herself from internalized masculine constructs and phallocentric ideologies. This poetry cries for freedom, for the necessity to bring to light ancestral repressions and oppression. Poetry is utilized as an instrument of communication to emphasize contents rather than the search for new forms of expression. Usually prosaic and anti-lyrical, this poetry combines the urge for self-awareness with a didactic and political function. Besides the poetry of older poets (Dacia Maraini's *Donne mie* and Mariella Bettarini's *Rivoluzione copernicana* represent two very significant cases), that of younger poets such as Marta Fabiani, Silvia Batisti, and Livia Candiani can be related to this feminist model.

The political and ideological force of the feminist movement activated, at the same time, the view of approaching poetry from a gender oriented discourse which ultimately turned into a debate around the specific identity of a feminine poetic writing. The anthology *Donne in poesia* (edited by Bincamaria Frabotta) is one of the most significant results of this perspective and debate. It provides a selection of women poets representing various generations, from Maria Luisa Spaziani and Margherita Guidacci to Rossana Ombres, Patrizia Cavalli, and Mariella Bettarini. Patrizia Valduga (a younger poet whose collections, such as *Medicamenta* and *La tentazione*, start to appear in the early 1980s) merges the search for a female identity with an engaging revisitation of old stylistic modes drawn from the poetic tradition.

Around the end of the eighties new poetic trends seem to emerge. They are represented by the poets grouped in the anthology *Poesia italiana della contraddizione* (edited by Franco Cavallo and Mario Lunetta in 1989) and by the young poets (in many cases born from the end of the fifties through the beginning of the sixties) who gave life in 1990 to the journal *Baldus*. With a clear allusion to the Neoavanguardia, the new movement has been named Gruppo 93; it consists of poets such as Biagio Cepollaro, Mariano Baino, Lello Voce (all editors of *Baldus*), Tommaso Ottonieri, Marcello Frixione, Lorenzo Durante, and Gabriele Frasca. Although some of the poets distance themselves from the group, they all seem to express the urge to shift toward a new form of poetry that pursues a fusion of disparate stylistic registers and languages (standard Italian, dialects, slang). In most cases, poetry seems to regain a critical and socially corrosive voice by becoming a defiant tool of everyday common sense communication. (Some of these poets have been grouped in an anthology that explores the possibility of a new "wave" of avant-garde poetry in Italy, *Terza ondata*, edited by Filippo Bettini and Roberto Di Marco). In the search for innovation, it should also be mentioned the intersemiotic poetry of a poet such as Enzo Minarelli who, with his "polipoesia," pursues a total poetic experience, multimedia synaesthetic performances that involve writing, sound, image and other sensory effects (for a theoretical orientation of his performances, see *Vocalitá & poesia*).

Among the younger poets there can be added the names of Paolo Gentiluomo (*Novene irresistibili*), Alessandra Berardi (see texts such as "Penelope nel Peloponneso", in Barilli, Ottonieri eds., *L'anello che non tiene*, which includes a selection of a number of young poets), Nadia Cavalera (by the latter, see *Brogliasso*; she is the editor of the poetry journal *Bollettario*). Generally for them, any new possibility of invention can take place only starting from the verbal forms. There emerges a sort of neo-baroque inventiveness, an hyper-semantization of the word pursued through philological investigations, ironic intertextuality, transgression and parody of genres, etymological games, obsessive and playful phonetic reverberations, the use of acrostic, abecedarius and innumerable other devises.

This mode of writing, as that of some of the poets included in *Terza ondata*, generally moves away from mimetic conceptions and advocates a view of poetry as a project centered around language. Deformation and displacement become the generative process of meaning. Poetry is a journey into the flesh of the word, into its material base with the intent to open up new paths of signification. As a disruptive and deviant force, it jolts the imagination and puts in motion new cognitive dimensions. It is an extreme effort to think the unthought and to design new cartographies of unchartered individual and collective subjectivities. The primacy of the signifier pushes the linguistic code to its limits. The boundaries of conventional language are viewed as a barrier to be surmounted for opening a passageway to new possible worlds.

WORKS CITED

Balestrini, Nanni. *Come si agisce*. Milan: Feltrinelli, 1963.

Barilli, Renato. Viaggio al termine della parola. *La ricerca intraverbale*. Milan: Feltrinelli, 1981.

Barilli, Renato and Ottonieri, Tommaso (eds.).*L'anello che non tiene. Sui limini della nuova enunciazione poetica*. Reggio Emilia: Elytra, 1992.

Berardinelli, Alfonso and Cordelli, Franco (eds.). *Il pubblico della poesia*. Milan: Lerici, 1975.

Bettarini, Mariella. *La rivoluzione copernicana*. Rome: Trevi, 1970.

Bettini, Filippo and Di Marco, Roberto (eds.). *Terza ondata. Il nuovo movimento della scrittura in Italia*. Bologna: Synergon, 1993.

Cacciatore, Edoardo. *La restituzione*. Florence: Vallecchi, 1955.

Cavalera, Nadia. *Brogliasso*. Modena: Gheminga, 1992.

Cavallo, Franco and Lunetta, Mario (eds.) *Poesia italiana della contraddizione*. Rome: Newton Compton, 1989.

Conte, Giuseppe. "Le istituzioni del desiderio." *Il Verri*, 2, 1976.

_____"La forma del fuoco: la visione e la conoscenza della poesia," in Kemeny, Tomaso and Viviani, Cesare (eds.). *I percorsi della nuova poesia*. Naples: Guida, 1980.

Di Nola, Laura (ed.). *La poesia femminista italiana*. Rome: Savelli, 1978.

Erba, Luciano. *Il male minore*. Milan: Mondadori, 1960.

Frabotta, Biancamaria (ed.).Donne mie. *Antologia della poesia italiana dal dopoguerra ad oggi*. Rome: Savelli, 1976.

Gentiluomo, Paolo. *Novene irresistibili*. Cosenza: Periferia, 1995.

Giudici, Giovanni. *La vita in versi*. Milan: Mondadori, 1965.

Giuliani, Alfredo (ed.). *I Novissimi. Poesie per gli anni '60*. Milan: Rusconi e Paolazzi, 1961; Turin: Einaudi, 1965.

_____*Povera Juliet, e altre poesie*. Milan: Feltrinelli, 1965.

_____ *Chi l'avrebbe detto*. Turin: Einaudi, 1973.

Lora Totino, Arrigo. "*Poesia concreta*," *Presenza Sud*, 1, 1968.

Luzi, Mario. *Quaderno gotico*. Florence: Vallecchi, 1947.

_____ *Primizie nel deserto*. Milan: Schwarz, 1952.

Maraini, Dacia. *Donne mie*. Turin: Einaudi, 1974.

Miccini, Eugenio (ed.). *Poesia e/o poesia*. Brescia-Florence: Sarmic, 1972.

Minarelli, Enzo. *Vocalitá & poesia*. Reggio Emilia: Elytra, 1995.

Montale, Eugenio. *Ossi di seppia*. Turin: Gobetti, 1925.

_____ *Le occasioni*. Turin: Einaudi, 1939.

_____ *La bufera e altro*. Venice: Neri Pozza, 1956.

_____ *Satura*. Milan: Mondadori, 1971.

_____ *Diario del '71 e del '72*. Milan: Mondadori, 1973.

_____ *Quaderni di quattro anni*. Milan: Mondadori, 1977.

Niccolai, Giulia. *Greenwich*. Turin: Geiger, 1971.

_____ *Russky Salad Ballads & Webster Poems*. Turin: Geiger, 1977.

Pagliarani, Elio. *La ragazza Carla e altre poesie*. Milan: Mondadori, 1962.

Pasolini, Pier Paolo. *Le ceneri di Gramsci*. Milan: Garzanti, 1957.

_____ *La religione del mio tempo*. Milan: Garzanti, 1961.

Pavese, Cesare. *Lavorare stanca*. Florence: Solaria, 1936; Turin: Einaudi, 1943.

Penna, Sandro. *Appunti*. Milan: La Meridiana, 1950.

_____ *Una strana gioia di vivere*. Milan: Scheiwiller, 1956.

Pignotti, Lamberto. *Istruzioni per l'uso degli ultimi modelli di poesia*. Milan: Lerici, 1968.

Pontiggia, Giancarlo and Di Mauro, Enzo (eds.). *La parola innamorata*. Milan: Feltrinelli, 1978.

Porta, Antonio. *Zero. Poesie visive*. Milan: 1963; now in *I rapporti*.

_____ *La palpebra rovesciata*. Milan: Azimuth, 1960.

_____ *Aprire*. Milan: All'insegna del Pesce d'Oro, 1964.

_____ *I rapporti*. Milan: Feltrinelli, 1966.

Quasimodo, Salvatore. *Giorno dopo giorno*. Milan: Mondadori, 1947.

_____ *La vita non é sogno*. Milan: Mondadori, 1949.

_____ *Il falso e vero verde*. Milan: Mondadori, 1956.

Risi, Nelo. *Pensieri elementari*. Milan: Mondadori, 1961.

Rosselli, Amelia. *Variazioni belliche*. Milan: Garzanti, 1964.

_____ *Serie ospedaliera*. Milan: Il Saggiatore, 1969.

Sanguineti, Edoardo. *Laborintus*. Varese: Magenta, 1956.

_____ *Erotopaegnia*. Milan: Rusconi e Paolazzi, 1961.

_____ "La letteratura della crudeltá" [1967], in *Ideologia e linguaggio*. Milan: Feltrinelli,1970.

_____ *Wirrwarr*. Milan: Feltrinelli, 1972.

_____ *Stracciafoglio*. Milan: Feltrinelli, 1980.

Sereni, Vittorio. *Diario d'Algeria*. Florence: Vallecchi, 1947.

_____ *Gli strumenti umani*. Turin: Einaudi, 1965.

Spatola, Adriano. *Zeroglifici*. Bologna: Sanpietro, 1966.

Ungaretti, Giuseppe. *Sentimento del tempo*. Florence: Vallecchi, 1933.

_____ *La terra promessa*. Milan: Mondadori, 1950.

_____ *Il taccuino del vecchio*. Milan: Mondadori, 1960.

Valduga, Patrizia. *Medicamenta*. Milan: Guanda, 1982.

_____ *La tentazione*. Milan: Crocetti, 1985.

Viviani, Cesare. Introduzione, in Kemeny, Tomaso and Viviani Cesare. *Il movimento della poesia italiana negli anni settanta*. Bari: Dedalo, 1979.

———— *Ostrabismo cara*. Milan: Feltrinelli, 1973.
———— *Piumana*. Milan: Guanda, 1977.
Zanzotto, Andrea. *La beltà*. Milan: Mondadori, 1968.
———— *Pasque*. Milan: Mondadori, 1978.
———— *Il galateo in bosco*. Milan: Mondadori, 1978.

RINALDINA RUSSELL

Coming of Age: An Overview of Women's Writing in Italy in the Last Half Century.

In the last fifty years of Italian history, Italian women writers have moved from a position of intellectual dependency and marginality into a new order of independence and professional responsibility. This progression, which I call the "coming of age," can be delineated in brief by referring to the links that connected women's literary practice to the changes occurring in the writing of male authors, and, with good cause, to the prevailing political, intellectual, and economic situation. In a country that moved rapidly, through protracted periods of political and social turbulence, from a pre- to a post-industrial economy, it is not surprising to see that major socio-cultural shifts have also taken place. Women's cultural activity has been part of this evolution, both as causal factor and as a result of it.

As Italy became an important partner in the European economy, its society moved away from traditional, inward-looking attitudes and customs to become more sensitive to cultural, religious, and gender differences. Once a country that considered emigration as a viable solution to its economic and social problems, it now witnessed a rapid flow of immigrants from all parts of the globe converge on its shores. Also, by the end of the century all of the country's religions had become equal before the law, while innovative social legislation regulated the work-place and a new family code reshaped intimate relationships. Unavoidably, intellectual and literary life underwent significant transformations as well. Since the advent of Fascism, Italian literature had been conditioned by political considerations; even in the war aftermath, literary creativity had been channeled into specific directions outlined by the dominant political intelligentsia. In a decade or so, however, a new affluent society and shifts in international alliances displaced the old socioeconomic polarization, rendering traditional political allegiances irrelevant. As a consequence, the link between politics and literary ideology became less obvious and less binding, and, for the first time, Italian writers found themselves alone having to negotiate a large variety of theoretical positions and literary forms coming from other European countries. Within this postmodern context of numerous, possible choices, women writers had become a very visible presence.

The connection between women's intellectual progress and their political and financial situation is also important to note. The general rise in family income made the access of daughters to higher education a collective reality, freeing a great number of young women from the mental restrains that had thwarted their mothers' and grandmothers' existence. At the end of the sixties, while literary men tended to become silent politically, feminists began to agitate for their civil rights and to advocate an openly interventionist type of literature. The pivotal point of their revolutionary program was expressed in the disquieting slogan "the personal is political, the private — the ultimate domain of publicly dispossessed men — is the public," and as such — women maintained — it had to be politically and publicly negotiated. What quickly became more disconcerting for older men was that feminist activism, with at first an undecided but in the end effective support of the left-wing parties, brought about momentous social reforms destined to reorient the life and mind of all Italians. Other social and cultural factors were also at work. As literary enclaves lessened their grip on editorial policies, the importance of male patronage for women became less decisive. At the same time, the much deprecated commercialism of the publishing industry, while limiting the effectiveness and authority of male intellectuals, meant for women better chances of publication and easier access to the reading public, which by now was relatively larger and comprised a higher percentage of female readers. The changes that marked women's writing can be schematically presented in three main stages, each distinguished by specific intellectual and literary assumptions, and ultimately leading to the self-assurance and independence of thought and choices that informs their current literary practice.

In the early 1950s, the ideologies of the political left and the poetics of neo-realism were a dominant force in Italian letters. The left-wing parties, which spearheaded the opposition to the Fascist regime and to the Nazi occupation in 1943-1945, endeavored to bring about a new political awareness and, drawing theoretical support from the writings of Antonio Gramsci, encouraged the creation of a literature at once 'national' and 'popular.' In the way the narratives of some women writers engaged moral and social issues, they could be seen to converge in such a plan. Among those women who left a record of partisan warfare in northern Italy were Ada Gobetti, who published a *Diario partigiano* (1956, The Diary of a Partisan), and Cesira Fiori who, in 1965, authored *Una donna nelle carceri fasciste* (A Woman in Fascist Prisons); while in *Deviazione* (1979), Luce d'Eramo related her experience in a concentration camp, just as Liana Millu had done in 1947 with *Il fumo di Birkenau* (*Smoke Over Birkenau*, 1991). But the narrative that most successfully applied the neo-realist model of populist epic was Renata Viganò's *L'agnese va a morire* (1946, Agnes Goes Out to Die). This is the story of a peasant woman who, after her husband's death at the hands of the Germans, slowly awakens to political consciousness, decides to throw her lot with the partisans, and finally one day, fully aware of the risks she is confronting, starts out on a mission from which she will not return. Descriptions of guerrilla organization and resistance[1] dovetail with the main story, and the gulf between the intellectual author and the inarticulate protagonist, which remained prominent in men's novels, is here bridged by the female narrator.

A fiction writer whose social conscience and subject matter could be neatly assimilated to the poetics of neo-realism was Laudomia Bonanni. An elementary school teacher in the remote areas of the Abruzzi mountains, Bonanni attained literary acclaim in 1954 with *Palma e le sorelle* (Palma and Her Sisters), to be followed by *L'imputata* (1960, The Accused), *Il bambino di pietra* (1979, The Stone Child) and *Le droghe* (1982, Drugs): all stories of poor women and children victimized by family and society in times of both war and peace. Another woman whose writing also seems at first to fall into the prescriptive parameters of neo-realism was Anna Maria Ortese (1914-1998). Her 1953 book *Il mare non bagna Napoli* (*The Bay is not Naples*, 1955) consists of four tales set in the poor quarters of Naples, while a fifth segment of the volume exposes the political disillusionment and conformism of what, in the aftermath of the war, had been a group of idealistic journalists. Ortese's pronounced sensibility for people sacrificed by the egotism of others was confirmed in her following books, of which *L'iguana* (1965, The Iguana) and *Il cardillo addolorato* (1993, The Grieving Finch) are best known. However, an unmotivated abundance of details, and many dream-like sequences, made her narratives difficult to grasp for critics and public alike. Despite their sustained literary output, Ortese and Bonanni remained on the fringes of Italian literature. Such was the case also of Livia de Stefanis, an aristocrat from Palermo, whose interest in both Greek tragedy and in the immutable structure of moral and mental degradation did not conform to the principle of political and moral advancement championed by Elio Vittorini, then the most authoritative Sicilian writer of the period.

At the time, and continuing through the 1970s, the literary limelight was shared by a few outstanding women novelists associated with influential literary magazines and intellectual circles. Gianna Manzini (1896-1974) contributed in the 1930s to the reviews *Solaria* and *Letteratura*, and maintained a relationship with the literary critic Enrico Falqui. Subscribing to the endeavor to bring Italian fiction within the sphere of the European experimental novel, Manzini produced, and continued to produce in the following decades, lyrical, stream-of-consciousness narratives, characterized by continuous change and analogy. Natalia Levi Ginzburg (1916-1991), born into a politically active family of Turin and married first to Leone Ginzburg, a socialist intellectual slain by the Nazis, and later to Antonio Baldini, a prominent literary historian, worked for many years as an editor for the prestigious publisher Einaudi. Her stories — among them *Tutti i nostri ieri* (1952, All Our Yesterdays), *Valentino*, 1957, *Le voci della sera* (1961, Voices of the Evening), *Caro Michele* (1973, Dear Michael) — exhibit a subdued realistic vein in their description of people beset by emotional want and moral ambivalence. Trapped in loveless marriages and cultivating attachments that are either of questionable nature or destined to remain unrewarded, her characters often approach a point of crisis but then either renounce their quest for fulfillment or find some form of routine accommodation. The shifting nature of family bonds is also the subject matter of Lalla Romano's novels. For decades a familiar figure in the artistic and intellectual scene of Milan, Romano's best known books, *La penombra che abbiamo attraversato* (1964, The Half-Light We Walked Across), *Le parole tra noi leggere* (1969, The Light Words We Exchanged) and *L'ospite* (1973, The Guest) are admired for their delicate touch in bringing mental and emotional states in and out of focus. Among these older writers, a most self-dramatizing personality is that of Elsa Morante (1918-1985). Born to poor Roman parents, and herself with little formal education, Morante was introduced to Roman literary circles, thanks to her successful children stories, and soon after became the wife of Alberto Moravia, the most prominent Italian novelist of the time. She gained critical acclaim with the publication of *Menzogna e sortilegio*, 1948 (*The House of Liars*, 1950), which was confirmed, ten years later, by *L'isola di Arturo* (*Arturo's Island*, 1959). Morante's consistent theme, the contrast between individual needs and the bitter facts of life, is carried into the context of the Second World War and given apocalyptic overtones in *La storia*, 1974 *(History: a Novel*, 1977). This long novel provided a fruitful field of historiographical investigation for feminist critics, as I shall mention, but in the volatile political atmosphere of the 1970s, the open, passionately ideological thrust of the narrative sparked a heated debate in regard to its literary value. While some hailed the book as a masterpiece, others were dissatisfied by what looked like the cynical exploitation of many sympathy-inspiring elements, as man-induced horrors and uncontrollable misfortunes are piled on the innocent and simple-minded protagonists, a half-Jewish teacher and her epileptic son, born from her being raped by a German soldier, and on their loyal dog, fiendishly shot in the end by the Nazi police.

A small number of women poets were also enjoying the critical recognition of prominent literary figures. Up to the moment of her death in 1977, Cristina Campo basked in the devoted admiration of a closed circle of Florentine poets and critics. With them she shared the hermetic notion of poetry as *raptus* to be experienced voluptuously through progressively deeper visionary states of being. Her verse, characterized by a high ritualistic tone and by intertextual allusions — and, according to Guido Ceronetti, as incandescent as that of seventeenth-century mystics (Campo, 301) — came out in the sixties and seventies and was collected posthumously in *La tigre assenza* in 1991. Maria Luisa Spaziani, an authoritative presence to this day in Italian poetry, made her debut in the shade of the post-hermetic school and of Montale's mounting reputation. Her verse, high and sententious in tone and sumptuously elegant, maintained an encoded quality throughout in treating such themes as the passing of time, death, the deceptive and illusory character of memory, and the possibility of recovery through poetry and fame. Her best known collections are *Le acque del Sabato*, 1954, *Luna lombarda*, 1959, *Il gong*, 1962, *Utilità della memoria*, 1966, *L'occhio del ciclone*, 1970. In subsequent years, Spaziani's notion of the poet as prophet and keeper of cultural values will allow her to turn from the abstract quest of essential truths to a feminist stance in a manner consistent with her character and intellectual orientation. In *Donne in poesia* she presents a roster of women poets ignored by literary historians, and in the long hendecasyllabic poem, *Giovanna d'Arco*, 1990, she creates a larger-than-life heroine of free will and determination. Another important poet of the sixties and the seventies was Margherita Guidacci (1921-1992). Unique in those days for her directness and clarity of expression, Guidacci, a Catholic who believed in the ultimate salvation of all human beings, was profoundly committed to a crusade of awareness of and atonement for the ills and the suffering of the world.

Their optimistic belief in the cognitive value of poetry placed

Campo, Spaziani, and Guidacci several steps removed from the neo avant-garde, whose poets — referred to as the *Novissimi* — avowed, in opposition to neo-realism, a credo of political and philosophical negativism, overturning completely the relationship of intellectuals to literature and society. The motivation usually given for their attitude is one of disillusionment with left-wing politics and alienation from the commercialism of modern Italian society. Labeling all the then current forms of poetic communication as morally stagnant, these 'new poets' engaged in a revolutionary program of linguistic obstructionism aimed at destroying all syntactical and lexical coherence. Women writers, who in general had occupied marginal positions in Italian intellectual circles, remained aloof from such linguistic experimentation, the exceptions being Mariella Bettarini, Milli Graffi, and Anna Oberto.

There were, however, other women poets who, although not totally identifiable with the ideological premises of the neo avant-garde, produced remarkably original and innovative verse which is to some degree indebted to the experimentalism of the Novissimi. Amelia Rosselli (1930-1996) and Giulia Niccolai are such poets. Rosselli's verse ignored lexical, syntactical, morphological, and even graphic norms. Mixing Italian, English, and French, it created a phonic, rather than a semantic, field of signification, whose reverberations are uncannily suggestive. In *Variazioni belliche* (1964, War Variations), *Serie ospedaliera* (1969, Hospital Series), and in her earlier poems collected in the *Antologia poetica*, of 1987, Rosselli creates a poetic discourse that moves on a vertical, rather than horizontal, axis to express the hallucinating reality of her inner self. By contrast, Giulia Niccolai's poetry exhibits good humor and wit, with a good measure of postmodern playfulness. Nonsense, puns, and allusions to an ever present ambiguity of meaning, suggest a reality in which sense and meaning are not found but constructed by the subject (West 1994, 303-304). Equally innovative, although more attuned to the more litigious strains of contemporary feminism, is the poetry of Iolanda Insana. Her aggressively contentious attitude is conveyed in a grotesque and abusive language, characterized by a mixture of Italian, Latin, Greek, and Sicilian words. Published under the significant titles of *Sciarra amara* (1977, Bitter Brawl), *Fendenti fonici* (1988, Phonic Slashes), *Il collettame* (1985, Collected Refuse), and *La clausura,* (1987, A Cloistered Existence), her poems revealed a persistent disquiet, due to conflict within the self, and between the self and the world. In the more recent *Medicina carnale* (1994, Carnal Medicine) and *L'occhio dormiente* (1997, The Sleeping Eye), Insana's aggressively emotional stance allows for a few moments of reprieve.

In all major Italian cities, the 1970s witnessed frequent student protest, strikes and street demonstrations, as well as disquieting episodes of terrorism and counter-terrorism. As the social agitation added to their disorientation, men writers looked to the psychoanalytic and philosophical theories of the decentered subject as justification for their non-commitment. The rejection of all representative functions of language that the neo-avant-garde in the early sixties had colored with political significance, now appeared to result from a general existential instability and from the intrinsic contradiction of all signifying acts. To women, however, the same political turmoil, together with an especially vociferous feminist movement, lent courage and innovative spirit. For the first time in history, Italian women were the spearhead of a social revolution that introduced the most radical reforms in Italy since the Counter Reformation. The establishment of divorce, the legalization of abortion, a new family code and extended civil rights would soon equalize the obligations of women and men in the family and in public life. This revolution would have profound (albeit different and often unconfessed) effects on the minds and behavior of present and future generations of Italians. The political momentum inspired women writers, strengthening their faith in the social and collective value of literature, which urged them to search for authoritative precedents in neo-realism and in nineteenth-century feminist texts.

Again the genres best suited to the conscience-raising aims of literary activists proved to be memoirs, fictionalized chronicles, and semi-documentaries, narratives that would effectively describe women's constraints in public and private life, allowing them to re-define female identity independently of patriarchal conceptions of womanhood.

The feminists' primary concern was to alter the mentality that shaped society's attitudes toward women. Their objective was to make women aware that the progress achieved in personal and social relationships, as well as in writing, was impaired by their own internalization of the same male prejudices against which they fought. Among the texts that best served that purpose were Dacia Maraini's *Due donne da buttare* (1974, Two Disposable Women) by Armanda Guiducci (1923-1992) and *Memorie di una ladra* (1972, *Memoirs of a Thief,* 1974). In a form that mixed the conventions of fiction, autobiography, reportage, and sociological tract, these books exposed all the motives that preserved and safeguarded women's exploitation in the family and society. From the 1970s to this day, many texts have been published that explore social phenomena and areas of experience previously ignored, providing valuable information on the history of Italian women. Giuliana Morandini's *E allora mi hanno rinchiusa* (1977, And So They Locked Me Up) is a collection of shocking stories of women committed to insane asylums. In *Vecchi* (1994, Old People), Sandra Petrignani investigates hospices, clinics and social centers, uncovering human fragility at all ages. In *Manicomio primavera* (1989, Spring-Time Asylum), Clara Sereni tells stories of wardens faced with the practical and ethical problem of balancing the care for others with the care of themselves. In *Mi riguarda* (1994, It Concerns Me) and in its sequel *Si può!* (1996, We can!), she deals with the difficulties encountered in society by the handicapped. Besides being conscience-raising narratives, these writings also contain compelling descriptions of personal confrontations with the suffering world.

The condition of women in middle class society was, since fascism, the concern of Alba de Céspedes. In a lucid and fluent style that eschewed the self-consciousness of contemporary literary prose, de Céspedes's stories addressed the alienation of women trapped in a patriarchal family and in politically and morally inert society. Solutions that could not be envisaged in the conservative climate of the forties and fifties were clearly suggested in the feminist narratives of the seventies and eighties. Emblematic of such a transition is again a work by Dacia Maraini, *Donna in guerra* (1975, *Woman at War*, 1988), a feminist Bildungsroman that charts the development of the main character from within a stifling bourgeois marriage to becoming a feminist protester who eventually rejects conventional gender constraints. But even if women authors did not participate directly in feminism, they displayed in their writings a new sensibility toward women's predicaments, and did so regardless of their political and literary beliefs. Gina Lagorio sets the lives of her female characters in unfamiliar and hostile cultural environments distant from their place of origin. Francesca Sanvitale, particularly responsive to issues of self-assertion and identity, has her protagonists confront problems of sex, love, and motherhood in a genteel middle class context. A most unusual book is Clara Sereni's *Casalinghitudine* (1987, Habits of House Wives). One hundred and five dishes prepared by the narrator for her husband and children at different stages of her life mediate her recollection of how her existence changed from one of essential separateness and dependency to one of autonomy and fulfillment, as wife, mother, and activist.

In *Quaderno proibito* (1952, Forbidden Notebook) Alba de Céspedes had also anticipated the much debated theme of women's subjectivity in relation to writing. Wife and mother living the drudgery of an existence thwarted by the demands of husband and children, de Céspedes's protagonist attempts to hold on to a separate identity by writing her thoughts in a secret diary. In the end, however, she is forced to renounce her furtive act and re-assumes the inarticulate role that her family expects of her. Women's estrangement from language and self-definition figured prominently in the repertoire of feminists in the 1970s and 1980s. The correlation of authorial voice and gender roles is the central theme of Dacia Maraini's epistolary novel *Lettere a Marina* (1981, Letters to Marina). This letter-writer discusses her relationship with her husband, family and a female lover, underlining the difficulties that she has in assuming an independent and distinctive voice, and arrives at the realization that her self-doubts are tied to her acceptance of the sexual and interpersonal roles imposed by others. Patriarchal restraints on women's bodies were also the focus of Armanda Guiducci's semi-autobiographical novel *La mela e il serpente* (1976, The Apple and the Snake). Noteworthy is also the attention given to the sexuality of children and adolescents by Elena Gianini Belotti, a teacher and essayist, who for twenty years was the director of the Montessori Center in Rome. Belotti received nation-wide attention in 1973 for her book length essay, *Dalla parte delle bambine* (On Behalf of Little Girls), which investigated the common attitudes toward sex and other prejudices that throughout the centuries have cramped women's lives. In *Ritratto di famiglia degli anni Ottanta* (1981, Family Portrait in the Eighties), Belotti analyzes the changes that have occurred in the Italian family in the aftermath of the new family code. Her first novel, *Il fiore dell'ibisco* (1985, The Hybiscus Flower), tells the story of a tender love between a young boy and an adult woman, while in *Amore e pregiudizio* (1988, Love and Prejudice) she critiques the representations of love and sex found in history, literature and film, while championing a woman's right to take on a younger partner and, like men, enjoy successive seasons of love. Women's sexual needs, consistently ignored by the elementary and coarse definitions of human eroticism that prevailed in official morality, are directly addressed in the novels of several other writers, as, for example, in Lidia Ravera's *Porci con le ali* (1976, Pigs With Wings), written in collaboration with Marco Lombardo Radice, and in Rossana Campo's *In principio erano le mutande* (1992, In the Beginning There Was Underwear). Truly remarkable, this last work describes the mental longing and sexual fancies of a young woman who at the very end of the narrative turns out to be the person who is writing. Particularly noteworthy is Campo's use of language which exhibits an unusual representational power in reproducing the sociolinguistic context of southern immigrant families transplanted into the slums of the industrial north.

After years dedicated to promoting women's progress in numerous essays, stories, and plays, Dacia Maraini obtained full critical recognition in the 1990s with the publication of *La lunga vita di Marianna Ucria* (*The Silent Duchess*, 1992), a novel which exemplifies the sought-after fusion of ideology and art. Set in eighteenth-century Sicily, it tells the story of a deaf-mute woman who, by various self-taught ways of communicating as well as by writing, is able to overcome the restrictions imposed on her by her physical handicap and by an abusive family system.

Underlying the representation of Marianna Ucria's mutism was the assumption, held by both French and Italian feminists, that psychoanalytic discourse legitimatizes the de-facto banishment of women to silence. The problem was then how to define a theoretical space from which women could speak and achieve autonomy. Jacques Lacan's idea of the subject as a linguistic construct was in this regard useful to feminists. While providing a blueprint for women's alienation from the world of man, it also suggested a possible solution. If the language that objectifies women comes into being in the symbolic order of the father, as Lacan maintained, women purportedly could return to the pre-symbolic, 'imaginary' phase of existence in which they could ground their striving for identity and self-expression. Such a theme is articulated both theoretically and creatively in the writings of Bianca Maria Frabotta and Elisabetta Rasy. Rasy's first work, *La lingua della nutrice* (1978, The Language of the Foster-Mother — with a preface by Julia Kristeva) grapples with the conflict between a woman's need to gain access to language and her confinement to man's definition of her physical being. Years later, in *La prima estasi* (1985, The First Ecstasy) — a fictionalized biography of Saint Teresa of Lisieux — Rasy resolves that conflict mystically and in terms compatible with Martin Buber's *Ecstatic Confessions*. The access to language and the world is represented as a discontinuous process of initiation, generating moments of being that transcend ordinary experience, in which all is one and one is all, free of the principles of noncontradiction and the linear progression of conventional logic (Rasy 1992, 81). An analogous model for female identity was proposed by Anna Maria Frabotta. In her collection of poems *Il rumore bianco* (1982, White Noise), Frabotta posits a state of being as a presence that is at the same time an absence, whose contact with the world of ordinary signification gives way to the "white noise" of the book's title. This concept informs the narrative of *Velocità di fuga* (1989, Speed of Flight), whose protagonist, victimized by men and estranged from her lesbian friend, learns to turn her body into a "subject" of pleasure and a base of creativity and writing. She imagines experience as an exhilarating flight away from the alienating world of "the father" into a kind of cosmic dimension, powered by a "jouissance," both linguistic and sexual, neither female nor male.

For the majority of writers, however, returning to the personal meant above all representing the coming into being of their own personalities within the context of the family and national history. A great many texts employing various techniques were then produced, which can be called "historical" because they all ground their narratives in historically definable settings. More significant than their transgeneric character are the representational and cognitive assumptions they embody.

Even though literary fashion was moving away from neo-realism, many historical narratives continued to employ straightforward mimetic techniques. With the advent of the feminist movement, some writers began to expound overtly feminist ideas or to embed them in the narrative structure of their works. Others moved away from feminist theorizing to a more puzzled speculation on female identity. Still others, influenced by theories of subjectivity, wrote historical fictions giving expression to a skeptical view of the social relevance of the individual and of her capacity to make history.

The response of a group of Roman intellectuals to the unfolding of national events during the most crucial year of the Second World War is forcefully depicted by Vittoria Ronchey in her novel *1944* (1992), while another of her stories, *Figlioli miei, marxisti immaginari* (1975, My Imaginary Marxist Sons) centers on the contemporary educational crisis and the unrest spread among the youth of the capital. In *Nucleo zero* (1981, Zero Unit) Luce d'Eramo focuses on the terrorist organizations that paralyzed the country in the seventies, while in *Prima del fuoco* (1993, Before the Fire) Camilla Salvago Raggi describes the public involvement of her aristocratic ancestors seen from the hunting lodge where they had all vacationed during one century of Italian history. The disruption that historical events have on people's lives was perceptively recorded years before by Natalia Ginsburg in *Lessico famigliare* (1963), and has been dramatized more recently by Isabella Bossi Fedrigotti in *Casa di guerra* (1983, House of War) and *Di buona famiglia* (1991, From a Good Family). The interest of these writers in the historical context of their characters' lives speaks to their need to address their own development in relation to family, class, and national history. As it has been noted, such an aim was better served by texts that mixed fiction and history, biography and autobiography. An eloquent example of this kind of narrative is Clara Sereni's *Il gioco dei regni* (1993, The Game of Kingdoms), a chronicle of the Italian Communist Party and of Zionism from the point of view of the members of the author's family who were active in them. The convergence of personal narrative and official documentation has the effect of bringing history into the sphere of the private, showing how public occurrences have a bearing on personal lives and, most importantly, how single individuals can intervene in the historical process.

History could also effectively be seen in terms of the present. Such a perspective was adopted in feminist texts designed to vindicate female figures that had been ignored by official chronicles. The model for this type of historical recovery is Anna Banti's *Artemisia* (1947), a novel that dramatizes the life of Artemisia Gentileschi, a sixteenth century portrait painter whose celebrity is owed to her having been raped by fellow artist Agostino Tassi and to the sensational trial that followed. By using the ploy of telling a fictionalized version of Artemisia's personal life, Banti is able emphasize at once Artemisia's gender-related struggle and her own marginalized position as twentieth-century woman writer. Much less self-referential, albeit equally effective, is Maria Bellonci's *Rinascimento privato* (1985, A Private Renaissance), in which she tells the story of Isabella d'Este, duchess of Mantua. Weaving together known historical events with Isabella's specific motivations, Bellonci shows how a woman at the service of her dynasty is capable of influencing momentous events in history. In Maria Rosa Cutrufelli's feminist novel, *La briganta* (1990, The Woman Outlaw), the use of history takes a direction opposite to that of Banti and Bellonci. The woman outlaw's adventures are told in the form of a memoir. Margherita, daughter of an aristocratic Sicilian family, in the aftermath of Italy's unification, joins a band of disenfranchised peasants rebelling against the newly established order; now in prison, she writes in order to claim her identity and rescue her act of revolt from obscurity. The author uses the peasant rebellion, and within it the isolation of the female protagonist, to illustrate the situation of Italian women who participated in the revolutionary events of the 1960s only to come face to face with their own difference and their position at the margins of the groups for which they had campaigned (Jeannet, 137-138). Cutrufelli's belief in the cognitive power of history is plain: her interest is much less than rescuing a woman from her forgotten past — there exists documentary evidence of the existence of such an outlaw — than re-telling a story for its capacity to shed light on current realities.

As the1980s progressed, an increasing number of works responded to the lure of post-modernity. The first to do so, however, takes us back to 1962, when scholar and literary critic Maria Corti published *L'ora di tutti* (Everybody's Hour). The novel tells the story of the southern Italian town of Otranto during its sack by the Turks in 1480. Corti describes the events from the point of view of four participants in the siege; a fifth account is then given by the bishop who arrives in the city after its liberation and who, transforming the events into miraculous occurrences, voids the significance of the actions and motivations of the men and women who participated in them. What the structure of this narrative emphasizes is the notion that ordinary people behave according to the customs, feelings, and attitudes that persist unchanged through the ages — a notion popularized by the French anthropologist Lévy-Strauss, whose structures of kinship, and, in parallel critical application, the synchronic literary systems of meaning, influenced much Italian criticism at the time (Corti/Segre 407-17). In an interview published some thirty years later, Corti confirmed the structural function of her characters' thoughts and memories, and, retrospectively, explained the popularity of the historical novel in Italy with what later became the widely popularized notion of historical recurrences, i.e., "the postmodern vision of history where past and present merge together"(Corti 71). Another novel with a strong meta-historical structure is Elsa Morante's *La storia*, which we have mentioned above. As the English title, *History: A Novel*, suggests, Morante sets apart history and fiction, the former relating to the official interpretations and the bulletins released in the capital during the Second World War, the latter to the experiences of her victimized characters. Whatever its much debated value may be, the novel continues to attract the interest of feminist critics who have compared its underlying view of history and maternal love to feminist psychoanalytical and historiographical theories. Lucia Re has suggested that the child Useppe's behavior and language, in ignoring all oppositional differences established in the symbolic order of the father, achieve a state of innocent being that circumvents the entrapment of humankind in history (368-69). Furthermore, the narrator's occasional remarks on the dubious character of her own emotionally charged version of what happened have been seen as anticipating the postmodern notion of the unreliability of all narratives and the "historicity of human psychic structures" (Della Coletta 1996, 131). The changes brought about by time and the ambiguous character of all interpretations of the past have also been thematized by Giuliana Morandini in *I cristalli di Vienna* (1977, *(Blood Stains*, 1978), *Caffè Specchi* (1983, Mirror Café), *Angelo a Berlino* (1987, Angel in Berlin), and *Giocando a dama con la luna* (1996, Playing Checkers with the Moon). The modern histories of Vienna, Trieste, Berlin, as well as that of ancient Egypt, provide the forever changing settings that reflect the character's search for an enduring identity. Marta Morazzoni's *La ragazza col turbante* (1986, Girl With a Turban) dramatizes instead the lack of communication between a female model and the artist who has the power to define her in his painting: an incomprehension that she returns to in her subsequent novel, *L'invenzione della verità* (1988, The Invention of Truth). Here Queen Mathilde, who planned the Bayeux tapestry and directed a throng of female workers to complete it, is empowered to create a truth which will remain elusive to posterity, represented in the novel by John Ruskin, the art historian who centuries later interprets the design.

Meta-historical implications are part of the texture of story-telling in narratives authored by Rosetta Loy and Silvana La Spina. In *Le strade di polvere* (1987, *The Dust Roads of Monferrato*, 1991), Loy recounts the life of a family of farmers in Monferrato from the end of the Napoleonic wars to the unification of Italy. Their story is told in a quick and gripping succession of births, loves, marriages, departures and returns, against the revolving backdrop of wars, invasions, and liberation. Sentences follow sentences that touch only on sensations and feelings, rarely on ideas and reasoning. Loy spins a vast sensory web which connects people to other people, to the land around them, to the weather, the food they eat; links the past to the present and, with frequent forward flashes, to analogous experiences in the future. Public events are brought into the description in an incidental manner and for the sensory impressions or emotional disorientation they produce. The resulting effect is that of an "organic"connection of people to places and times, whose significance must be sought by the reader in the "long duration." As it is, Loy's characters have only an indirect relationship to the linear progression of history; they are rather subservient to, never agents in, the perennial pattern of happenings which transcend and dominate them. A similar view of history, but with insistent moral overtones, is at the core of Silvana La Spina's novels, for example, the historical narratives *Un inganno dei sensi malizioso* (1995, An Artful Deception of the Senses) and *L'amante del paradiso* (1997, The Lover from Paradise) or such multi-layered, skillfully plotted thrillers as *Morte a Palermo* (1988, Death at Palermo) and *L'ultimo treno da Catania* (1992, The Last Train from Catania). *Un inganno dei sensi malizioso* is remarkable for the suspenseful way in which it intertwines the adventurous meandering of many highly individualized characters, a sister of Saint Clare endowed with visionary powers, a priest with a vocation for martyrdom, and an array of high functionaries and aristocrats driven by obsessions and magic. Their lives are depicted against a sixteenth-century background that varies from abject poverty to voluptuous splendor, and transport the reader — as the blurb on the book-cover promises — from the sun-drenched beaches of Sicily to the enchantments of Spain, from a sumptuous and clamorous Naples to the burning stakes of the Roman Inquisition, to a Prague seduced by alchemy, and to the labyrinthine streets of Istanbul. People and places come to life in a continuous unfolding of images, concepts and cultural allusions. La Spina captures the minds and instincts of her characters in such a way as to create a collective story of a picaresque human existence in all its multicultural variety. All human beings appear as pawns of history, floating particles in an indefinite time dimension, equally subjected to, but, at the same time, all personally implicated in its making.

By the 1980s, the new theorizing on subjectivity was reflected in the works of all Italian writers. An entire generation of poets became engrossed in the self and its relation to the world. Among those who sought to bring poetry closer to nature, favoring, in the words of

Giuseppe Conte, a "joyous practice of the dissemination of the I or of its total vanishing"(quoted by Picchione 1999, 254) was Rosita Copioli. In the collection *Splendida lumina solis* (1979, *The Blazing Light of the Sun*, 1996) — a title drawn from Lucretius's *De rerum natura* — Copioli, a scholar of myth and of natural symbolism in literature, gives a demonstration of "myth as a form of knowledge" (Conte in Vicentini, 56) in a spellbinding depiction of the transmutation of being at a time prior to the appearance on earth of man and animals, picturing for us primordial existence: an origin that, in Renata Treitel's words, bespeaks "a vision of female auto-erotic fantasies of generation without copulation" (Copioli 11). The recreation of the origin of life is also the subject of Copioli's subsequent volume of poetry, *Furore delle rose* (1989, The Fury of Roses). Here she depicts the dawn of human life on earth as exemplified by the sites of primitive religious rituals which Copioli manages to envelop in a visionary, Orphic atmosphere. Her evocation of the primeval past continues in *Elena,*1996, a verse drama in which Helen of Troy's monologue is interspersed with dream sequences inhabited by archetypal and mythical characters. What is noteworthy in Copioli's verse is the fusion of classical and mythical images — frequently evoked by quotations in Latin from Virgil and Lucretius — and modern speech, in such a way that her visions acquire legendary authority and contemporary relevancy.

The loneliness of the self is the subject matter of the work of Patrizia Cavalli, Vivian Lamarque and Patrizia Valduga. In *Le mie poesie non cambieranno il mondo* (1974, My Verse Will Not Change the World) and *L'io singolare proprio mio* (1992, My Singular Very Own Self), Cavalli expresses a dreaded condition of separateness in lucidly written poems that are deeply aversive in their apparent serenity and simplicity of diction. Lamarque's poetry has an uncanny manner of transposing her emotions into a pre-adult imaginary — she is also the author of several books for children — never failing to underscore the presence of controlled anguish. Foremost among her best collections is *Poesie dando del Lei* (1989, Poems in the Courtesy Form of Address), written while she was ongoing psychoanalytic therapy and dedicated to her doctor. Here the Italian use of the polite form of address is a painful reminder that love is unattainable. The 74 poems of the collection are composed of commonplace, whimsical imagery in short rhymes in which a single word startles the reader by providing expected entry into the poet's desires. Inaccessible love gives way to a variety of themes in *Una quieta polvere* (1996, A Quiet Dust), a title derived from Emily Dickinson's "This Quiet Dust was Gentlemen and Ladies." Here Lamarque guilelessly reveals the life around her in metropolitan Milan. Patrizia Valduga is the author of two noteworthy collections. *Donna di dolori* (1991,

Suffering Woman) is a chilling monologue of a dead woman crying out from the grave. The woman's mind is tortured by the recollection of a life of disappointment and wasted passions, as her body slowly decomposes and her lamentations turn into prattle. This is a powerful piece whose impassioned language creates a chilling sense of desolation. In the other collection is *Cento quartine e altre storie d'amore* (1997, One Hundred Quatrains and Other Love Stories). Valduga delves into the physical and mental aspects of sex, dauntlessly exposing the undersides of eroticism in a juxtaposition of literary language and sex talk, designed to convey the dominance and subjugation of woman. In representing the loss of selfhood, Valduga, perhaps better than any other modern Italian writer, has drawn from the richness of the lyric tradition with original and powerful effects.

The "coming of age" of Italian women writers is no doubt demonstrated by the high quality of their achievements. Less evident are the factors that made that quality possible. The larger part taken by women in public life has given them a self-assurance that has led to their conceiving of human realities creatively in a way that addresses issues of moral and philosophical importance. In their writing, the self is no longer exclusively the locus of female identity and the springboard of feminist protest. Even when the protagonist is a woman, living in an individualized womanly environment, her concerns are of general significance. The self has rather become the point from which a certain vision of the world is constructed; a vision that bears, at each moment, the conditions and the responsibility of its own making.

The human subject as a source of moral action is the subject matter of a group of novelists who made their debut or came to literary prominence in the eighties and nineties: Francesca Duranti, Fabrizia Ramondino, Carla Cerati and Paola Capriolo. Their probing of the human condition is conducted in a manner that, regardless of point of view, transposes all autobiographical references and personal conviction into the web of fiction. Implied in their narratives is the idea that the subject, rather than being a point of stable identification and authoritative certainty, is at best the locus of continuous adaptations and challenges, and, at worst, the origin of illusions and prevarication.

On the surface, the protagonists of Francesca Duranti's many novels are men and women intent on pursuing new images of themselves. From the beginning of their stories, changing circumstances force them to make difficult adjustments. In *La casa sul lago della luna* (1984, The House on Moon Lake), for instance, the male protagonist, desirous of establishing his reputation as a scholar, embarks on a search for the unpublished manuscript of a forgotten author. Imperceptibly, the search becomes an ontological quest for identity and, in the end, the character finds himself a prisoner in the web of his own imaginings and misconceptions. In *Effetti personali* (1988, Personal Effects) the quest for personal identity takes on sociological and political overtones. A literary woman travels beyond the iron curtain to interview a writer and discovers that the name of the person she is looking for refers to a collective of authors. The elusiveness of her search is further stressed when she realizes that the man among them with whom she becomes emotionally involved is fleeing both the collective and the civil authorities, institutions that require the denial of identity and personal possessions. So even writing, seemingly our most inalienable possession and the very essence of our identity, can cease to be ours and become something other than ourselves. Fabrizia Ramondino takes us from Duranti's restrained northern upper class background and its literary milieux to the animated urban life of the Neapolitan bourgeoisie. Ramondino's narrator analyzes human relationships from many points of view within complex narrative structures. The characters she places under her merciless gaze may be family members (*Althénopis*, 1981 and *Storie di patio*, 1983) or strangers (*Un giorno e mezzo*, 1988). In each case, the effect is the destruction of some of our most sacred myths: the validity of fatherly authority, the generosity of parental love, children's innocence, and the integrity of manhood. The titles of the novels Carla Cerati has written in a span of thirty years — *Un amore fraterno* (1973, A Brotherly Love), *Un matrimonio perfetto* (1974, A Perfect Marriage), *La condizione sentimentale* (1977, An Emotional Condition), *La cattiva figlia* (1990, The Bad Daughter), *Legami molto stretti* (1994, Very Close Ties), and *L'amica della modellista* (1996, The Fashion Designer's Friend) — all indicate the focus of her narrative: namely, that human bonds, whether created by love, familial affection, intellectual admiration, or emotional dependency, come undone under the impact of incomprehension, concealment, and evasion; and loyalties, seemingly unassailable, crumble under the impact of new experiences.

By contrast, Paola Capriolo's fiction hovers imperceptibly between realistic exactitude and fantasy. In *La grande Eulalia*, her first collection of stories written at the age of twenty-six, we find for instance a homely young woman, who after seeing the image of a handsome man in a mirror, becomes beautiful and enters the mirror in pursuit of him. There is also a prisoner who by playing a violin in his cell is able to bend the will of a woman living beyond his prison's walls and coach her to accompany him at the piano. These are characters who haunt their objects of desire, prey on them until the end are destroyed by them. The surreal light in which they are cast eases their way down the path of their desires, revealing the intangible chains that enslave them to one another. Capriolo, however, does not write escapist narratives. There is a strong moral undertone in all her stories, a significance which is not preached but rather absorbed into the very fabric of fiction. It concerns the choices we make in life, the mutual implication of seducer and seduced, the co-responsibility of prey and predator. As the prisoner in the tower says: "The hand that inflicts the blow and the flesh that receives it are one and the same." (*La grande Eulalia*, 122) After her first success, Capriolo went on to publish many other novels that illustrated her unusual talent for creating suspense. In *Un uomo di carattere* (1996, A Man of Character) she turns her surrealism into metafictional allegory. The scene is set in a country villa whose obsessive owner is waging war on the weeds and stones that threaten the perfect symmetry of his orderly garden. Slowly but surely, he succumbs to the charms of a female visitor called Zeta — "zero" or nothingness — whose relaxed, irrational ways lead him to a life of carelessness and mediocrity. Art, seen here as order imposed on disorder, is the object of a lifelong pursuit, which is heroic because doomed to succumb to the forces of nature and to the loss of the self that comes with dying.

On my view, Capriolo's novel is an allegory of the positioning of the writer in the world of writing. As such, it can be taken as a fitting closure to the above summary. Speaking for many of the younger authors, it views the writer's work as a craft, rather than an act of initiation to art, as it was for many literati of previous generations; it reveals a full awareness of the difficulties and the responsibilities of the profession, while pointing out the negative effects of evasion. In virtue of the diminished role of the male intellectual in Italian literary life and the increased commercial concerns of the publishing industry, women authors are today numerous and diverse in background and formation. Because of this, and because of their greater integration in the life of the country, they now feel confident about entering the profession and remaining involved in it at a parity with men. Proof of this new state of affairs is Susanna Tamaro's *Va dove ti porta il cuore* (1994, *Follow Your Heart*, 1995) which has achieved record sales world-wide, comparable only to Umberto Eco's *The Name of the Rose*. And it has done so without academic backing, and against the expectations of prestigious critics. Interestingly, the book was at the center of another literary controversy in Italy, where critical approval and financial success are not necessarily commensurate. Tamaro is a talented story teller who can turn a graceful phrase, show wisdom, and create suspense, while wandering in that uncharted territory she calls "the heart." It would not be surprising, therefore, if comparable public favor should grace her subsequent book, *Anima Mundi* (1997), in which a hostile, psychologically troubled male protagonist is scrutinized with the same suspense-creating skill. Indeed, if women can experience the satisfactions of authorship in the way men do, they too must face the same risks and responsibilities. Exemplary of the variety of different talents and choices made by women writers today are two books I would like to mention in closing: Elena Gianini Belotti's most recent novel, *Apri le porte all'alba* (1999, Open the Doors to the Dawn), an overtly ideological work that favors the prospect of a multicultural and multiracial society; and Carmen Covito's *Benvenuti in questo ambiente* (1997, Welcome to This Environment), a book that welcomes the new technologies and the virtual realities in which its characters live, provided they are used in considerate and rational ways. The coming of age of women's writing speaks to an interpretation of the world, to values the authors would like to see upheld and the extent to which they are ready to commit themselves to their craft as an expression of those values.

BIBLIOGRAPHY

Agosti, Stefano. *Poesia italiana contemporanea*. Milano: Bompiani, 1995.

Allen, Beverly, Muriel Kittel and Keala Jane Jewell, eds. *The Defiant Muse. Italian Feminist Poems from the Middle Ages to the Present*. New York: The Feminist Press, 1986.

Barañski, Zygmunt G. and Lino Pertile, eds. *The New Italian Novel*. Toronto: University of Toronto Press, 1993.

Barañski, Zygmunt G. and Shirley W. Vinall, eds. *Women and Italy: Essays on Gender, Culture and History*. London: Macmillan, 1991.

Bertoletti, Isabella. "Feminist Theory: France" and "Feminist Theory: Italy." In *The Feminist Encyclopedia of Italian Literature*, Rinaldina Russell ed., New Haven: Greenwood Press, 1997.

Brooke, Gabriella. "'Si sente la mano femminile?' Feminine Writing and the Concept of History in the Historical Fiction of Silvana La Spina." In *Gendering Italian Fiction. Feminist Revisions of Italian History*, Maria Ornella Marotti and Gabriella Brooke eds., Madison, N. J.: Farleigh Dickinson University Press, 1999.

Caesar, Michael. "Contemporary Italy (since 1956)." In *The Cambridge History of Italian Literature*, Peter Brand and Lino Pertile eds., Cambridge: Cambridge University Press, 1996.

Campo, Cristina. *Gli imperdonabili*. Milano: Adelphi, 1987.

Capozzi, Rocco. "Un incontro elettronico con Carmen Covito." *Forum Italicum* 33, 1 (1999): 263-272.

Capriolo, Paola. *La grande Eulalia*. Milano: Feltrinelli, 1988.

Copioli, Rosita. *The Blazing Lights of the Sun*. Translated from the Italian by Renata Treitel. Los Angeles: Sun & Moon Press, 1996.

Corti, Maria. "Interview" in *The Review of Contemporary Fiction* 12, 3, (1992): 70-75.

Corti, Maria and Cesare Segre. "La critica e la vita letteraria (consuntivo in forma di dialogo)." In *I metodi attuali della critica in Italia*, Maria Corti and Cesare Segre eds. Torino: ERI, 1970.

Dedola, Rossana. "La poesia del transfert: La poesia innamorata di Vivan Lamarque" in *Studi novecenteschi*. 81 (1991): 223-38.

De Giovanni, Neria. *Carta di donna: Narratrici italiane del Novecento*. Torino: Società Editrice Internazionale: 1996.

Della Coletta, Cristina. *Plotting the Past. Metamorphoses of Historical Narrative in Modern Italian Fiction*. West Lafayette, Indiana: Purdue University Press, 1996.

_____ "Scrittura come utopia: la lente scura di Anna Maria Ortese" *Italica* 78, 3 (1999): 371-388.

Di Nola, Laura, ed. *Poesia femminista italiana*. Rome: Savelli, 1978.

Frabotta, Biancamaria, ed. *Donne in poesia. Antologia della poesia femminile in Italia dal dopoguerra ad oggi*. Roma: Savelli, 1976.

Gatt-Rutter. John. "The Aftermath of the Second World War (1945-1956)." In *The Cambridge History of Italian Literature*, Peter Brand and Lino Pertile eds. Cambridge: Cambridge University Press, 1996.

Gugliamone, Paola. *Conversazione con Susanna Tamaro. Il respiro quieto*. Roma: Omicron, 1996.

Jeannet, Angela. "Between Document and Fiction: Maria Rosa Cutrufelli's *Voices*." In *Italian Culture* 16, 1 (1998): 129-141.

Lazzaro-Weis, Carol. *From Margins to Mainstream: Feminist and Fictional Modes in Italian Women's Writing 1968-1990*. Philadelphia: University of Pennsylvania Press, 1993.

_____ "Stranger than Life? Autobiography and Historical Fiction." In *Gendering Italian Fiction. Feminist Revisions of Italian History*, Maria Ornella Marotti and Gabriella Brooke eds. Madison, N. J.: Farleigh Dickinson University, 1999.

Luti, Giorgio, ed. *Narratori italiani del secondo Novecento*. Rome: La Nuova Italia, 1985.

Miceli-Jeffries, Giovanna, ed. *Feminine Feminists: Cultural Practices in Italy*. Minneapolis: University of Minnesota Press, 1994.

Marotti, Maria Ornella, ed. *Italian Women Writers from the Renaissance to the Present*. University Park, Pa.: The Pennsylvania University Press, 1996.

_____ "Literary Historicism and Women's Tradition." *Italian Culture* 13 (1995): 261-271.

O'Brien, Catherine. *Italian Women Poets of the Twentieth Century*. Dublin: Irish Academic Press, 1996.

Pallotta, Augustus, ed. *Dictionary of Literary Biography. Volume 177: Italian Novelists Since World War II, 1945-1965*. Detroit: Gale Research, 1997.

_____ *Dictionary of Literary Biography. Volume 196: Italian Novelists Since World War II: 1965-1990*. Detroit: Gale Research, 1999.

Parati, Graziella. *Public History, Private Stories: Italian Women's Autobiography.* Minneapolis: University of Minnesota Press, 1996.

Petrignani, Sandra. *Le signore della scrittura. Interviste.* Milan: La Tartaruga, 1984.

Picchione, John. "Poesia al femminile: rabbia, gioco e terapia." In *Donna. Women in Italian Literature*, Ada Testaferri ed. Toronto: Dovehouse, 1989.

_____ "Poetry and the Human Sciences in Italy. (The 1970s and 80s)."*Forum Italicum* 33, 1 (1999): 249-261.

Rasy, Elisabetta. "Interview." *The Review of Contemporary Fiction* 12, 13 (1992): 79-81.

Re, Lucia. "Utopian Longing and Constraints of Racial and Sexual Difference in Elsa Morante's *La Storia.*" *Italica* 70 (1993): 361-375.

Russell, Rinaldina, ed. *Italian Women Writers. A Bio-Biographical Sourcebook.* New Haven: Greenwood Press, 1994.

_____ ed. *The Feminist Encyclopedia of Italian Literature.* New Haven: Greenwood Press, 1997.

Speciale, Emilio. "Post-modern o Neo-classicismo? Patrizia Valduga e il ritorno alle forme metriche nella recente poesia italiana." *Annali d'Italianistica* 9 (1991): 254-270.

Testaferri, Ada, ed. *Donna: Women in Italian Studies.* Ottawa: Dovehouse Editions, 1989.

Vicentini, Isabella. *Colloqui sulla poesia.* Torino. Nuova Eri/Edizioni RAI Radiotelevisione italiana, 1991.

Wedel De Stasio, Giuliana, Glauco Cambon and Antonio Illiano, eds. *Dictionary of Literary Biography. Volume 114: Twentieth-Century Italian Poets. First Series.* Detroit: Gale Research, 1992.

_____ *Dictionary of Literary Biography. Volume 128: Twentieth-Century Italian Poets. Second Series.* Detroit: Gale Research, 1993.

West, Rebecca and Dino S. Cervigni eds. *Annali d'Italianistica: Women's Voices in Italian Literature*, 7 (1989).

West, Rebecca."Giulia Niccolai." In *Italian Women Writers. A Bio-Biographical Sourcebook*, Rinaldina Russell ed. New Haven: Greenwood Press,1994.

Wilson, Katharina M, ed. *An Encyclopedia of Continental Women Writers.* 2 vols. New York: Garland, 1991.

Wood, Sharon. *Italian Women's Writing 1960-1993.* London: Athlone, 1995.

Zecchi, Barbara. "Il corpo femminile tra trampolino e volo. Enif Robert e Biancamaria Frabotta: settant'anni verso il tempo delle donne." *Italica*, 69, 4 (1992): 505-518.

_____ "Maria Luisa Spaziani." In *Italian Women Writers. A Bio-Biographical Sourcebook*, Rinaldina Russell ed. New Haven: Greenwood Press, 1994.

JOSEPH FRANCESE

The Italian Postmodern:
A Comparative Perspective

The incorporation of pastiche and parody, the principal features of postmodern writing, into contemporary Italian literature seems to accurately reflect Italy's reception of postmodern culture as a whole. As one critic has pointed out, no country other than Japan has taken to the new reality of postmodernity with a greater appearance of spontaneous and casual ease than Italy (Ceserani, 146). Yet, while many areas of social and cultural experience have proven to be willing participants in postmodern culture, Italian criticism has been much less eager to contribute to the debate on postmodernism. In fact, there has been an unyielding refusal of many intellectuals to consider the question at all. Part of this may be due to deep-seated intellectual and literary traditions, part from the rejection of an overly zealous and unquestioning appropriation of a cultural identity not its own, which is a continuation of a long-standing tendency in Italy toward self-deprecation when it comes to questions of modernization and Europeanization. When considering how Italian writers respond to a shared condition of postmodernity, we cannot speak of an indigenous movement with specific Italian characteristics, but of a conscious effort on the part of some to transcend a perceived inferiority, a sense of perennially lagging behind the times. Thus, we are confronted on the one hand with a sincere desire to put an end to a lengthy cultural isolation, on the other with an attempt at imitating dominant modes of modernization, a 'weak' response to the rapid expansion of industrialization and technological progress.

Post-modernity is the life condition in Western societies that corresponds to the economics of flexible accumulation and globalization. As such, it effects our experience of identity, time, and space. In postmodernity there

> is no overarching totality, rationality, or fixed centre to human life, no metalanguage which can capture its endless variety, just a plurality of cultures and narratives which cannot be hierarchically ordered or "privileged," and which must consequently respect the inviolable "otherness" of ways of doing things that are not their own. Knowledge is relative to cultural contexts, so that to claim to know the world "as it is" is simply a chimera - not only because our understanding is always a matter of partial, partisan interpretation, but because the world itself is no way in particular. (Eagleton, 201)

As result, our shared condition of post-modernity is defined by shortened temporal horizons and spatial disorientation to which postmodernism (the philosophical belief in the end of the "grand narratives" of truth, reason, science, progress and universal emancipation and the culture corresponding to them), and the postmodern (the esthetic expression of this belief) respond.

Post-modernity is often characterized as a change in common sense, a "paradigm shift" from globalizing to localizing tendencies. The Enlightenment myth of linear progress and the belief that reality can be known because it is fundamentally univocal have lost all currency. Knowledge can no longer be deduced from amorphous chaos; similarly, understandable and interpretable fact and reality can no longer be represented in narrative. While the Modernist writer, who believed that the world could be known and explained, stood above events that were rooted in historical time and viewed their unfolding, the postmodernist constructs and modifies reality through language.

The lack of faith in all metanarratives finds a literary counterpart that has no recourse to essential beliefs and customs. Instead, it searches for ways to represent the complexity of reality. Characters and plots surrender their explanatory significance while the center of narrative gravity shifts away from the author, diminishing the epistemological and cognitive importance of a fixed center of consciousness, now seen as nothing more than an arbitrary construct. The conception and representation of multiple social and existential realities are now subject to the infinite play of language.

Despite the similarities in current Western literary trends, and because of the subaltern manner in which postmodern culture has been imported, any overview of the Italian literary postmodern cannot avoid a consideration of Italy's specific literary tradition. The task we have set ourselves here is that of providing a selective overview of representative present-day Italian writing against the backdrop of the Italian literary tradition as it developed over the second half of the twentieth century. It is necessary to do so because two trends in Italian postmodern writing are the logical outgrowth of the two major tendencies that have remained constant over the past half-century. Italian literature has tended to either look to its realist past and attempt to engage and transform society or to acquiesce in the status quo, seeking refuge in pure literariness. Italian postmodernist writings are characterized by similar responses.

As World War II drew to a close, the need to join the European cultural mainstream was not a matter of overwhelming importance to the majority of Italian literati. Instead, after twenty years of cultural isolationism imposed by fascism, their primary concern was coming to grips with the country's immediate past: specifically, with the refusal of intellectuals as a group to actively engage and oppose the dictatorship. After the War and in response to the a-political stance of the Hermetic poets, neo-realism, a loosely organized movement inspired by the writings of Antonio Gramsci came into being. While neo-realists never united under a manifesto, they embraced an explicit program of total social engagement for artists and intellectuals alike. Within this context, Gramsci's thought became a crucial element in the cultural debates of the early 1950s. It was used to rebut the idealism of Benedetto Croce and his followers, for whom culture and politics were independent activities of the human mind that had to be kept separate. However, the subsequent hardening of positions — aggravated by the advent of the Cold War — led to a simplification of the arguments. Gramsci's concept of a "national-popular literature" lost its complexity and was reduced to a slogan. As a result, many of Italy's more progressive intellectuals returned to the national tradition, now seen as an antidote to intellectual cosmopolitanism, a trend that paradoxically reinforced the isolation from the European mainstream imposed by the Fascist regime. Although the assimilation during the 1950s of Gramsci's thought into the Italian cultural mainstream may be today considered to be a misappropriation, it constituted an important first step in a process of self-awareness that was necessary in order to de-provincialize Italian literature and mark its entry into a European context as a legitimate interlocutor.

Despite the political and social commitment of the neo-realist writers, loosely knitted as a group, the works they produced were largely naturalistic in form and paternalistic in subject matter. They lacked the ideological clarity needed to confront Italy's intricate social ills, and lost all cohesiveness when their narrative shortcomings were underscored by the very critics whose support they actively sought.[1] By mid-decade, the neo-realists' belief in social rebirth was shattered in the wake of the watershed events of 1956,[2] after which new cultural and esthetic tendencies began to gain in prominence.

This was particularly the case with the novelist Italo Calvino whose first novel, *Il sentiero dei nidi di ragno*, recounts the author's experience as Communist Resistance fighter, told from the vantage point of a young boy. Calvino's career as a writer is highly germane to our topic because, as we have stated, it can be taken to exemplify the shift in literature from the modern to the postmodern. Calvino's writings demonstrate a shift from a Modernist faith in enlightened reason, with its almost utopistic belief in progress and in the perfectability of the future, in favor of a reflection of the post-cognitive doubt that characterizes post-modernity.

Calvino's debut as a writer occurred shortly after the end of World War II, within the framework of neo-realism. During the early- and mid-1950s he began to distance himself from neo-realism and move in the direction of the fantastic, publishing in 1952 *Il visconte dimezzato*, and editing in 1956 a collection of Italian folk tales. But even before the critical events of 1956, which over time would result in a general disaffection with politics, Calvino championed the need for de-provincializing Italian literature. During the first half of the decade he sparked a debate among Leftist intellectuals when he raised the question of the value of a Communist cultural politics designed to represent the age-old poverty and exploitation of the Italian South. According to Calvino, the PCI's more-or-less official support for neo-realism and its "cult of the national tradition" effectively constituted an "anti-cosmopolitan campaign." He argued that excessive cultural significance was being given to a national literary tradition that over the previous three centuries had proven to be minor in comparison to other European traditions" (Calvino, *Nord e Roma-Sud* and *Il midollo del leone*). Thus, by raising the "Northern Question," as opposed to the "Southern Question," Calvino hoped to spark new creativity which would lead to new forms of narrative, distinct from the representations of popular traditions and cultures idealized by neo-realism.

In 1964 Calvino left Italy for Paris, where he strengthened his ties with the major exponents of French Structuralism, and participated in the literary experiments of the Oulipo group led by Raymond Queneau.[3] With *Le cosmicomiche* (1965) and *Ti con zero* (1967) he then concluded his fantasy cycle. *Le cosmicomiche* takes us to the origins of the universe in an attempt to understand the essence of our humanity. The novel's protagonist, Qfwfq, tells of his experiences as a microscopic bit of matter present at the "Big Bang," and then, in molecularly transformed appearance, at various evolutionary junctures in the history of our galaxy and planet. *Ti con zero* delves further into this problematic, again observing humanity from a non-anthropocentric vantage point, focussing on themes such as the self and the other, chaos and order, and untaken pathways in human evolutionary history. Calvino's interest in combinatory literature led him to *Le città invisibili* (1972), a re-writing of Marco Polo's *Il Milione*. Emblematic of basic human character traits, the urban landscapes represented in this work allow Calvino to depict a totality of multiple, heterogeneous societies. A year later, with *Il castello dei destini incrociati*, Calvino uses two decks of tarot cards to investigate the deep structures of narrative. The tarots, which represent both atavistic human character traits and basic units of narrative, are woven together into a neat fabric to produce tales that, while new, are reminiscent of canonical stories.

As he pursued his experimental fiction, Calvino kept in mind the work of Jorge Luis Borges, particularly two of the *Ficciones*, *Pierre Menard, Author of Don Quixote* and *The Library of Babel* — the same two narratives cited by John Barth in "The Literature of Exhaustion," in an attempt to describe postmodern literature. Barth speaks of the need to "transcend narrative finitude" by reconfiguring the elements of tales already told. Borges had suggested to both Barth and Calvino the metafictional recyclings of basic, a-temporal narrative units within an exclusively bibliographic universe.

In 1979 Calvino carried his experiments with the meta-novel to the extreme in *Se una notte d'inverno un viaggiatore*, a work in which he, as author, feigns his own "death" and subsequent "re-incarnation" in the reader. In an essay titled "I livelli della realtà in letteratura" ("The Levels of Reality in Literature") Calvino identified four levels of subjectivity hidden beneath the author's name and conveyed by means of the writer: the author ("a voce, a style, a self-projection, a psychological position, a rapport with the world" that did not by necessity exclusively coincide with specific aspects of the writer's personality), the "character-protagonist" (or narrating self), and the plot. However, such distinctions become blurred when the act of creating characters affects the author's original identity, causing him/her to disappear within his/her creation. Calvino's scheme corresponds for the most part to narratological theory (Benedetti, 97-99), to which, by dividing writer and author, and thereby nullifying what Foucault called the "author-function," Calvino makes an original contribution to the general principles of narratology (Benedetti, 99-102).

In *Se una notte d'inverno un viaggiatore* Calvino collects within a frame-tale the beginnings of ten different novels all written for the benefit of his Model Readers, in search of the ultimate reading experience. The identity of Calvino the writer cannot be distinguished from that of the implied narrator of the frame-tale, who addresses the reader from a meta-narrative vantage point. Then, the implied narrator turns the tables on Calvino the author by directly addressing the reader in order to reveal the secrets of the writer's trade. In doing so, the implied narrator is able to flatter the reader — the narrator's tone invites the reader to participate in an erudite coterie of select readers – and to gain his confidence by making reference to the unwritten agreement that predetermines how novels are written and read. The middle-level reader, the object of Calvino's affectionate gaze, is the "true" protagonist of the work. At the novel's end, we are taken into a library full of "pure" readers for whom books are a means of escape from the world.[4]

After *Se una notte d'inverno un viaggiatore* Calvino begins to question the foundations of perceived reality, moving toward the post-cognitive skepticism characteristic of postmodernism. His final work, *Palomar* (1983), is the culmination of this shift in perspective. *Palomar* is a collection of detailed isolated descriptions. The implied narrator of this work fixes his gaze on the minute aspects of the world around him hoping that by looking at specific aspects of empirical reality, "as if for the first time," he will be able to understand their essence, and then use that understanding to comprehend human existence in general. However, his attempt fails when he is unable to harmonize the existence of individual, society, and world. Hence, a general theory of knowledge is impossible. The writer is left with perplexity and doubt.

While Calvino moved from meta-fictional representations of totality toward the fragmentation of knowledge, the experimentalists of Gruppo '63 or neo-avant-garde sought to address the complicated and contradictory reality of modern Italy in a manner that posed radical linguistic and structural challenges to traditional forms of narration. Adopting the French *nouveau roman* as a model of complicated, refractory prose, the Gruppo '63 produced obscure and often indecipherable texts that negated the humanistic value of literature as an interpersonal experience (Ferretti, 508). Although relatively heterogeneous, the Gruppo '63 shared the desire to return to the linguistic experimentation advocated by the historical avant-garde of the early twentieth century. Its members all believed in the importance of poetic language as a means of engaging the world. The more politically committed of them thought it possible to combat linguistically the alienation typical of industrialized society, some advocating the use of a vocabulary and style usually associated with technology and science (Manacorda, 469-70, 474). It goes without saying that the linguistic experimentation of the Gruppo '63 contrasted sharply with neorealism's interest in the local dialects of the country's illiterate and semi-illiterate classes.

The rise of the neo-avant-garde was closely linked to radical transformations in Italian society brought on by rapid industrial development in the late-1950s and early 1960s, and the growth of the "culture industry." Umberto Eco, an author considered to be emblematic of the Italian postmodern and one of the group's most prominent members, theorized the positive aspects of the culture industry, and the utility of "literary engineering." In *Opera aperta* he argues that works are free from the writer's authority, hence open to an infinite number of interpretations. The reader takes precedence over the writer, who willingly abdicates his authority over the text, and through interpretation, collaborates to "complete" the "open" literary work. However, for Eco the open text decides the extent to which reader collaboration must be controlled, encouraged, directed, and transformed. The writer appears to relinquish control when he declares himself superfluous to the appreciation of the text and asks for the interpretive collaboration of the reader. But in point of fact, he is in firm control of the narrative process, through which he re-orders the apparent chaos of the universe.[5] As Eco affirms in *Lector in fabula*, the meta-fictionist feigns his death in order "to repressively direct reader cooperation" (60).

It was not by accident that Eco became the greatest practitioner of the literary engineering he theorized. Literary engineering denotes a process of writing whereby erudite works of high literary value are pre-packaged to meet (and create) the needs of a mass reading public. Such planning and construction of the literary product takes into account, from the outset of the creative process, reader tastes and desires (Ferretti, 54-55). While writing the author carefully creates a public for his works by positing a model reader, who is both capable of identifying the erudite citations and other linguistic codes to be deciphered, and is responsive to the flattery inherent in such a proposal. The reader's expectations are unchanged for there is nothing new to be found in the work that might cause him to change his views. Instead, as a consumer of the text he uncovers the probable and the foreseeable (the skillful blending of old and new within the plot, the pre-ordained truths, etc. (Ferretti, 56). The explicit intention of Eco's *Apocalitici e integrati* is that of analyzing a "craft whose goals are consumption, escapism, and the popularizing of acquisitions." In other words, he sought to legitimize the utility of the "mediation" and "vulgarization" of elite cultural experience to a mass audience. To that end, Eco juxtaposed popular pulp novels of the day to novels capable of transferring "avant-garde" experiences to a higher level of consumption in an intelligent and productive way. Thus, as Terry Eagleton has written, the model reader proposed by Eco and other Structuralist theoreticians is merely "a function of the text itself" (105).

If it is true that the author does not renounce his authority over the text and that his purpose is to impose order on a chaotic world, Eco's historical meta-fictions actively strive to overcome the post-cognitive perplexity that is said to be endemic to our postmodern condition. Eco argues in *Opera aperta* that contemporary art must deal with the chaos caused by the breakdown of the traditional Order set out a millennium ago by the great Medieval *summae*. The world codified by such writers as Thomas Aquinas has collapsed. Modern artwork does not reflect a conception of the cosmos as a hierarchy of clear and pre-established orders. Eco's purpose is that of investigating how contemporary art and artists give form to a world dominated by "chance, indeterminacy, probability, and ambiguity" (5, 50, 16-17).

Eco's novel *Il nome della rosa* is emblematic in this regard. A murder-mystery which has the characteristics both of a Gothic novel and an historical meta-fiction, it evokes a multitude of canonical literary texts while presenting itself as a sort of *conte philosophique* designed to illuminate the theological disputes that took place within Scholasticism during the late Middle Ages. Its techniques range from the imitation of medieval writings to satire. Verifiable historical figures are mixed with fictitious ones in what purports to be a personal memoir dealing with the events that transpired in a monastery during a week in November of 1347. But the effect of Eco's parodic undermining of the literary tradition through the use of erudite quotations of canonical texts is the condensation of the past into the reader's present. On the one hand, we are offered the fragmentation of a chaotic world, on the other its domination by means of the conventions of the detective story. Although in fact the detective fails to solve the case while the murderer destroys himself.

The enormous success of *Il nome della rosa* gave rise to what has been termed the "Eco effect" (Perosa), namely a proliferation of works by novelists who hoped to follow in Eco's footsteps. These writers strove to overcome what they saw as the three principal weakness of much contemporary Italian writing: the illegibility of neo-avant-garde experimentalism, the emphasis on subject matter typical of realistic fiction, and the consumerist orientation of much contemporary writing. In their attempt to give Italian narrative an international profile, some writers, Gianni Celati for example, turned to biography; others, such as Daniele Del Giudice, adopted a style of writing more commonly associated with the physical sciences.

At this same time, the women's movement raised in Italy the question of the existence of a uniquely female literary perspective. The novels of Rosetta Loy are important in this regard as they may be read as the direct expression of a feminine sensibility that refuses to adapt to a male-dominated world and to a literary canon conceived by men. Her prose concentrates on the intimate psychology of female characters and their family life. In *Le strade di polvere,* Loy uses the traditional model of the historical novel but avoids the grand sweep of events characteristic of classic realism of the nineteenth-century. She writes from an intentionally narrower, more intimate, domestic perspective. Narration is neither carried forth nor concentrated on one character, but revolves around the home. The family residence, evoked at the outset of the book, conditions and defines all individual identities, and at the novel's conclusion outlives all family members, who leave the house alone to face an uncertain future. Her historical narrative is without a center of consciousness, thereby denying the reader access to a unified perspective with which to identify.

Because of post-modernity's loss of faith in *grands récits* and its preference for intimate narratives, a minimalist trend, paralleling that identified by John Barth in America, gained impetus in Italy. As one commentator has written, the "form of the short story, indeed of the short, unrelated, fragmented narrative, [came to be] cherished and practiced in a way that was unthinkable" prior to the 1980s (Perosa). As theorized by John Barth, literary minimalism adopts the terseness usually associated with the short story ("A Few Words about Minimalism"). And according to Frederick Barthelme, minimalist works may be considered small poems in prose designed to provide, rather than the microcosmic essence of reality, an intimate representation of a shared world. The reader is thus called, not to witness the representation of the world, but to experience and participate in local events that are "palpable, compelling, frightening." His close depictions of the world are "somehow remarkably *real* because the context and components [are] not obviously fantasies, abstractions, assertions about the language, arguments dressed up as fictions, but ordinary things, ordinary places that allow the reader to insert his/her world in the blank spaces" (Barthelme, "On Being Wrong," 26, 27). Barthelme's own *Bob the Gambler* is a highly significant example of this trend.

Perhaps the most significant Italian exponent of this trend is Gianni Celati. His *Narratori delle pianure* provides a series of direct reproductions of oral accounts of everyday life in the Po Valley, offering an immanent rendering of events that focus on the conflict between modernity and traditional ways of thinking and acting. The brief narratives of Celati (whose debut as an author was sponsored by Calvino) are primarily concerned with the meta-temporal reasons that catalyze narration, and the specific forms narration takes. His *Avventure in Africa* is a cross between a prose documentary and an expressionistic rendering of the experiences of a European tourist during his first trip to Africa. To explain his penchant for minimalist narrations, Celati has stated that in order to combat the separateness inherent in the writer's condition, he seeks out a "feeling" or link between words and the archetypal or mythological origins of humanity, which is lost in contemporary society. His writings "confront words and the time of words" while seeking a narrative "tone" that might bind him to others at a pre-linguistic, a-temporal level (Lapenna, 54). Following Barth, Celati believes that since the world is organized according to our narration of it, all human praxis is a fiction; a fiction, however, which we must think is true. His rejection of globalizing perspectives reflects the postmodern move toward localized knowledge and underwrites the basic notion that we cannot understand reality in its entirety because we are part of it and thus subject to all its languages, possibilities, and uncertainties.

Gesualdo Bufalino's inquiry into the loss of wholeness, into the instability that has replaced ordered systems of knowledge, and into a multi-dimensional and mutable reality defines well the postmodern *Zeitgeist*. Peter Hainsworth has pointed out that while Bufalino is very much concerned with the Sicilian character, he "has no vision of history" (21). Instead his focus is on the instability and insubstantiality of human life, whose ultimate meaning, if there is one, may be found in death. His first work, *Dicerie dell'untore*, tells the story of a plague-spreader, quarantined in a tuberculosis sanitarium, who is searching for the ultimate reasons to his life. Yet, for Bufalino "there is no one foundation or transcendent objective order to which we can refer, but rather many." Moreover, "these entities or modes of existence are without metaphysical legitimation; instead they are created by human beings and are realized in a play of forces" (Dombroski, "Re-writing Sicily," 271). In *Dicerie*, the narratives of the plague-stricken are meant to forestall death. Similarly, in *Le menzogne della notte* the four main characters are political prisoners scheduled for execution at sunrise. Each tells of the events which led to his imprisonment on prompting from the warden, who hopes one of them will inadvertently reveal the identity of the leader of their conspiracy. The hope expressed by one of the captives — that from their stories (significantly, the "menzogne" or lies of the title) some justification for their destiny might emerge — is ill-founded. This result was to be expected, as one critic has written, "given the total absence of theological meaning from Bufalino's perspective and his distinctly postmodern tendency to a surface or constructed reality" (Dombroski, "Re-writing Sicily," 272). The prisoners in effect choose death over betrayal, frustrating all expectations of attaining an even fictional truth.

In addition to the formal responses to the postmodern condition given by such writers as Calvino, Eco, Celati, and Bufalino, Italy has produced numerous "strong" narrative responses as well. The work of Vincenzo Consolo, for example, investigates forms of individual memory that engage civil history, with the purpose of bringing to the surface the complexities of a civilization buried in time. Consolo confronts his reader with historical documents and facts on the one hand, and, on the other, with the poetic retrieval of archaic, primordial and mythical remembrance. This "double register" always goes forward "with an eye — that of the weak and downtrodden — turned toward the present (Burgaretta)" to whom memory restores a lost temporal depth. Consolo's recent *Lo spasimo di Palermo* concludes a cycle of works that investigate the history of Italy since the Unification, depicting the travails of a generation that came of age during the Resistance. The novel's protagonist, the father of a post-1968 terrorist, is tormented both by instances of his own less-than-heroic behavior and by his son's frustrated dreams of a new society. Consolo investigates the labyrinthine meanderings of his memory while attempting to negotiate life in a present dominated by the collusion of Church, State and Mafia.

Daniele Del Giudice's characters also investigate issues of pressing actuality such as the crisis of reason, the relationship of science to literature, and the prospect of a united Europe (Ferroni, 726). As was the case with Celati, Del Giudice's literary debut (*Lo stadio di Wimbledon*) was endorsed by Calvino, and, like Calvino's, Del Giudice's work has prospered from contact with the physical sciences. Del Giudice adopts a clear and concise form of expression to conceal emotions and anxieties behind a seemingly imperturbable language and meticulous description reminiscent of the *école du regard* (Manacorda, 912).[6] His works are also metafictional in that they are concerned with the act of writing. *Lo stadio di Wimbledon* investigates the reasons behind a writer's decision to stop writing in order to devote himself to the people around him; while his *Atlante occidentale* is the story of the friendship that develops between an elderly writer on the verge of a professional crisis and a young scientist who is close to discovering a new theory of the atom.

From the beginning of his career Sebastiano Vassalli has striven to assign a practical function to literature, placing special emphasis on political confrontation. He rejects the idea that literature has a nature of its own distinct from the social world and has underlined the writer's responsibility to retrieve sense from the surrounding world (Manacorda, 548-49). As Zygmunt G. Barański has indicated, Vassalli

> is quite explicitly shifting the focus of his writing away from the narcissistic, self-indulgent, ultimately vacuous aestheticism of so many of his peers. Instead he is intent on re-proposing the age-old question regarding the relationship between writers and the world; he is bent on underlining the necessary contacts between literature and experience, between art and the mundane; most of all, he is highlighting the social dimension of writing, and thus the responsibilities this entails. (243)

Over the past three decades Vassalli has continued to "construct a vision of himself as an author" (Barański, 242). His use of metaliterary quotations is never an end unto itself, but is "always and principally concerned with some sort of "reality" beyond that of the written word" (Barański, 243). Vassalli has distinguished himself with historical metafictions such as *La notte della cometa* (which retells the life and times of the poet Dino Campana) and *La chimera*, an ironic overturning of Manzoni's classic *I promessi sposi*. His concern in both these works is that of giving voice to figures silenced by history. In *La chimera* Vassalli historically reconstructs the story of an innocent young woman found guilty of witchcraft and burnt at the stake. It has been pointed out that *La chimera* effectively demonstrates how very different conclusions about the 17th century can be reached by authors with radically diverse perspectives such as Manzoni and Vassalli (Barański, 254). Like the American novelist E. L. Doctorow, Vassalli looks beyond historical "truths," which are always subjectively constructed, to the "spirit of truth," which is accessible if one is scrupulously honest" (Barański, 254).

The call for the reader's collaboration in the writings of Antonio Tabucchi has little to do with the notion of the "death of the author" postulated by Roland Barthes in the mid- and late- 1960s.[7] Instead, Tabucchi's need to de-center the perspective of narration is behind his desire to engage the reader in the writing process. This in turn has caused him recently to compose works in his second language, Portuguese, which he then has had translated by others into his native Italian. He has argued that writing in a language other than one's own highlights aspects of the self that are not associated with what he calls the "hegemonic I." Such "linguistic schizophrenia" permits irreconcilable traits of a non-monolithic ego to co-exist within the text. The mediation of the translator then prevents direct writer-reader communication, and thus diminishes the writer's authority. The reader is forced to fill in the blanks left by the now disarticulated and irretrievable authorial self.

Tabucchi borrowed this strategy from the heteronymic theory of the Portuguese Modernist Fernando Pessoa. Pessoa's heteronyms were not mere *noms de plume*, but poet-characters invented in minute detail, including biographies, somatic features, esthetic preferences, cultural backgrounds and idiosyncrasies. They all wrote with distinct styles, and succeeded in establishing themselves as self-sufficient individuals. Tabucchi takes this means of radical self-analysis from Pessoa, not simply to analyze repressed aspects of his own personality, but to overcome the monadic isolation of the modernist subject. The examination of the otherness within allows his subjects to better understand and interact with what is external.

This freeing of what has been suppressed is part of an attempt to bring artistic experience out of the realm of the "I" to the objectifying perspective of the "We." Therefore, the dialogic complicity of the reader is a necessary complement to the writer's desire to be inscribed in the world. For Tabucchi, writing is no longer a symptom of human alienation, as was the case with Joyce, Proust, Svevo, Musil, Pessoa, Pirandello, Kafka and Beckett, but a means of dealing with life's most elementary problems and with a hostile reality.

Tabucchi's *Sostiene Periera* (1994) and *La testa perduta di Damasceno Monteiro* (1997) are important examples of socially engaged prose. Like his earlier *Notturno indiano* (1984), and his *Il filo dell'orizzonte* (1986), these works can be described as mysteries or detective stories that in a typically postmodern fashion fail to achieve closure. What is perhaps unusual in these novels is the object of the quest: rather than the murderer, Tabucchi's protagonists are looking for their alter egos. On the other hand, his *L'angelo nero* (1991) juxtaposes seemingly occasional, mosaic representations of local realities. Their implied narrators give voice to the suppressed trauma of Italians, more or less of Tabucchi's generation, those whose birth coincided approximately with World War II and who came of age during the social unrest of the 1960s. Thus, we can say that all of Tabucchi's protagonists seek to transcend their own individuality and speak to the need of Italian intellectuals to confront the literary, social, and political inheritance of the twentieth century.

As the second millennium drew to a close Italians lived a period that witnessed the "end of ideologies" (in this context the term "ideology" is not intended to denote forms of false consciousness, but is associated with its traditional value of "moral compass," a global instrument for world visions and for critical intervention), a process accelerated by the collapse of the Berlin Wall and of the Soviet state. In Italy, as in the rest of Europe, exponents of "negative thought" questioned the viability and the correctness of the origins and any "end" of history. Italian postmodernist writings responded to this "crisis of reason," either seeking to stylistically reflect the fragmentation installed by postmodernity or by moving to narrow the gaps postmodernity rent in the social fabric. As we have seen, Italy has produced in recent years significant samples of postmodern writing that refuse to abstain from interrogating the present. In some instances the free play of language allows the disassembling of the dominant cultural policy (totality). In others, the refusal to surrender literature's right to interrogate the present is an explicit interrogation of the future of what has yet to be lived and written. They seek to transform and redirect the flux of post-modernity, by installing a narration of narrations that transcends local knowledge while seeking to restore to the present its lost dialogic cohesiveness.

NOTES

1. It must be noted that neo-realism as a movement had other, much more potent enemies than Leftist literary critics. First and foremost, it had to contend with the highly conservative Italian government and State apparatus. There one found great support for a partisan clerical cultural politics that eschewed neither crude forms of censorship and economic pressure nor the crass use of its dominance of public radio and television broadcasting to silence what it considered negative depictions of social reality.

2. Such as Kruschev's denunciation of Stalin, the subsequent Soviet invasions of Poland and Hungary, and the Anglo-French invasion of the Suez Canal.

3. The poetic research of the Oulipo group aimed at the integration of mathematical procedures into literature. The application of mathematical symmetry and combinatorial analysis would enrich literary creativity by forcing authors to write *sous constrainte*: the creative act reposed in the choice of self-imposed limitations.

4. Calvino, *Se una notte d'inverno un viaggiatore*, 92, 47. See also, Calvino, "Se una notte d'inverno un narratore." Concealed here is the first "level of reality in literature" — the Cartesian "I write, therefore I am" — on which Calvino's construct is founded (I. Calvino, "I livelli della realtà in letteratura," 383).

5. In this regard see Eco, *Opera aperta*; and his "Postille" to *Il nome della rosa*.

6. As Manacorda indicates, in *Atlante occidentale*, Del Giudice's two protagonists "summarize the problem and the drama of contemporary humanity: the assumption of responsibility for the ultimate choices on which the future of humanity depends, along with the possibility of articulating those choices" in narrative (913).

7. Barthes writes that since "the generating center of linguistic time is always the present of the speech-act [énonciation]" (14); however, "the subject of the speech-act can never be the same as the one who acted yesterday: the I of the discourse can no longer be the site where a previously stored-up person is innocently restored." In other words, the I expresses itself and dies. As Barthes explains, "once a fact is recounted — for intransitive purposes, and no longer to act directly upon reality" a "gap appears, the voice loses it origin, the author enters into his own death, [and] writing begins" (49). Therefore, the reader is the true writer of the text: since the I is dead, the reader appropriates the "dead" author's tale and recounts it.

WORKS CITED

Barañski, Zygmunt G. "Sebastiano Vassalli. Literary Lives," in *The New Italian Novel*, 249-57.

Barth, John. "The Literature of Exhaustion," in J. Barth, *The Friday Book. Essays and Other Non-fiction*, New York: Putnam, 1984. See also, in *The Friday Book*, "The Literature of Replenishment."

_____ "A Few Words About Minimalism," *New York Times Book Review*, December 28, 1986, 1.

Barthelme, Frederick. "On Being Wrong: Convicted Minimalist Spills Bean," *New York Times Book Review*, April 3, 1988, 1; 25-27.

_____ *Bob the Gambler*, Boston: Houghton Mifflin, 1997.

Barthes, Roland. "To Write: An Intransitive Verb?" and "The Death of the Author" in R. Barthes, *The Rustle of Language*, trans. R. Howard, 1984, New York: Hill and Wang, 1986; 11-21, 49-55.

Benedetti, Carla. *Pasolini contro Calvino. Per una letteratura impura*, Turin: Bollato Boringhieri, 1998.

Borges, Jorge Luis. *Ficciones*, Buenas Aires: Emecé Editores S.A., 1956.

Bufalino, Gesualdo. *Dicerie dell'untore*, Palermo: Sellerio, 1981.

_____ *Le menzogne della notte*, Milano: Bompiani, 1988.

Burgaretta, Sebastiano. "Mito e ragione nell'opera di Vincenzo Consolo," *Otto/novecento*, V. 17, N. 1, January-February 1993, 171-80.

Calvino, Italo. *Il sentiero dei nidi di ragno*, Turin: Einaudi, 1947.

_____ *Il visconte dimezzato*, Turin: Einaudi, 1952.

_____ "Il midollo del leone," *Paragone*, N. 66, June 1955, now in I. Calvino, *Saggi*, 9-27.

_____ "Nord e Roma-Sud," *Contemporaneo*, March 31, 1956, now in I. Calvino, *Saggi*, 2183-87.

_____ *Fiabe italiane*, Turin: Einaudi, 1956.

_____ *Le cosmicomiche*, Turin: Einaudi, 1965.

_____ *Ti con zero*, Turin: Einaudi, 1967.

_____ *Le città invisibili*, Turin: Einaudi, 1972.

_____ *Il castello dei destini incrociati*, Turin: Einaudi, 1973.

_____ *Se una notte d'inverno un viaggiatore*, Turin: Einaudi, 1979.

_____ *I livelli della realtà in letteratura*, in I. Calvino, *Saggi*, 381-98.

_____ "Se una notte d'inverno un narratore," *Alfabeta*, December, 1979, 4-5.

_____ *Palomar*, Turin: Einaudi, 1983.

_____ *Saggi. 1945-1985*, Ed. M. Barenghi, Milan: Mondadori, 1995.

Celati, Gianni. *Narratori delle pianure*, Milan: Feltrinelli, 1988.

_____ "Finzioni a cui credere," *Alfabeta*, N. 16, December 1984.

_____ *Avventure in Africa*, Milan: Feltrinelli, 1998.

Ceserani, Remo. *Raccontare il postmoderno*, 1997, Milano: Bollati Boringhieri, 1998.

Consolo, Vincenzo. *Lo spasimo di Palermo*, Milan: Mondadori, 1998.

Del Giudice, Daniele. *Lo stadio di Wimbledon*, Turin: Einaudi, 1983.

_____ *Atlante occidentale*, Turin: Einaudi, 1985.

Dombroski, Robert S. "Re-writing Sicily: Postmodern Perspectives," in *Italy's "Southern question": Orientalism in One Country*, Ed. Jane Schneider, New York : Berg, 1998, 261-76.

Eagleton, Terry. *Literary Theory*, 1983, Minneapolis: U of Minnesota P, 1996.

Eco, Umberto. *Opera aperta*, 1962, Milan: Bompiani, 1976.

_____ *Apocalittici e integrati*, Milano: Bompiani, 1965.

_____ *Lector in fabula. La cooperazione nei testi narrativi*, Milan: Bompiani, 1979.

_____ *Il nome della rosa*, Milan: Bompiani, 1980.

Ferretti, Gian Carlo. *Il best seller all'italiana. Fortune e formule del romanzo «di qualità»*, Milan: Masson, 1993

Ferroni, Giulio. *Storia della letteratura italiana. Il Novecento*, Turin: Einaudi scuola, 1991.

Foucault, Michel. "Qu'est-ce qu'un auteur?," *Bulletin de la Société francaise de Philosophie*, July-September, 1969.

Hainsworth, Peter. "Gesualdo Bufalino: Baroque to the Future, in *The New Italian Novel*, 20-34.

Lapenna, Antonietta. "Conversazione con Gianni Celati," *Gradiva*, 4 (1987): 53-57.

Loy, Rosetta. *Le strade di polvere*, Turin: Einaudi, 1987.

Manacorda, Giuliano. *Storia della letteratura italiana contemporanea. 1940-1996*, Nuova edizione aggiornata, Roma: Editori Riuniti, 1996.

The New Italian Novel, Ed. Z.G. Barański and L. Pertile, Edinburgh, Edinburgh UP, 1993.

Perosa, Sergio. "The Heirs of Calvino and the Eco Effect," *New York Times Book Review*, August 16, 1987, 1; 24-25.

Tabucchi, Antonio. *Notturno indiano*, Palermo: Sellerio, 1984.

_____ *Il filo dell'orizzonte*, Milan: Feltrinelli, 1986.

_____ *I volatili del Beato Angelico*, Palermo: Sellerio, 1987.

_____ *L'angelo nero*, Milan: Feltrinelli, 1991.

_____ *Sostiene Pereira*, Milan: Feltrinelli, 1994.

_____ *La testa perduta di Damasceno Monteiro*, Milan: Feltrinelli, 1997.

Vassalli, Sebastiano. *La notte della cometa*, Turin: Einaudi, 1990.

_____ *La chimera*, Turin: Einaudi, 1990.B

ELLEN NERENBERG

Pulp Fiction, "Italian Style"

"Conrad come sta? Chiede ancora di me? Ha minacciato di tagliarsi le vene, bere il suo sangue e spedirmene un po' dentro una fialetta di soluzione fisiologica? Ho letto tutti i manga che mi hai regalato e ho visto le tue foto su *Playboy* di Ottobre. Se vuoi rispondere alla mia lettera, e se ne hai voglia incolla sotto il francobollo un acido Beta Kappa, che tanto sai già a cosa mi serve. Mi piace il tuo nuovo naso e dovresti venire a trovarmi prima di Natale. Esci ancora con il negro della pubblicità degli spermicidi?"

Isabella Santacroce, *Destroy*[1]

[How's Conrad? Does he still ask about me? Has he threatened to open his veins, drink his own blood and send me some in a pipette? I read all the stuff you gave me and I saw your photos in the October *Playboy*. If you want to write back and if you could, send me some Beta Kappa blotter acid underneath the stamp on the envelope: you already know what I want it for. I like your new nose and you should come visit before Christmas. Are you still dating the black guy from the spermicide ads?]

I. *Primi delitti*, or, how I learned to love the (literary) bomb

Historically, "pulp fiction" derived its name from the paper source on which this popular literature was printed in the United States: the stock was recycled, extracted from the paper pulp of a variety of sources, something that distinguished it from the more expensive paper stock used for the printing of "proper" literature purveyed by publishing houses and magazines with the deeper pockets required for these finer endeavors.[2] Of common (read: low) origin, "pulp" was always a matter of taste: it was popular, not necessarily "good", and its success — understood as both financial and aesthetic, inasmuch as its diffusion was concerned — depended on sales, not the opinions of publishers, editors, critics, or academics. The tastes of the reading public consuming this phenomenon ran lurid and along lower lines than those of canonical, aulic literature; "pulp" told the stories of hard-boiled detectives, gumshoes, gamblers, con artists, prostitutes, and others just outside the law.[3]

The recent fiction published in Italy, in Italian, with the interchangeable names of "splatter" and "pulp," shares some of these properties. Like the American publishing phenomenon, Italian pulp is popular, it tends to showcase those beyond the pale of law and order, and it, too, is a matter of taste. Paying homage to a more contemporary practitioner of "pulp" praised by nearly every young Italian writer (*viz.*, Quentin Tarantino, the director of the 1994 Miramax film *Pulp Fiction*), the Italian articulation of "pulp" is suffused by violence.[4] Violence — like the horror this body of work describes — is extreme, unrestrainable, and perhaps above all else, it is cool. A search for cool propels these young Italian writers (henceforth I will call them "pulpisti") into investigations of late-twentieth-century, often urban entanglements. The scenarios they devise are complicated by (among other things) drugs, self-mutilation, the commodification of culture, and global media. The characters of this literature are on the move; like Misty, the protagonist of Isabella Santacroce's short novel *Destroy* whose letter home from London makes up my epigraph, they leave the Peninsula (either literally or virtually) for other outposts in the European Union, the US, and beyond.[5]

Imminent violence characterizes all the sub-genres I mentioned just above, and alternately takes the form of patricide, matricide, homicide, genocide, the killing of pets, the killing of strangers, the killing of *extracommunitari* (illegal aliens), and so forth. This violence, particularly when serialized, is understood as the progeny of an increasingly anonymous society in which the law's capacity to curb violence and aggression is impaired and derided.[6] Although some critics differ, no precise boundaries demarcate phenomena like "*noir* italiano," "pulp", "splatterpulp," "cyberpunk," "trash," "narrativa grunge," and the written production of the "cannibali"; indeed, the common interest in (cool) violence that characterizes all these divisions draws them into a common rubric.[7] As concerns the extant critical assessments, like those of Luca Gervasutti, Fulvio Panzeri, Raffaele Cardone, Franco Galato, and, to a lesser extent, Filippo La Porta, these sub-genres feature as many commonalities as they do distinct attributes.[8] The broadlines of this common genealogy reveal how catholic are the tastes (and production) of Niccolò Ammaniti, Silvia Ballestra, Alessandro Baricco, Luisa Brancaccio, Enrico Brizzi, Rossana Campo, Mauro Covacich, Giuseppe Culicchia, Marcello Fois, Raffaella Krismer, Marco Lodoli, Carlo Lucarelli, Giulio Mozzi, Aldo Nove, Andrea Pinketts, Isabella Santacroce, and Tiziano Scarpa, to list a few authors associated with these genres.[9] With the increased rapidity of global communications and the attendant development of worldwide markets for the representation of violence (about which I will say more directly), "influences" on the cadre of young writers are uncovered by the mere click of a switch (or mouse). Like *bricoleurs*, young Italian authors respond to influences where they happen upon them. Enrico Brizzi, young Bolognese author of the bestselling 1993 *Jack Frusciante è uscito dal gruppo* (*Jack Frusciante Has Left the Group*), describes his influences this way: "le mie letture sono disordinatissime . . . come riferimenti culturali . . . sono molto più vicino a *Supertifo, Mountain Biking* che a good ol' Carlo Emilio Gadda."[10]

This genealogy of influences embraces pop culture (particularly from the Seventies onward), youth consumerism and commodity culture, an interest in *cronaca* (or journalistic reportage), and a global outlook bolstered by such transnational multimedia influences as popular music, cinema, television, and the Internet. This, a preliminary consideration of the "pulp" phenomenon in Italy, will concentrate on the confluence of the various uses of different media and ask how an interest in global or transnational culture plays out in an Italian context.

Signal in a discussion of these different media is their relation to *literary* production, my focus in these pages. Different from the linguistic signification of literary texts, in visual media violence effaces linguistic negotiation. The body in extreme pain, as Elaine Scarry has argued, is located outside of linguistic parameters and mediation.[11] Cinema provides a particularly useful case in point. In action movies, martial-arts films, pornography (in film or video format), or (the notorious, legendary) snuff films, what the actors *say* has next to no meaning: the body as the vector for violence effortlessly trumps the *enoncée*.[12] Following a brief examination of the impact of non-linguistic media on Italian authors of "pulp fiction," I will explore Raffaella Krismer's 1997 novel *Il signore della carne*, which subscribes to some "pulp" conventions and subverts others.

II. Transnational Multimedia

A. Rock: Variations on a Theme

> Chi oggi ha meno di vent'anni ha conosciuto i *clip* di MTV e di Videomusic più che il vecchio rock monolitico dei grandi gruppi. Forse i *teenager* di oggi non hanno coordinate musicali molto chiare (la

mercificazione elimina la prospettiva), ma anche se parliamo di *kids* che ascoltano veramente musica e non fans dei Take That, credo che la definizione "rock" sia ormai troppo stretta; anche i due minuti dei Sex Pistols, da soli, non bastano più. Credo che l'immaginario della mia generazione, e dunque anche degli scrittori che ne fanno parte, sia colonizzato dal *crossover*, dal mescolarsi di suoni diversi coi fondamentali del punk. Considero dunque estremamente indicativo il fatto che tra le *band* più significative e influenti ci siano nomi come i Red Hot Chili Peppers, Green Day, o i mai abbastanza esaltati Primus.

Enrico Brizzi[13]

[Anybody under twenty knows videos from MTV and Videomusic better than the music from the classic groups. Maybe teenagers today don't have clear musical coordinates (commodifcation reduces their perspective), but even if we're talking about kids who actually listen to music and not Take That fans, I think the definition of what rock is is too limited; even two minutes of the Sex Pistols, on their own, isn't enough anymore. I think the imagination of my generation, and of the writers of my generation, has been colonized by the crossover phenomenon, of mixing different sounds with the fundamentals of punk. I find it really indicative that among today's most significant and influential groups are the Red Hot Chili Peppers, Green Day, or a band like Primus, which is never praised highly enough.]

Popular music serves a function at once thematic and formal in contemporary "pulp" fiction. Rock n' roll has the power to swiftly and undeniably ground narrative in youth culture and a history of social change. Giuseppe Caliceti's novel about clubbing, *Fonderia Italghisa* (1996), thematizes popular music through the citation of such recording artists as Vasco Rossi, Luciano Ligabue, Articolo 31, and Frankie Hi Nrg. However, the music that pervades this literature is not so Peninsular as this list of recording groups might lead us to believe. Giorgio van Straten's citations of Bob Dylan in his novel *Generazione* (1987) as well as the comments of Brizzi, given in the passage just above, testify to the presence and cachet of a distinctly international musical menu. Of course, the passage from Dylan to the Red Hot Chili Peppers, Green Day, and Primus tells another story and one of just as much import. The solo singer songwriter has been superseded by the grunge group, and songs of social protest have given way to the jeremiads bellowed painfully by such groups as Nirvana, Pearl Jam, Fiona Apple, or Hole. At the same time, a nostalgia for the stadium rock of classic bands like Led Zeppelin shimmers on the horizon, evident in a work like Andrea Demarchi's *Sandrino e il canto celestiale di Robert Plant* (1996), where the title really says it all.

But more than flag common cultural referents (anomie, AIDS, suicide, and Ecstasy, to name but a few), the presence of popular music

also signifies formally for the *pulpisti*. Outside of any consideration of its thematic content, cultural critic Enzo Siciliano observed,
> music is a mercurial element that brings together different levels of meaning. For example, it links psychology and history . . . . Following the long tenure of minimalist literature . . . . perhaps we're beginning to feel again a need for novels that recuperate a more reflective narrative stance, that revive a dimension of thought. Music can help because it is the perfect form of the thought that thinks and the representation that is aware of itself as such. You could say that music draws wordlessly into the orbit of thought without the tiring deliberations of philosophy.[14]

Music's ability to form connections between otherwise discrete disciplines, as Siciliano notes, is but one of the manifestations of its formal influence on pulp narrative.[15] Judging from Sandro Veronesi's 1995 collection of essays interspersed by fiction, popular music may be used as a structuring device for prose fiction: this volume of (non-fictional) essays, entitled *Live*, is compiled as though it were a concert album. In fact, we may consider the short story, the prose genre of choice of the Italian Gen-Xers, as a reflection of album-like compilation. Giuseppe Culicchia recalls that the idea for organizing *Tutti giù per terra* (also made into a film in 1997) came to him while listening to the Ramones: "mi proponevo di riprendere la struttura di quei dischi, elaborando capitoli brevi, come fossero pezzi di un album."[16] Gabriele Romagnoli's 1994 collection, *Videocronache*, is compiled in like fashion, complete with a proposed "soundtrack" that suggests specific songs and recording artists (Tears for Fears, Sting, Stadio, Springsteen, Jovanotti, Vasco Rossi, the Rolling Stones, Fiorella Mannoia, among others) to accompany the reading of particular chapters.

Another formal property that comes to bear on prose of this genre concerns the practice of "sampling" ("remixaggio" in the Italian), popular in Rap and Hip Hop (which, in turn, make appearance nightly in clubs throughout the Peninsula).[17] "Sampling" works by lifting a recognizable portion of a popular song (percussion, the musical line of a particular instrument, a specific melody, the trademark sound of a particular artist, etc.) and interpolating it into a new and different song. "Sampling" is intrusive, deliberate, and exacts recognition; consequently, it should not be confused with copyright infringement or, worse, plagiarism. The standard operating procedure of DJs in clubs beginning sometime in the mid-Eighties, sampling became, in the decade that followed, *de rigeur*, a commonplace. (Though it has become by now an omnipresent phenomenon in popular music, vintage examples of "sampling" include the rap group Run-DMC's rendition of Aerosmith's "Walk this Way," or the Beastie Boys' use of AC-DC's "Back in Black.")[18]

Material for the "sampling" put to use in "pulp" fiction derives from a rich array of pop cultural expressions including popular music itself, cinema, comic books (these authors routinely praise Tiziano Scalvi's serial comic *Dylan Dog*) and graphic novels, commercials and advertisements, television, and so forth.[19] Writer for television Tommaso Labranca, Gervasutti informs us, convinced Aldo Nove, Rossana Campo, Isabella Santacroce, and Tiziano Scarpa to revise some of their own texts along the lines of "sampling" and "scratching," another DJ-club practice common in the Eighties which consisted in the manual backspinning of a record under the stylus, resulting in a considerable amount of static, hence its name. "[A] dire il vero," Gervasutti confesses, the experiment "è abbastanza deludente, però dimostra una volta di più il desiderio di fondere la musica e la letteratura."[20]

B. I Like to Watch: Violence and Visual Media

> Perchè il suo mondo, la luce di quel mondo, è nel video. In lui non c'è stato pendolarismo, diffidenza o cauto approccio. No, quello è il suo luogo di nascita, il suo continente, il punto cardinale. È un Tom Sawyer elettronico che ha perduto il suo amico Huck e si è inabissato in un mondo virtuale e sconosciuto.
>
> Nico Orengo, *Una lieve impressione*[21]
>
> [Because his world, the light of that world, is in the video. For him there had been no commuting for him, no diffidence nor cautious approach. No, that was his birthplace, his continent, the focal point. He is an electronic Tom Sawyer who has lost his friend Huck and has fallen into a virtual and unfamiliar world.]
>
> > In macchina io e Sergio facciamo sempre "Tàtta tàra tattà tatàtta."
> > Facciamo così all'inizio di Ok il prezzo è giusto.
> > Iva Zanicchi entra e c'è quella specie di festa, prima della publicità.
> > Tutti saltano e gridano: — OK il prezzo è giusto!
> > Aldo Nove, "Il mondo dell'amore"[22]
> >
> > [In the car Sergio and I always go "Tàtta tàra tattà tatàtta."
> > Like at the beginning of "The Price is Right."
> > Iva Zanicchi comes in and it's always like a party, before the commercials.
> > Everybody jumps up and yells: — OK, The Price is Right!]

Like popular music, visual media informs "pulp narrative" from both a thematic and formal perspective. The visual representation of violence of myriad kinds has become pervasive. Whereas cinematic violence, on the rise in the last thirty-year period, once required an act of will (buying a ticket, entering the theater), expanded television reportage has made global violence as near as the living room, as visible as one inaccurate click of the telecommand. Writer Fulvio Abbate (*Oggi è un secolo, Dopo l'estate, La peste bis*) remembers the chilling effect of watching on Tele Montecarlo the 1989 Rumanian tribunal that sentenced the Ceausescus, an event that produced an even greater impression once he realized that a synchronous world watched proceedings with him *dal vivo*.[23] But the visual witness of even more accidental (or random) violence has also become more common.

The spectacle of the catastrophic accident with its prerequisite jumble of dead and mutilated bodies problematizes the relation between representation and violence, whether accidental or, as in serial killing, calculated.[24] Theories concerning the mass spectacle of violence study the degree of potential "containment" of the violence witnessed, either in person or by way of media technologies. Containment theories establish that witnessing violence parries the menacing content of the spectacle: I am grateful for the *participation* of the not-me in the violence whose results I have just visually *witnessed*. The problem with this tack, Mark Seltzer argues, is that it "reduces mimesis or simulation or mediation to a distancing or loss of the real, and reduces contagious relations between bodies and reproductive technologies to distanced or voyeuristic representation."[25] The containment theory reifies the false binary between the natural and the artifactual, between matter and representation, between bodies and technologies, between internal and external configurations of the self.

Suffused by violent acts, Italian "pulp" fiction attests to the spread of the representation of violence throughout the global marketplace, and marks the passage from the visual to literary representation. Visual representation of violence, as I stated earlier, does not rely on linguistic comprehension and, consequently plays as well in Peoria, Illinois, as the old saw has it, as it does in Pisa. Thus, an assessment, like Fabio Giovannini's and Antonio Tentori's in their introduction to the collection *Cuore di pulp*, where they train on the national origins of the pulp movement, seems problematic. "Pulp," they want to assert, is Italian, instead of one component of an ever-globalizing market for splatter-pulp-horror.[26] What of the repeated testimonials of young writers who point to such extra-Peninsular cinematic influences as David Cronenberg, Danny Boyle, Martin Scorsese, Francis Ford Coppola, Brian DePalma, Gus Van Sant, Wim Wenders, Quentin Tarantino, and Steven Soderbergh, to mention but a few? Giovannini's and Tentori's chauvinism aside, their approach does feature the advantage of pointing out some of the ways that the early incarnations of "pulp" in Italy took shape and root.

It is worth noting that Quentin Tarantino points to Italian directors

Dario Argento, Luigi Fulci, and Mario Bava as early influences on his filmmaking. This also complicates any genealogy of influences; it becomes a problem of a sort of chicken and egg causality: contemporary writers point to extra-Italian influences, among them Tarantino, who points back to Argento who, in turn, has always claimed that his films are better received outside of Italy. Traumatic vision dominates Argento's cinematic *oeuvre*. Argento's structuring of the scenes of seeing repeatedly underscores the act of looking. Throughout his first film, *The Bird with the Crystal Plumage*, the writer Sam Dalmas (Tony Musante) flashes back to the vision of a murder being committed in a gallery of modern art in Rome.[27] The title for his 1971 film, *Four Flies on Grey Velvet* refers to the last image contained on a murder victim's retina and offers the only clue to the identity of the person stalking jazz musician Roberto Tobias (Michael Brandon). In an autopsy scene, a laser is projected onto the eyeball which is then able to reproduce the image. In *Profondo Rosso/ Deep Red* (1975), pianist Marc Daly (David Hemmings) is haunted by a missing clue he saw at the scene of the hatchet murder of a psychic. The clue disappears when he needs to track down the killer, only to reappear as a kind of *trompe l'oeil* at the film's climax. One of *Suspiria's* victims exhibits the darts that pierce her eyeballs. And the list does not stop there.[28]

Cinema may provide the *pulpisti* with thematic content, but they also borrow from it certain narrative techniques. Editing techniques proper to visual media clearly inform recent fiction; we can see the relation of the jump cut, quick cutting, and the standard length of a cinematic shot in a mainstream film, to the use of techniques like the "sampling" and "scratching" of popular music. We can also relate the more dilettantish notion of "zapping" (channel surfing) to the quick pace and (truncated) length of this fiction. Poet and novelist Edoardo Albinati confesses that "Guardo parecchio la TV, per quanto maldicendomi, e ne traggo spunti per trasformarla, materiale grezzo da lavorare.... Io mi lascio trafiggere dalla TV e spero che ne nasca qualcosa."[29] Aldo Nove dedicated his first collection of ultra-short fiction to the 1970s television character Woobinda. (He entitled still another collection, hilariously, *Superwoobinda*.) Whether or not television informs their writing in the same way or to the same degree, both Silvia Ballestra and Andrea Pinketts reveal it as a staple in their daily media diet.

Raffaella Krismer's first novel, *Il signore della carne*, exercises some of the themes I have advanced. Although video of the Internet variety is not conspicuous, cinema (especially some of the cinema I discussed earlier) is celebrated, and references to a legion of pop cultural influences is a chief trait. A graduate of the Università di Bologna, she was "discovered" like many other young writers in the Transeuropa-Mondadori stable, by Pier Vincenzo Tondelli for the second *Papergang* anthology, published in 1990.[30] Krismer is an accomplished stylist and this short novel offers some singing sentences in a gripping story. Moreover, in the sea of testosterone that characterizes the field of young writers of horror in Italy, this novel seems all the more refreshing for its embrace of wider themes and frames.[31] Exemplary of certain trends of the "pulp" genre as I have outlined it, *Il signore della carne* also strikes out in new directions.

III. Raffaella Krismer's *Il signore della carne*

Misi l'audio a mezzo volume.

Il talento magico di Cronenberg riusciva a ispirare gli attori sulla scene con tale visionaria sapienza, che ogni minimo dettaglio comunicava terrore. Poi, questo *Scanners* l'avevo già visto tipo trenta volte, non scherzo, ma a nessun costo avrei rinunciato alla replica di Canale Tele Nord.

Dubito molto ci siano persone preparate che ancora non conoscono 'sto capolavoro di genere. Comunque, quei pochissimi digiuni della faccenda dirò almeno che gli effetti speciali del film erano di un realismo agghiacciante: a un certo punto gli attori si gonfiava la testa fino a esplodere; i protagonisti erano dotati di formidabili facoltà telepatiche, credo potessero agire sui tessuti cellulari a colpi di volontà. Bastava un niente, per ritrovarsi con delle cisti esplosive su guance, tempie, e zigomi, alterazioni tremende dei tratti fisiognomici . . . .

Mi sistemai comoda sul divano, lasciai che la magia dello schermo mi facesse prigioniera e la visione degli incubi telepatici vincesse il piccolo velo di sonno.

Le due e venti.

Avevo ancora a disposizione un'ora e mezzo di alterazioni cellulari strepitose, prima di raggiungere camera mia. Okay, mi dissi. Mettiamoci ancora *più* comode e cerchiamo di tenere gli occhi bene aperti. Il mio problema principale era prestare attenzione ai punti di snodo del racconto, far tesoro delle soluzioni narrative che consentivano il crescendo della suspense. Si poteva imparare parecchio da un maestro così (12-13).

[I lowered the volume to half.

Cronenberg's magical talent succeeded in inspiring the actors with such visionary wisdom that each small detail telegraphed terror. But then, even though I've seen *Scanners* something like thirty times, no joke, for no price would I miss the rerun on Canale Tele Nord.

I doubt that there are "educated" people that still don't know this masterpiece of the genre. At any rate, for those very few starved of the phenomenon I will say at least that the special effects in the film are numbingly real: at a certain point the actors' heads swell to the point of bursting; the protagonists are graced with formidable telepathic skills: they could use them at will on cellular tissue, I think. Nothing was needed for tremendous physiognomic alterations to appear with exploded cysts on their cheeks, their temples, their cheekbones.

I made myself more comfortable on the couch, I let the magic of the screen take me prisoner and the vision of the telepathic nightmares dispel my slight sleepiness.

2:20.

I had another hour and a half of amazing cellular transformation before going to my room. Okay, I said to myself. Let's get even more comfortable and let's try to keep our eyes really open. My chief problem was attending to the clues in the story, mining the narrative solutions that yielded a crescendo for suspense. You could learn a lot from a maestro like this.]

As the novel begins, Rita is ensconced on her sofa, watching a late night rerun of David Cronenberg's *Scanners* on television. Rita shares an apartment in Bologna with Angela, and the first-person point of view alternates between them in the close to twenty chapters making up the novel's four sections. As the passage above makes clear, Rita is a young writer who has apprenticed herself to masters like Cronenberg, from whom she hopes to learn ways to sculpt and perfect the crafting of her stories, borrowing especially "effetti speciali . . . di un realismo agghiacciante." The influence of American film does not disappear at the close of the first episode, and later in the novel Rita defends her recourse to Hollywood and American independent cinema, praising Zemeckis, Spielberg, and her favorite, Tarantino. The more devoted, though less gifted, student of the pair, Angela, tries desperately to achieve two goals: to pass her course on International Law and to lose weight. Like many young women in Italy and elsewhere in the industrialized world, Angela's body falls far away from her desired body image. Her failed efforts to reduce dismay her. So convinced is she of this failure that she believes Dr. Milan, her nutritionist, has scheduled her appointments later and later in the evening so that she will not run into his other patients in the waiting room. Although Rita does not share her roommate's compulsiveness toward food, she watches (perhaps obsessively) horror reruns for inspiration for her "extreme" short stories.

One evening after Rita leaves for a party, Angela invokes il Signore della Carne, believing he will strip from her the unwanted weight. Rita, en route to the party in town, gets caught in a deluvial rainstorm, a flood we take as a cue for what is about to occur. Soaked to the skin when she arrives, Rita immediately goes to the bathroom to repair her "look." In the shower she is struck by a powerful, completely extraordinary, and extraordinarily painful menses. At the same time, Angela, back in the apartment, also experiences a sudden onset of menses. In the bathroom at the party, Rita hears voices (easily recognized as Italian either spoken backwards or supplemented with extra, irregular syllables) and, through space and time, detects Angela's pleas and warnings. Angela implores Rita not to return home, lest she encounter Osgood il Ripugnante (also Il detestabile), the emissary of Il signore della carne. Rita returns to find Angela in the thrall of a monstrous demon, whom she (Rita) subdues sexually and they eventually exorcise. Or so they believe.

Blood is the *sine qua non* of splatter (it is, after all, what splatters). And although blood has made a variety of appearances in horror literature and fiction, its appearance in the form of menstruation is rather uncommon. One significant appearance of menstruation in the genre occurs in Brian DePalma's 1976 film *Carrie*.

Close to the beginning of the film, Carrie White (Sissy Spacek) finishes gym class at her high school. The shower scene that follows is pleasant, warm, rosy, and — it is possible — an occasion for the private pleasure of masturbation. Shot in slow motion, this scene rhythmically corresponds to the climactic prom scene, where blood also figures prominently. Significantly, it is with the onset of menses that Carrie develops powers of telekinesis that form the basis of DePalma's film.

The problem with the film *Carrie*, at least for feminists, and at least according to Barbara Creed, is the way it signals misogynistic and conflictual views of women's bodies without really extricating itself from the sign system that vilifies women's bodies and women's blood.[32] However much Carrie may tell her mother, a religious fanatic played by Piper Laurie, that it is "natural" that women have breasts and that they menstruate, the film also makes it seem natural that menstruating women, when physically and emotionally abused, will cause immolation, general mayhem, and the crucifixion of their mothers. Rather than live as a powerful witch, Carrie kills her classmates, her mother, and herself.

In her influential work on horror, Julia Kristeva discusses the tight weave of revulsion and the abject, of revulsion at the abject.[33] Those things expelled (abjected) from the body (e.g., excreta, feces urine, pus, blood, and so forth) are the things that sicken us the most. Kristeva believes that the cadaver is the example par excellence of the abject since it is the corporeal shell that the soul has expelled or left behind.

Menses, like other bodily fluids, are expelled, the body rids itself of them, but they tend not to cause revulsion in the women whose bodies bleed monthly. (I will not rehearse the ways in which menstruation has been reviled in Western culture. Let us remember only the practice of the mikva in Judaism as well as the work of the late-nineteenth and early-twentieth-century forensic psychiatrist Cesare Lombroso, who capitalized the notion that women's criminality was predicated on menstruation.) Significantly, in DePalma's non-feminist film, Carrie is initially terrified and made hysterical at the appearance of her own blood.

The objectification of women DePalma is renowned for (e.g., in *Body Double,* and *Dressed to Kill*) certainly finds correspondence in some of the violent new fiction emanating from Italy. Emblematic of this tendency in contemporary Italian "pulp" fiction is "Rispetto," a dark and successful story from Niccolò Ammaniti's 1996 collection of short fiction, *Fango.* ("Fango" [mud] itself seems to herald something slippery, primordial, and potentially abject.) Ammaniti's delineation of the violence against women is more menacing than usual. The narrative voice of this short story is a collective "we," the force of which the reader finds undeniable. This is savage masculinity in numbers, and its aim is to satisfy its hunger. As the collective narrator says, "E quanto siamo affamati. Affamati di fica. Affamati di fica ruvida."[34] The aggregate of the verbal forms is remarkable for its ability to indicate a tribal voice and to capture the surge of collective power. The absence of a speaking "I" marks a progression, begun, perhaps, by Jay McInerney in his novel *Bright Lights, Big City,* who popularized once more the "you" characteristic of Hemingway's stories of the *Snows of Kilimanjaro* vintage.[35] MacInerney's and Hemingway's "you" is more intimate and personalized; theirs would be a "tu" rather than Ammaniti's indiscriminate, blurry "voi." The Italian flags this explicitly in a way the English cannot.

Ammaniti's successful and disturbing fiction tells the story of anonymous, tribal fun at a rave (near the coast, perhaps Rimini, though Ammaniti doesn't care to make this more precise). The evening turns nightmarish for the three female victims. While the young women are named (Maria, Paola, and Amanda), the young men are part of that indistinct group that makes up the famished "noi." The young men and women leave the dance club, drive to the beach, and, in an alcoholic blur (though these young men are not beholden to a power greater than they are, Ammaniti suggests), two of the women are viciously raped, one is beaten and killed outright, and another is left for dead.

Krismer's sense of humor is a great corrective to the potential violence against women that always seems near to hand in this genre. Menstrual blood, so reviled in *Carrie,* signals in Krismer's novel a solidarity between women that should make most feminists thrill. Not only have Angela and Rita demonstrated the very real biochemical phenomenon of human pheromones, which help synchronize hormonal cycles in a bounded community where more than one woman lives, but the sudden onset of menstruation is brought on sympathetically, a commiserative act. Other young women at the party try to help Rita and, importantly, no one maligns her.

DePalma uses menstruation to show a rupture in time. Reminiscent of the syncope figure advanced by Catherine Clément, Carrie is out of time: she and she alone is in the shower, long after the other young women have finished. DePalma calls attention to Carrie's syncopation, her rupture of time, through the use of the obtrusive cinematic device of slow-motion. There are other ruptures in this scene as well: the soap falling down along a vertical axis, interrupting what has been a uniform presentation of the body in space along the horizontal axis. The falling soap presages the appearance of the menstrual blood, which also descends vertically. Similarly, though the music does not end mid-note, it does end abruptly, finishing at the precise moment that blood appears. In a precise visual echo, blood descends dramatically along a lengthened vertical visual in the climax at the prom. Like its counterpart in the shower, the climax, as I have already noted, is also shot in slow-motion. Different from Carrie's freakish isolation, for she is both out of place and out of time, Krismer uses menstruation to draw into temporal proximity Rita's and Angela's conditions, and this is only the beginning of her revision.

Comically, when Rita returns home, she is greeted by the aroma of smoked trout and celery (remember, this was Angela the Plump's incantation) and finds her roommate barricaded, naturally, in the bathroom. I say naturally for where else should one encounter the abject save for the bathroom, the appropriate place for soil and that which expelled from the body? Tormented by Osgood, Angela requires her roommate's intercession. Rita sexually subdues Osgood who, depleted, begins to resume his non-bestial and mortal identity. Osgood's shedding of scales and regaining of human form exactly recalls one from the film *Hellbound*, the second of the *Hellraiser* film series inspired by Clive Barker's terrifying short story, *The Hellbound Heart*, and strengthens the connection between Krismer's "pulp" and visual culture. In fact, had Krismer not flagged Barker as an influence in the novel's first epigraph, one might be tempted to call this rendition more plagiarism than allusion.

Briefly, in *Hellraiser* Kirstie does battle with her fiendishly curious uncle, Frank, who, by way of a device he bought in the Orient, opens the portal to Hell. But Hell turns out to be even worse than Frank imagined, a place where his body is ceaselessly tormented, flayed, ripped asunder, stitched back together, only to be flayed and ripped apart once more. With the help of Kirstie's evil stepmother, Julia, Uncle Frank seeks to become corporeal once again. Julie lures anonymous men to her house, kills them, drains their blood and gives it to Frank who, with the blood of each new victim, acquires one more dermal layer. He kills Kirstie's father, whom she tries to retrieve from the underworld in *Hellbound*. Her conspirator in the second film in the series (there are, to date, four, though Barker's deal to direct ended with the first) is Tiffany, a traumatized, autistic young woman with a knack for puzzles. The (fiendishly curious) head physician of the insane asylum where the hysterical Kirstie has been placed at the end of the first film is, like Uncle Frank, slightly too interested in the parallel universe. He believes that Tiffany can help solve the riddle of Frank's rune and open the portal to hell. It is not what he expects, either, and a diabolical battle (with the trademark *Hellraiser* character, "Pinhead," familiar to Barker fans everywhere from the film's promotional campaign) ensues between the Doctor and Julia and the two young women.

Barker and Krismer both resist what Carol Clover identifies as the "last girl" strategy. Tracing a genealogy of slasher pictures mostly from Hollywood, Clover identifies the "last girl" who defies the demonic forces of evil.[36] Krismer, like Barker, doubles the "last girl," and they both locate her salvation in solidarity, for Barker between Kirstie and Tiffany, for Krismer between Angela and Rita. Kirstie in *Hellbound* will no more leave her friend Tiffany in hell than Rita will leave Angela to the domination of Osgood the Repugnant.[37]

Rita's allegiance to Angela and their friendship is the sort of thing that sets *Il signore della carne* apart from the random acts of violence so characteristic of the "pulp" genre. Not all "pulp" is violent in the way of visual media, especially, perhaps, pornography, where the representation of violence against women is the norm. By way of humor, *pulpiste* like Krismer and Santacroce, with whose work I began, subvert current notions of "pulp" and "cannibal" fiction in Italy. The components that make of this novel an exemplum of the "pulp" genre include the menace of violence, copious amounts of blood, and repeated references to an international market for horror. However, differing from so much of the contemporary testosterone-driven fiction, this particular novel distinguishes itself, much in the way that Clive Barker's fiction and films do, by refusing to vilify women, their blood, and their relationships to other women.

NOTES

The author thanks Noah Isenberg, Giancarlo Lombardi, Sean McCann, and Diana Sorensen.

1. Isabella Santacroce, *Destroy* (Milan: Feltrinelli, 1996), back cover copy. This and all translations are my own unless otherwise noted.

2. Classic pulp fiction authors include Raymond Chandler, Dashiell Hammett, et. al. Significant in this context is the work of James M. Cain, whose *The Postman Always Rings Twice* served as the blueprint for Luchino Visconti's 1942 film *Ossessione*.

3. For the publication history of pulp in the US market, see Sean McCann, *Gumshoe America* (Chapel Hill, NC: Duke U P, 2000).

4. See, among others, Alcide Paoline, "Tarantineide," *Messaggero Veneto* 29 June 1996 and the anonymous "I nipotini di Tarantino specchio di un'Italia 'cannibale'." URL: http://www.cyberlogic.it/abitare/Dic96/libri.htm#uno.

5. A hallmark of the language of some of these texts might be called "brand name fiction," an interest in connecting the characters (crafted in the Italian language, it goes without saying) with their fellow consumers worldwide. Silvia Ballestra offers a great example of this, interested by, as she says, a "'lingua di plastica' che sembra distribuita a Standa." See Giusi Ferré, "Questi romanzi vietati ai maggiori," *L'Europeo*, 8 February 1995. This kind of heightened attention to consumerism is a trait of the fiction of Bret Easton Ellis (especially in *American Psycho*), an often-cited influence on the *pulpisti*.

6. I explore the figuration of serial killing and the law in the literature of the "cannibali" in "Monstrous Murder: Serial Killers and Detectives in Contemporary Italian Fiction," in *Italian Literary Monsters*, ed. Keala Jewell (Wayne State U P, 2000).

7. Indeed, strictly speaking, some critics think the category of "pulp" should be limited to two collections of short stories, Niccolò Ammaniti's collection *Fango* and Aldo Nove's *Woobinda e altre storie senza lieto fine*.

8. I refer to Gervasutti's essential *Dannati e sognatori. Guida alla nuova narrativa italiana*. (Paisan di prato: Campanotto Editore, 1998), the essays collected and edited by Panzeri, Cardone, and Galato in *Altre storie. Inventario della nuova narrativa fra anni '80 e '90*, ed. Raffaelle Cardone, Franco Galato, Fulvio Panzeri (Milan: Marcos y Marcos, 1996). Filippo La Porta's assemblage of material in *La nuova narrativa italiana. Travestimenti a stili fine secolo* (Turin: Bollati Boringhieri, 1995), differs notably from the other two thematically organized collections and stretches beyond the received categories in the way it establishes critical links between different groups of writers. For an English language introduction to Italian "cannibal" literature see my "Monstrous Murder" and the forthcoming *Italian Pulp Fiction: The "Giovani Cannibali" Literary Movement*, ed. Stefania Lucamante (Fairleigh-Dickinson U P).

9. The bibliography that follows contains a partial list of the titles of these writers. When possible, I include reference to English translations.

10. Qtd. in Gervasutti, 55.

11. See Elaine Scarry, *The Body in Pain: The Making and Unmaking of the World* (NY: Oxford U P, 1985) and *Literature and the Body: Essays on People and Populations* (Baltimore: The Johns Hopkins U P, 1988).

12. Joel Schumacher's 1999 film *8mm* credibly represents the black market of

snuff films in a variety of formats (home video, the 8 mm format referred to in the title, 16mm, etc.).

13. Qtd. in Gervasutti, 25.

14. The original reads: "la musica è un elemento mercuriale, che mette in relazione piani diversi. Per esempio, congiunge la psicologia e la storia [....] Dopo la lunga fase della letteratura minimalista [....] forse ricominciamo a sentire con forza il bisogno di romanzi che recuperino l'aspetto più riflessivo di narrare, che riaccolgano la dimensione del pensiero. La musica può aiutare perché è la forma perfetta del pensiero che pensa e della rappresentazione che sente se stessa. Si potrebbe dire che avvicina al pensiero senza le parole e i percorsi faticosi della filosofia." Qtd. in Elisabetta Rasy, "Scritti sul pentagramma," *Panorama* 12 September 1996.

15. To my knowledge, pulp serves as a category for prose only. It is worth noting that the poetry "slams" that came into vogue in the US around the late Eighties have appeared in Italy. The degree to which this format has been taken up in Italy is beyond the scope of this essay.

16. Qtd. in Gervasutti, 24.

17. On Rap and Hip hop in a global setting see Prevos, André J.M. "Communication through Popular Music in the Twenty-first Century? The Example of French Rap Music and Hip Hop Culture," in *Language and Communication in the New Century*, ed. Jesse Levitt. New York: Cummings and Hathaway. 137-48; William Perkins, "Youth's Global Village," in *Droppin' Science: Critical Essays on Rap Music and Hip hop Culture*, ed. W. Perkins (Philadelphia, PA: Temple UP, 1996), 257-73.

18. See Nelson George, *Hip hop America* (New York: Viking, 1998).

19. See also Daniele Barbieri, *Il linguaggio del fumetto* (Milan: Bompiani, 1991).

20. Gervasutti, 29.

21. Nico Orengo, *Una lieve impressione* (Milan: Garzanti, 1991).

22. Aldo Nove, "Il mondo dell'amore," *Gioventù cannibale*, ed. Daniele Brolli (Turin: Einaudi, 1996), 53.

23. For Abbate's remembrance, see Gervasutti, esp. 40-45. Even before the Ceausescu television event, some chroniclers of television remember mesmerizing broadcast coverage sometime in 1980 or '81 of an Italian child trapped in a well for approximately 24 hours as teams attempted a rescue and the press (not unlike the scene of the coverage of the "miracle" in Federico Fellini's 1959 *La dolce vita*) watched. See Gianpaolo Capretini, *La scatola parlante*.

24. Sylvestre Matushka's 1932 staged railway accidents, or natural disasters, plane crashes, J.G. Ballard's novel *Crash* — and Steven Soderbergh's film of it — make this evident.

25. Mark Seltzer, *Serial Killers: Death and Life in American Would Culture* (New York and London: Routledge, 1998), 37.

26. *Cuore di pulp: antologia di racconti italiani* eds. Fabio Giovannini and Antonio

Tentori (Rome: Stampa alternativa, n.d.), 5.

27. The duplicitousness of the visual image in Argento's film is probably an homage to Antonioni's 1966 *Blow-up*, where repetition (series of scenes of the making of the photographs, the series of the photographs themselves) leads to no resolution.

28. See Alan Jones, *Mondo Argento* (Cambs, England: Midnight Media, 1997) and Fabio Maiello, *Intervista a Dario Argento: L'occhio che uccide* (Naples: Edizioni scientifiche italiane, 1996).

29. Qtd. in Gervasutti, 42.

30. Tondelli was among the most influential of writer-editors on this school of young writers until his death from AIDS in 1991. His influence on the *pulpisti* warrants longer consideration than I have space for here.

31. This is not to suggest that there are not other *pulpiste*— women writers engaged in the crafting of "pulp" fiction. In addition to Krismer, Alda Teodorani, Luisa Brancaccio, Isabella Santacroce, and perhaps even Silvia Ballestra are all engaged in this sort of minimalist literature that flirts with violence.

32. See Barbara Creed, *The Monstrous Feminine: Film, Feminism, and Psychoanalysis* (London: Routledge, 1993).

33. See Julia Kristeva, *The Powers of Horror: An Essay on Abjection*, tr. Leon Roudiez (New York: Columbia University Press, 1982).

34. Niccolò Ammaniti, *Fango* (Milan: Mondadori, 1996), 125.

35. Alongside McInerney, Hemingway, and, as we noted, J.D. Salinger, *pulpisti* steadily cite the influence of Easton Ellis, Philip K. Dick, Raymond Carver, Grace Paley, John Fante (we might note here the series of Italian American writers brought to the Italian reading public by Marcos y Marcos, including classics like Fante and Pietro Di Donato, among others), Lori Moore, Samuel Beckett, F. Scott Fitzgerald, Hubert Selby, Céline, and Robert Musil.

36. See Carol Clover, *Men, Women, and Chain Saws: Gender in the Modern Horror Film.* (Princeton: Princeton U P, 1992) and "Her Body, Himself: Gender in the Slasher Film," *The Dread of Difference. Gender and the Horror Film.* ed. (Austin: U of Texas P, 1996), 66-113.

37. Krismer clearly nods to her Anglo-American influences at as early a point as the novel's epigraphs, one from Barker and the other from Salinger.

BIBLIOGRAPHY

Abbate, Fulvio. *Oggi è un secolo.* Rome: Theoria, 1992

_____ *La peste bis.* Milan: Bompiani, 1997.

_____ *Dopo l'estate.* Milan: Bompiani, 1995.

Ammaniti, Niccolò. *Branchie!* Ediesse, 1994.

_____ *Fango.* Milan: Mondadori, 1996.

____ *L'ultimo capodanno*. Milan: Mondadori, 1998.

Baldini, Eraldo. *Bambine*. Rome: Ritmi Theoria, 1995.

Ballestra, Silvia. *Il compleanno dell'iguana*. Milan: Transeuropa Mondadori, 1991.

____ *La guerra degli Antò*. Milan: Transeuropa Mondadori, 1992.

Baricco, Alessandro. *Oceano mare*. Milan: Rizzoli, 1994.

____ *Seta* Milan: Rizzoli, 1996.

____ *Silk*, tr. Guido Waldham. London: Harvill P, 1997.

____ *Ocean Sea*, tr. Alastair McEwen. New York: Knopf, 1999.

Brancaccio, Luisa and Niccolò Ammaniti. "Seratina," *Gioventù cannibale*, ed. Daniele Brolli. Turin: Einaudi, 1996.

Brizzi, Enrico. *Jack Frusciante è uscito dal gruppo*. Milan: Transeuropa, 1993, Baldini & Castoldi, 1994.

____ *Bastogne*. Baldini & Castoldi, 1996.

____ *Jack Frusciante Has Left the Group*, tr. S. Luczkiw. New York: Grove, 1995.

Caliceti, Giuseppe. *Fonderia Italghisa*. Milan: Marsilio, 1996.

Campo, Rossana. *Il pieno di super*. Milan: Feltrinelli, 1993.

Covacich, Mauro. *Colpo di lama*. Vicenza: Neri Pozza, 1993.

Culicchia, Giuseppe. *Tutti giù per terra*. Milan: Garzanti, 1994.

____ *Bla bla bla*. Milan: Garzanti, 1997.

Demarchi, Andrea. *Sandrino e il canto celestiale di Robert Plant*. Milan: Transeuropa Mondadori, 1996.

Fois, Marcello. *Ferro recente*. Granata, 1992.

____ *Sempre caro*. Milan: Frassineli, 1998.

Krismer, Raffaella. *Il signore della carne*. Milan: Zelig Editore, 1997.

____ *Storia della mia vita sulla terra*. Milan: Transeuropa, 1998.

Lodoli, Marco. *I fannulloni*. Turin: Einaudi, 1991.

____ *Grande circo invalido*. Turin: Einaudi, 1993.

Lucarelli, Carlo. *Lupo mannaro*. Rome: Edizioni Theoria, 1994.

____ *Almost Blue*. Turin: Einaudi, 1997.

Mozzi, Giulio. *Il male naturale*. Milan: Mondadori, 1997.

Nove, Aldo. *Woobinda e altre storie senza lieto fine*. Rome: Castelvecchi, 1996.

____ *Superwoobinda*. Turin: Einaudi, 1998.

Pinketts, Andrea. *Il vizio dell'agnello*. Milan: Feltrinelli, 1994.

____ *Il senso della frase*. Milan: Feltrinelli, 1995.

____ *Lazzaro, vieni fuori*. Milan: Feltrinelli, 1996.

Romagnoli, Gabriele. *Videocronache*. Milan: Mondadori, 1994.

Santacroce, Isabella. *Fluo*. Rome: Castelvecchi, 1995.

____ *Destroy*. Milan: Feltrinelli, 1996.

Scarpa, Tiziano. *Occhi sulla graticola*. Turin: Einaudi, 1996.

Sclavi, Tiziano. *Nero*. Camunia, 1992

____ *Apocalisse*. Camunia, 1993.

____ *Dylan Dog* n.d.

____ *Nel buio*. Camunia, 1993.

____ *Mostri*. Camunia, 1994.

Tondelli, Pier Vincenzo. *Camere separate*. Milan: Bompiani, 1989.

____ *Un weekend postmoderno. Cronache degli anni Ottanta*. Milan: Bompiani, 1990.

van Straten, Giorgio. *Generazione*. Milan: Grazanti, 1987.

PETER BONDANELLA

Italian Cinema from the 1950s to the Present

Postwar Italian Neo-realism: The Background to the 1950s.
With the fall of Mussolini and the end of the war, international audiences were introduced to Italian films through a few great masterpieces by Roberto Rossellini (1906-77), Vittorio De Sica (1901-74), and Luchino Visconti (1906-76). Italian neorealism stressed social themes (the war, poverty, the Resistance, unemployment); they seemed to reject traditional dramatic and cinematic conventions associated with Hollywood; they stressed on-location shooting rather than studio work, as well as the documentary photographic style favored by many directors under the former regime; and they often employed non-professional actors in original ways. Film historians have unfortunately tended to speak of neo-realism as if it were an authentic movement with universally agreed-upon stylistic or thematic principles. The basis for the fundamental change in cinematic history marked by Italian neo-realism was less an agreement on a single, unified cinematic style than a common aspiration to view Italy without preconceptions and to employ a more honest, ethical, but no less poetic cinematic language in the process.

The masterpieces of neo-realism are Rossellini's *Roma città aperta* (*Rome Open City*, 1945) and *Paisà* (*Paisan*, 1946), two parts of what are known as his "anti-fascist trilogy"; De Sica's *Ladri di biciclette* (*Bicycle*

Thieves, 1948); and Visconti's *La terra trema* (*The Earth Trembles*, 1948). *Roma città aperta* so completely reflected the moral and psychological atmosphere of the immediate postwar period that its international critical success alerted the world to the rebirth of Italian cinema. With a daring combination of styles and moods (due in great measure to brilliant script-writing by Sergio Amidei [1904-91] and a young Federico Fellini [1920-94]), Rossellini captured the tension and the tragedy of Italian life under German occupation and the partisan struggle out of which the new democratic republic was subsequently born. *Paisà* reflects to a far greater extent the conventions of the newsreel documentary, tracing in six separate episodes the Allied invasion of Italy and its slow process up through the boot of the peninsula. Yet, the grainy film, the awkward acting of the non-professional actors, the authoritative voice-over narration, and the immediacy of subject matter we associate with newsreels do not completely explain the aesthetic qualities of the work. Rossellini depicts the historic encounter of two alien cultures, resulting in initial incomprehension but eventual kinship and brotherhood.

De Sica's *Ladri di biciclette* represents the finest example of non-professional acting in neorealist cinema. While De Sica employs non-professionals, on location shooting, and social themes (unemployment, the effects of the war on the postwar economy) typical of many neorealist films, the appeal of *Ladri di biciclette* cannot be explained completely by its superficially realistic style. The mythic structure of the plot — a quest for a bicycle, ironically a *Fides* (Faith) brand, that has been stolen — suggests to the viewer that De Sica is not merely offering a political film denouncing a particular socio-economic system. Social reform may change a world in which the loss of a mere bicycle spells economic disaster, but no amount of social engineering or even revolution will alter the basic facts of life in De Sica's universe — solitude, loneliness, and alienation.

Visconti's *La terra trema* is a far more ambitious ideological and aesthetic undertaking. An adaptation of the 'veristic' novel by Giovanni Verga, *I Malavoglia* (*The Malavoglias*, 1881), it is colored by the Marxist theories of Antonio Gramsci (1891-1937). In many ways, the film fits the traditional stereotypical definition of Italian neo-realism better than other equally famous films from the same period. No studio sets or sound stages were used, and the cast was selected from the Sicilian fishing village of Aci Trezza, the novel's setting. Visconti even refused to dub the film to standard Italian, preferring the more realistic effects of Sicilian dialect and synchronized sound. The film's visuals underline the cyclical, timeless quality of life in Aci Trezza. Visconti's typically slow panning shots with a stationary camera, or his long, static shots of motionless objects and actors, produce a formalism that bestows dignity and beauty on humble, ordinary people.

These four masterpieces by Rossellini, De Sica, and Visconti, all original contributions to film language, were, with the exception of *Roma città aperta*, unpopular within Italy and achieved critical success primarily among audiences, critics, filmmakers, and intellectuals abroad. One of the paradoxes of Italian neo-realism is that the ordinary people such films set out to portray were relatively uninterested in their screen self-image: Italians preferred to see Hollywood products. Of the approximately 800 films produced between 1945 and 1953 in Italy, only a relatively small number (about 10%) can be classified as neo-realist, and most of these films were box-office failures. Italian audiences were reluctant to abandon popular Hollywood codes, and a number of less original but more successful neo-realist films were able to achieve greater results at the box-office by incorporating traditional Hollywood genres within their narratives about Italian subjects. Such films as *Vivere in pace* (*To Live in Peace*, 1946) by Luigi Zampa (1905-91), *Senza pietà* (*Without Pity*, 1948) by Alberto Lattuada (1914-), *Riso amaro* (*Bitter Rice*, 1948) by Giuseppe De Santis (1917-), and *Il cammino della speranza* (*The Path of Hope*, 1950) by Pietro Germi (1914-74), expanded the boundaries of Italian neo-realism by shifting away from semi-documentary treatments of social problems toward conventional Hollywood themes and film genres, such as the western or *film noir*. As a result of their combination of neo-realist style with Hollywood subject matter, such works managed a respectable performance at the box office.

The "Crisis" of Neo-realism in the 1950's and the Birth of a New Italian Cinema.

It soon became obvious that while Italian leftist intellectuals and social critics preferred the implicitly political and sometimes even revolutionary messages of neo-realist cinema, the public was more interested in Hollywood films or Italian films with a Hollywood spirit. Even the greatest neo-realist directors (Rossellini, Antonioni, Visconti) soon became uncomfortable with the restrictive boundaries imposed upon their subject matter or style by such well-meaning but ideologically motivated critics. In Italian film history, the transition beyond neo-realism is often called the "crisis" of neo-realism. In retrospect, the period from 1950-53 to 1968 can be more accurately described as a natural evolution of Italian film language toward a cinema concerned with psychological problems and a new aesthetic style no longer dominated by non-professional actors, on-location shooting, documentary style, and social problems. Crucial to this historic transition are a number of early works by Michelangelo Antonioni (1902-); several works starring Ingrid Bergman by Rossellini; and the first films directed by Federico Fellini. In *Cronaca di un amore* (*Story of a Love Affair*, 1950), Antonioni's first feature film, the director employs a plot indebted to James Cain's novel, *The Postman Always Rings Twice* and to American *film noir*. But his distinctive photographic signature is already evident: characteristically long shots, tracks and pans following the actors; modernist editing techniques reflecting the slow rhythms of daily life; and philosophical concerns with obvious links to European Existentialism. In *Viaggio in Italia* (*Voyage to Italy*, 1953), Rossellini abandons his documentary style to embrace an abstract psychological realism that also reflected the emphasis upon alienation typical of contemporary postwar European philosophy.

It is with Fellini's early films that the Italian cinema moved resolutely beyond a preoccupation with social problems, although his works certainly reflect a deep understanding of Italian culture that no other Italian director can match. In *I vitelloni* (*The Vitelloni*, 1953), for example, Fellini provides a classic portrait of six provincial characters which a neo-realist director would have presented in an indictment of provincial backwardness. But Fellini is more interested in exploring the private fantasy worlds of his creations than he is in making polemical statements about Italian society. Fellini's concern with private fantasy worlds and his belief in transcendental experiences beyond mere humdrum reality find their greatest expression in two masterpieces, both of which were to receive an Oscar for Best Foreign Film: *La strada* (*The Road*, 1954) and *Le notti di Cabiria* (*The Nights of Cabiria*, 1956). In each film, Fellini moves beyond a strictly realistic portrayal of provincial life to reveal a new poetic dimension, one motivated by a personal vision and a particular Fellinian mythology concerned with spiritual poverty and the necessity for grace or salvation (defined in strictly secular terms but owing an obvious debt to Catholicism).

New Directions After Neo-realism:
From Psychological Realism to Ideological Commitment.

In the decade between 1958 (a time when the so-called "crisis" of neo-realism had clearly passed) and 1968 (a year of violent social and political upheavals all over Europe which shook Italy to its foundations), Italian cinema reached a level of artistic quality, international popularity, and economic strength it had never before achieved. Film production continued at well above 200 films per year in Italy, while a prolonged crisis in Hollywood reduced American competition within the Italian market and abroad. Not only did Italy boast a number of distinguished *auteurs* (Antonioni, Fellini, Rossellini, Visconti) whose names had become household words everywhere and whose greatest films were being produced at this time, but the Italian cinema witnessed the arrival of a second generation of brilliant young directors who had apprenticed with their masters: Pier Paolo Pasolini (1922-75); Bernardo Bertolucci (1940-); Marco Bellocchio (1939-); Gillo Pontecorvo (1919-); Ermanno Olmi (1931-); Francesco Rosi (1922-); Elio Petri (1929-82); Paolo (1931-) and Vittorio Taviani (1929-); and Sergio Leone (1921-89). Italian films regularly won major prizes at the world's most important festivals (Cannes, Venice, Berlin, New York); Italian films, their directors, and their actors were the toast of international critics and film historians who privileged the so-called "art film"; and perhaps most importantly, the industry made huge profits in the international market by exporting not only the traditional film comedies that had always been the staple product of the Italian industry, but also other genre films, such as the "spaghetti" western (a genre usually associated with Hollywood but which Italians revolutionized, making a star out of Clint Eastwood in the process) or the peplum film, costume films set in the classical period that recalled Italy's initial success with this genre during the silent period.

Italian Film Comedy and Social Criticism in the 1960's.

Film comedies (the so-called *commedia all'italiana*) and "spaghetti" westerns dominated the Italian market during this decade. The Italian cinema was blessed with a number of excellent comic directors, such as Mario Monicelli (1915-); Luigi Comencini (1916-); and Dino Risi (1917-). Even more important, Italian cinema boasted a wealth of great actors — Alberto Sordi (1919-); Vittorio Gassman (1922-); Marcello Mastroianni (1923-96); Nino Manfredi (1921-); Ugo Tognazzi (1922-90); Monica Vitti (1931-); Claudia Cardinale (1939-); Sophia Loren (1934-); and Stefania Sandrelli (1946-) — which no national cinema outside of Hollywood could match. Many critics of the left during the period denigrated *commedia all'italiana* as merely "commercial" cinema without artistic value, just as they ignored the Italian contribution to the western genre. Their ideological bias ignored the fact that Italian comic films often contained more trenchant social criticism than the more acceptable ideologically oriented "art films" of the period. The great comic films of the decade from 1958 to 1968 provide an amusing but often accurate mirror of changing Italian customs and values. They helped to force the average Italian into a greater awareness of conflicting moral standards; they attacked age-old prejudices; and they questioned the rule of inept governing elites and institutions. The film which best reflects the combination of humor and social criticism typical of the *commedia all'italiana* is Pietro Germi's *Divorzio all'italiana* (*Divorce, Italian Style*, 1961). Made before Italian law permitted legal divorce, Germi's satire of Sicilian sexual mores chronicles the comic attempts of a Sicilian nobleman to force his hated wife into adultery, so that he can murder her, receive a light sentence for a crime of honor (hence the film's title), and marry his mistress. Utilizing a complex narrative juxtaposing the director's critical view of this affair with the Sicilian's biased justifications of his misdeeds, Germi recreates the oppressive atmosphere of Sicilian provincial life that forces men and women to commit violent crimes in order to obtain sexual fulfillment.

The Spaghetti Western and the Peplum Film:
Italian Cinema and the Hollywood Genre Film.

The other remarkably successful commercial genre during this period was the western, dominated by a single man: Sergio Leone. The Italian "spaghetti" western owes a debt to another popular genre, the so-called neo-mythological or peplum film, which accounted for 10% of Italian production between 1957 and 1964. Set vaguely in classical times and populated by mindless musclemen and buxom damsels in distress, these works appealed to a predominantly male audience that thrived on violent action and strong, anti-intellectual heroes such as Steve Reeves (only one of a number of American actors employed by the Italian industry during this period). The peplum film's characteristic emphasis upon action was continued by the spaghetti western. Between 1963 and 1973, over 400 such westerns were produced in Italy, but none of them had the impact of Leone's first work, *Un pugno di dollari* (*A Fistful of Dollars*, 1964). This film revolutionized what was at the time an almost exhausted Hollywood genre by a conscious departure from what had come to be known as the "classic" western formula. Leone plunges us into a violent and cynical world far removed from the traditional West of John Ford or Howard Hawks. The hero is motivated by the same greed as the evil bandits, and graphic violence is accompanied by grotesque comic gags and mannered close-ups indebted to Eisenstein. A crucial artistic element is the skillful music of Ennio Morricone (1928—) who first received international recognition from his collaboration with Leone, and whose unusual sound track composed of gunfire, ricocheting bullets, cries, trumpet solos, Sicilian folk instruments, and whistles became an international best-selling record. The classic western showdown becomes in Leone's hands a ritualistic act concluding a narrative cycle and employs a crescendo of music not unlike the conclusion of an aria in grand opera. Though few in number, Leone's influential western films that followed *Un pugno di dollari* were not merely hugely profitable: they also revived the most famous of all American film genres.

Auteurs and the "Art Film": Visconti, Antonioni, Fellini.

If film comedy, Roman pot-boilers, and western epics produced the industry's most lucrative returns, the so-called "art films" directed by *auteurs* proved to be almost equally good investments during the decade. In fact, one of the remarkable features of this period in Italian film history was its ability to produce great art that also turned a handsome profit. Works such as Fellini's *La dolce vita* (*The Sweet Life*, 1959), Visconti's *Il Gattopardo* (*The Leopard*, 1962), or Antonioni's *Blow-Up* (1966) were not only major artistic creations, but they gained a large share of the international film market. Fellini's best work during the period emphasized his introspective fantasy world and brilliant, Baroque imagery in his masterpiece *Otto e mezzo* (8 ½, 1962), *Giulietta degli spiriti* (*Juliet of the Spirits*, 1965), and *Fellini Satyricon* (1969). Visconti's best films — *Rocco e i suoi fratelli* (*Rocco and His Brothers*, 1960); *La caduta degli dei* (*The Fall of the Damned*, 1969); and *Morte a Venezia* (*Death in Venice*, 1971) — analyze European decadence and owe a great debt both to grand opera and to the European novel. Antonioni's brilliant modernist photography finds its best expression in the black and white trilogy of *L'Avventura* (*The Adventure*, 1960), *La Notte* (*The Night*, 1961), and *L'eclisse* (*The Eclipse*, 1962), or in his innovative treatment of color in *Il deserto rosso* (*The Red Desert*, 1964).

Otto e mezzo, *Il deserto rosso*, and *La caduta degli dei* reflect the highly complex stylistic shifts which had occurred in the work of these three dominant *auteurs*, each of whom had his origins in the Italian neo-realist era. Visconti usually aimed at establishing a link between his films and a broader historical context. *La caduta degli dei* provides a powerful visual metaphor for the infernal nature of moral degradation, a pathological case history of Nazi Germany underlined by the violent and hellish colors that dominate the film's visuals. In Antonioni's *Il deserto rosso*, color photography pre-empts the central function of traditional plot and character by concentrating upon the relationship between characters and their environment, represented by the machinery and contemporary technology of a modern oil refinery in Ravenna. Antonioni's color photography is thoroughly modernist (only a single scene, a dream of a desert island, is shot in what we have come to consider as "natural" film color). Its hues come from the world of industrial plastics, chemicals, and artificial fabrics. In some case, the director even changes the colors of natural objects (grass, fruit) to reflect the psychological states of his disturbed characters. And he frames each shot as if he were a contemporary abstract painter, asking us to consider objects from the world of technology primarily as art forms and only later as objects with a utilitarian function. Fellini's *Otto e mezzo* embodies its creator's belief that the cinema exists primarily for the purpose of individual self-expression, not historical investigation or abstract photography: fantasy, rather than reality, is its proper domain, because only fantasy falls under the director's complete artistic control. The harried protagonist of the film, the director Guido, possesses many of Fellini's personal traits. Fellini's narrative moves rapidly and seamlessly between Guido's "reality," his fantasies, and flashbacks to the past of his dreams — a discontinuous story line with little logical or chronological unity. The influence of psychoanalysis is obvious in the view Fellini presents of sexuality in the film, as personal problems prevent Guido from achieving artistic fulfillment. In no other film by Fellini was there to be such a perfect synthesis of his personality, his introspective style, and cinematic bravura.

A New Generation of Auteurs in the 1960's:
Exploiting the Heritage of Neorealism.

While Visconti, Antonioni, and Fellini dominated Italian cinema during the period, their international prestige coincided with the rise of an extremely talented group of younger men whose first works were indebted to neo-realism but who reflected what might be called a critical realism with ideological implications. The best examples of such precociously brilliant works are Pasolini's *Il vangelo secondo Matteo* (*The Gospel According to Matthew*, 1964); Pontecorvo's *La battaglia di Algeri* (*The Battle of Algiers*, 1966); Bernardo Bertolucci's *Prima della rivoluzione* (*Before the Revolution*, 1964); Marco Bellocchio's *La Cina è vicina* (*China Is Near*, 1967); Francesco Rosi's *Salvatore Giuliano* (1962); and Ermanno Olmi's *Il posto* (*The Job*, 1961).

In *Il posto*, Olmi's use of non-professional actors, and his emphasis upon expressive deep-focus shots in office interiors reflects an obvious debt to De Sica's poetic Neo-realism. Rosi, following Visconti's example in his belief that film must make an ideological statement, moves beyond neo-realist presentation of "facts" to what he terms a "documented" method of making films *in Salvatore Giuliano*. This treatment of a Sicilian bandit's career and death is less a work of fiction than an investigation (*film inchiesta*) into the ambiguous historical circumstances of this figure, and the film uncovers corrupt connections between the Christian Democratic Party and the Mafia, establishing the first of many Italian "political" films that would flourish in the period. Pontecorvo employs a documentary style in *La battaglia di Algeri*, with a narrative structure that uses flashbacks and flash forwards to provide critical commentary on the "facts" the film presents. His careful recreation of a case history of Third-World revolution owes an important debt to the early war films and techniques of Rossellini. Pontecorvo's highly mobile, hand-held cameras employ fast film stock; the telephoto lenses common in television news reporting simulates a documentary style; duplicating the negative of his film in the lab recreates the grainy, documentary texture of Rossellini's *Paisà*.

Bertolucci, Bellocchio, and Pasolini — all influenced by the aesthetics of Brecht and the cinematic practice of Godard — exhibit a far more ambiguous relationship to the heritage of Italian neo-realism. Pasolini accepted many of the superficial characteristics of neo-realist style — non-professional actors, on-location shooting , contemporary themes, natural lighting — but he rejected any attempt to employ cinema to present a naturalistic view of life. For Pasolini, realism included mythology and dream. The cinematic signature he developed in *Il vangelo secondo Matteo*, a Biblical film made by a Marxist atheist, can be described as pastiche, mixing the most disparate cultural and thematic materials. Bertolucci and Bellocchio present a fresh view of Italian politics in their youthful works. With *Prima della rivoluzione*, Bertolucci adapts *Stendhal's The Charterhouse of Parma* (1839) in a poetic and highly lyrical study of a young bourgeois intellectual from Parma (Bertolucci's home) who toys with Marxism but eventually prefers a safe, middle-class marriage to revolution or an incestuous love affair with his aunt. Bellocchio's artistic perspective is angry and provocative rather than lyrical and elegiac. While Bertolucci's Fabrizio retreats into the protective womb of the Italian nuclear family, Bellocchio's protagonists in *La Cina è vicina* attack the very notion of a provincial, middle-class family in a satire of Italian political corruption. The result is a political allegory attacking the 'historic compromise' between the right and the left in Italy, viewed from the microcosm of a small, provincial family.

Post-1968 Cinema: Politics and Ideology in the Dramatic Film.

Between the upheavals in Italian society that took place around 1968 and immediately afterwards, and the mid-1980's, when a period of "normalcy" was re-established in Italian society, a number of major critical trends can be traced in the evolution of Italian cinema. Politics and ideology continued to play a major role, moving even normally apolitical directors (such as Fellini) to treat political themes. Nevertheless, it is also fair to say that the emphasis on ideology in the cinema is also responsible for some of the most boring and pretentious cinematic works of the period that are best left unmentioned. Films that combined political themes with intriguing and original cinematic styles (hardly an exhaustive list) include: *Medea* (1969) and *Il Decameron* (*The Decameron*, 1971) by Pasolini; Bertolucci's *Il conformista* (*The Conformist*, 1970); Fellini's *Amarcord* (1976); Elio Petri's *Indagine su un cittadino al di sopra di ogni sospetto* (*Investigation of a Citizen Above Suspicion*, 1970); *Padre Padrone* (1977) and *La notte di San Lorenzo* (*The Night of the Shooting Stars*,

1982) by the Taviani brothers; and Olmi's *L'albero degli zoccoli* (*The Tree of the Wooden Clogs*, 1978).

With *Medea*, Pasolini employs the classic tragedy by Euripides as a metaphor to explore the confrontation of Western, industrialized society with the pre-industrial cultures of the Third World. In *Il Decameron*, Pasolini transforms Boccaccio's panoramic portrait of the rise of middle-class, mercantile culture in an age dominated by the city of Florence into an amusing portrayal of the sub proletariat of Naples and its sexual adventures. The film underlines not only the class-oriented nature of the original literary source, but also proposes liberated sexuality as a characteristic of non-industrialized cultures and uses this innocent sense of sexuality to critique modern, Western values.

Bertolucci's *Il conformista* and Fellini's *Amarcord* provide two very different interpretations of Italy's Fascist heritage. Bertolucci employs a complicated plot with frequent flashbacks, portraying the creation of a Fascist assassin. Bertolucci's mature grasp of his craft is evident in the famous tango scene between two women, with its quickly shifting camera angles, positions, graceful motions, and skillful editing, a virtuoso performance due, in large measure, to the brilliant cinematography of a young Vittorio Storaro (1940-). Fellini's *Amarcord* is much less stridently ideological but is no less a condemnation of Fascist restrictions of individual freedom. In an unforgettable evocation of life in a sleepy provincial town, Fellini combines a nostalgic view of his childhood with a searing indictment of Italian conformity during the Fascist period.

Two directors became identified almost exclusively with trenchant critiques of Italian political life in this period: Elio Petri and Francesco Rosi. Petri's works, blending his ideological message with suspense and slick, commercial presentation, have always been popular abroad. *Indagine di un cittadino al di sopra di ogni sospetto*, winner of an Oscar for Best Foreign Film, presents contemporary Italian politics in an abstract, almost philosophical manner, akin to Kafka's parables, and Petri's message applies not only to power in Italy but to power in general. Rosi's many interesting political films are less comprehensible abroad, since they contain a more specific connection to actual events in Italian daily life. The richly documented briefs against the system he began with *Salvatore Giuliano* are continued in a series of interesting works: *Lucky Luciano* (1973), a probing look into the link between American politicians and the Sicilian Mafia; and *Cadaveri eccellenti* (*Illustrious Corpses*, 1975), a chilling parable of the connection between political power and corruption in Italy, adapted from a novel by Leonardo Sciascia, where the image of the Mafia is transformed into a universally comprehensive metaphor for corrupt power all over the world; or *Tre fratelli* (*Three*

Brothers, 1981), a view of contemporary Italian life seen through the lives of three brothers who return to southern Italy for the funeral of their mother.

L'albero degli zoccoli by Olmi is one of the many good Italian films financed by the state-controlled television network (the RAI), an increasingly important source of funding for Italian works or co-productions with other European national cinemas. In it, Olmi offers a patient recreation of peasant life on a farm near Bergamo at the turn of the nineteenth century and adopts a style recalling the conventions of neorealism, employing non-professional peasants from the area who speak their local dialect. The three-hour length of the film allows Olmi to duplicate the slow rhythms of life in a pre-industrial peasant culture.

The Taviani brothers are perhaps the most interesting of the so-called "political" directors. Their *Padre Padrone* is an autobiographical account of how an illiterate Sardinian shepherd struggled to become a professor of linguistics. The acquisition of standard Italian thus becomes a metaphor for the acquisition of full citizenship in modern Italian society. *La notte di San Lorenzo* is a postmodern reinterpretation of Italian neo-realism and its central theme, the partisan Resistance and the liberation of Tuscany in August 1944.

Bittersweet Laughter: A Satirical Critique of Contemporary Italy in the Commedia all'Italiana.

While films with predominantly political or ideological content tended to dominate the production of "art films" between 1968 and the mid-1980's, traditional film comedies continued to provide the backbone for the Italian industry and were consistently the most popular works in the peninsula but frequently dealt with important social issues. Taken as a group, comedies during this era embody a black, even grotesque vision of contemporary Italian society, and the laughter in these works rings bittersweet. An excellent example of the creative combination of humor and social criticism in this modified *commedia all'italiana* is *Pane e cioccolata* (*Bread and Chocolate*, 1973) by Franco Brusati (1922-), a devastating indictment of the conditions experienced by Italian "guest workers" in what is depicted as a racist Switzerland.

The dominant director of this bittersweet kind of film comedy is Ettore Scola (1931-), who began working in the cinema as a scriptwriter on dozens of comic films produced in the 1950's and the early 1960's. In a number of memorable works — *C'eravamo tanto amati* (*We All Loved Each Other Very Much*, 1974); *Brutti, sporchi e cattivi* (*Dirty, Mean and Nasty*, 1976); *Una giornata particolare* (*A Special Day*, 1977); and *La terrazza* (*The Terrace*, 1980) — Scola employed a metacinematic narrative to treat the history of Italian cinema itself, examining not only the heritage of neo-realism (especially his model, Vittorio De Sica) but also the assumptions of the *commedia all'italiana,* a film genre with which his work has long been identified since his early beginnings as a successful comic screenwriter. *C'eravamo tanto amati* is the most complex of these films, combining a consideration of the many social and political changes through which Italy has undergone since the fall of the Fascist regime with an equally comprehensive survey of major developments in the history of postwar Italian cinema. In a series of excellent films — *Mimì metallurgico ferito nell'onore (Mimì the Metallurgist Wounded In His Honor,* 1971); *Film d'amore e d'anarchia (A Film About Love and Anarchy,* 1972); *Travolti da un insolito destino nell'azzurro mare d'agosto (Overcome by an Unusual Destiny in the Blue Sea of August,* 1974) — Lina Wertmüller (1928-) combines an exuberant imagery indebted to Fellini with a concern for topical political issues, all set within the conventions of traditional Italian film comedy, with its vulgarity, stock characters, and frontal attack upon society's values. Wertmüller's films aroused the ire of many feminists, as her works did not conform to what many Anglo-American academics considered to be proper for a woman's film.

Italian Portraits of the Holocaust.

Wertmüller's comic masterpiece, *Pasqualino Settebellezze (Pasqualino Seven Beauties,* 1975) was attacked by some critics as irreverent, even though there was a clear cinematic precedent for such a perspective in Chaplin's *The Great Dictator* (1940). However, its tragic-comic treatment of such sensitive subject matter within a comic framework and her memorable portrait of the hellish life inside a concentration camp found important critical defenders, while the virtuoso performance of its protagonist, Giancarlo Giannini (1942-) made him an international star.

Another controversial portrait of the Holocaust was *Il portiere di notte (The Night Porter,* 1974), a work by another woman director, Liliana Cavani (1936-). In sharp contrast to feminist hostility to Wertmüller's films, Cavani's morbid portrait of a love affair between a woman in a death camp and a sadistic German officer, a relationship which was renewed in the postwar period after a chance encounter between the two in Vienna, was praised by a number of feminist critics though damned by others for its revisionist view of evil in the camps. The treatment of the Holocaust during this period in the Italian cinema that elicited almost unanimous praise (except from Giorgio Bassani, the novelist whose book was its source) was Vittorio De Sica's *Il giardino dei Finzi-Contini (The Garden of the Finzi-Continis,* 1971), a lyrical, elegiac portrait of the Jewish population of prewar Ferrara which was awarded the Oscar for Best Foreign Film in 1972.

Perhaps the most successful portrayal of the Holocaust in the Italian cinema was provided by La vita è bella (Life Is Beautiful, 1997), a tragicomedy about the Holocaust that most certainly is indebted to Chaplin rather than the vaudeville music-hall kind of comedy employed by Wertmüller's *Pasqualino Settebellezze*. Director and actor Roberto Benigni (1952) received special recognition at the Cannes Film Festival, three Oscars, and nine Italian Oscars (the David di Donatello award) for the film, which broke every American record for box office returns for a foreign film in the postwar period.

The Italian Cinema and the Hollywood Blockbuster Epics:
1900, Once Upon a Time in America and The Last Emperor.

At the height of the Italian cinema's international success, two directors — Bertolucci and Leone — produced three films that seemed more typical of Hollywood blockbusters than of Italian cinematic production. Bertolucci's 1900 (1977), describes the history of the class struggle in Italy from the death of Verdi to our own times through the intertwined accounts of two boys from different classes. It may well be described as a Marxist *Gone With the Wind*. A much more successful epic film was Bertolucci's L'ultimo imperatore (The Last Emperor, 1987), the story of Pu Yi, China's last emperor who ended his days as a humble gardener. With a brilliant flashback/flash forward structure, this work swept the Oscar awards for the year, winning in nine categories (including Best Picture, Direction, Cinematography, Costumes, Editing, and Music), an unprecedented honor for an Italian director and for a film indebted primarily to Italian technicians. Perhaps the most fascinating epic film to come from Italy was Sergio Leone's last work, C'era una volta in America (Once Upon a Time in America, 1984) — an ambitious attempt to change the generic conventions of the Hollywood gangster film as Leone had already done with the Hollywood western with Jewish, not Italian, gangsters.

New Faces at the Dawn of the Millennium.

By the time Fellini received a fifth Oscar in 1993 for his career shortly before his death, Italian cinema seemed to be immersed in an economic and artistic crisis. Its rich tradition of great directors, actors, and films, on the other hand, was universally recognized by a number of international awards. In the late 1980's and 1990's, a new generation of young directors rose to prominence within Italy and some even garnered important recognition abroad, holding out the promise of yet a third "Renaissance" of Italian cinema that would follow those of neo-realism and of the generation of Bertolucci and Pasolini. These include such figures as Maurizio Nichetti (1948-); Nanni Moretti (1953-); Gabriele Salvatores (1950-); Giuseppe Tornatore (1956-); Gianni Amelio (1945-); Roberto Benigni; Francesca Archibugi (1960-); and Carlo Carlei (1961-).

Amelio's *Le porte aperte* (*Open Doors*, 1990), nominated for an Oscar, is an adaptation of a novel by Leonardo Sciascia about justice in Fascist Italy. His *Il ladro di bambini* (*The Thief of Children*, 1992), winner of a Grand Jury Prize at Cannes, is a moving treatment of children reminiscent of De Sica's classic neo-realist works. In *L'america* (*America*, 1994), Amelio focuses upon Albanian emancipation from Communism and looks at a poor country (Albania) from the novel perspective of a nation (Italy) that was once poor and chronicled its poverty in neo-realist film, but which is now rich and intent on exploiting the poor in Albania.

Unlike Amelio, many of the younger faces in the Italian cinema prefer the comic genre, and the variety of styles they employ is impressive. Nichetti's *Ladri di saponette* (*Soap Thieves*, 1989), a brilliant spoof of De Sica's neo-realist classic, *Ladri di biciclette*, employs techniques the director learned from working in television and advertising, while his *Volere volare* (*To Desire to Fly*, 1991) mixes actors and cartoon characters in a technique exploited most notably in Robert Zemeckis's *Who Framed Roger Rabbit?* (1987). Tornatore's tremendously popular *Cinema Paradiso* (*The Paradise Cinema*, 1988) owed much of its success to its bittersweet look at contemporary Italy through the prism of its cinematic past. It was awarded a special Jury Prize at Cannes in 1988 and the Oscar for Best Foreign Film in 1989. Salvatores' *Mediterraneo* (*Mediterranean*, 1991), another Oscar winner for Best Foreign Film, employs the old formula of the *commedia all'italiana* to portray World War II from the perspective of Italian soldiers marooned on a Greek island. While its director (Michael Radford) is certainly not Italian, everything about *Il postino* (*The Postman*, 1994) has links to the Italian film industry and the perennially popular *commedia all'italiana*. The film brought actor Massimo Troisi to the attention of international audiences, but Trosi died shortly after shooting was completed for the film. *Il postino* was a smashing critical and commercial success, receiving five Oscar nominations and one award in the category of Original Musical Score. While practically unknown outside of Italy, Leonardo Pieraccioni's recent comic films have made spectacular gains at the box office within the lucrative Italian market: *Il ciclone* (*The Cyclone*, 1995) and *Fuochi di artificio* (*Fireworks*, 1996).

Two actors who script and direct their films, Nanni Moretti and Roberto Benigni, have enjoyed considerable success in the last decade. With *Caro diario* (*Dear Diary*, 1994), Moretti — the favorite director of Italians under forty — won the Grand Prize at the Cannes Film Festival for an autobiographical portrait that led some critics to label Moretti as "the Italian Woody Allen" for his cerebral brand of comedy. Roberto Benigni first achieved international attention as the strange Italian learning English in Jim Jarmusch's *Down by Law* (1986) and as the heir to Peter Sellers' role of Inspector Clouseau in Blake Edwards' *Son of the Pink Panther* (1993). His *Johnny Stecchino* (1991), a spoof on the gangster genre, broke all records for Italian or American grosses inside Italy, foreshadowing the record-breaking critical and commercial success of *La vita è bella* both inside Italy and abroad.

The list of the critical and commercial successes of films by younger directors during the last decade seems to promise positive developments during the next millennium. Whether a few important and universally praised top-quality films per year produced by a small handful of directors can sustain an industrial base for the Italian cinema in the future is, however, less certain. Producing films requires more and more capital, something the Italian industry sadly lacks. No amount of government subsidy or intervention into the sector can easily make up for the lack of the kind of industrial organization that makes Hollywood such a formidable competitor. Like the phoenix, the postwar Italian cinema seems to have arisen from the ashes of the past in a succession of creative generations since 1950. Whether figures such as Tornatore, Benigni, Moretti, and their contemporaries will be capable of directing their creative energies toward yet another such rebirth in the future remains an open question.

SUGGESTIONS FOR FURTHER READING

Armes, Roy. *Patterns of Realism: A Study of Italian Neo-Realism*. Cranbury, N. J.: A. S. Barnes, 1971.

Bazin, André. *What Is Cinema? II*. Berkeley: University of California Press, 1971.

Bondanella, Peter. *The Cinema of Federico Fellini*. Introduction by Federico Fellini. Princeton: Princeton University Press, 1992.

_____ *The Films of Roberto Rossellini*. New York: Cambridge University Press, 1993.

_____ *Italian Cinema: From Neorealism to the Present*. 2nd rev. ed. New York: Continuum, 1990; New Devon: Roundhouse Publishing, 1999.

_____ "Recent Work on Italian Cinema." *Journal of Modern Italian Studies* 1, #1 (1995), 101-23.

Brunetta, Gian Piero. *Storia del cinema italiano*. 4 vols. Rome: Editori Riuniti, 1993.

Gieri, Manuela. *Contemporary Italian Filmmaking: Strategies of Subvervion — Pirandello, Fellini, Scola, and the Directors of the New Generation*. Toronto: University of Toronto Press, 1995.

Landy, Marcia. *Fascism in Film: The Italian Commercial Cinema, 1931-1943*. Princeton: Princeton University Press, 1986.

Marcus, Millicent. *Filmmaking by the Book: Italian Cinema and Literary Adaptation*. Baltimore: The Johns Hopkins University Press, 1993.

Sidney, P. Adams. *Vital Crises in Italian Cinema: Iconography, Stylistics, Politics*. Austin: University of Texas Press, 1995.

Sorlin, Pierre. *Italian National Cinema 1986-1996*. London: Routledge, 1996.

COUNCIL ON NATIONAL LITERATURES

(Orders)
GRIFFON HOUSE PUBLICATIONS
P.O. BOX 468
SMYRNA, DE 19977
TEL/FAX: 302-659-1791 / griffonhse@aol.com

(Editorial)
68-02 METROPOLITAN AVE.
MIDDLE VILLAGE, NY 11379-1622
TEL: 718-821-3916 / FAX:718-767-8380
ISBN: 0-918680

Review of National Literature. A forum for scholars and critics concerned with literature as the expression of national character and the repository of national culture in its most vital and readily communicable form. (Vols. 1 through 21: ISSN: 0034-6640)

Series Editor: Anne Paolucci

New Series: **Review of National Literatures and World Report** initiated in 1998
(ISSN:1521-7337)

Machiavelli '500. Vol. I, No. 1. Spring, 1970. Ed. Anne Paolucci. Contrib.: Leo Strauss, Giuseppe Prezzolini, Joseph A. Mazzeo, John C. H. Wu, Gian Roberto Sarolli, Richard C. Clark.
(ISBN: 0-918680-56-5)   paper $6.95 + $3 s&h)

Hegel in Comparative Literature. Vol I, No. 2. Fall 1970. Spec. Ed. Frederick G. Weiss. Contrib.: Albert Hofstadter, Henry Paolucci, Daisy Fornacca Kouzel, Robert L. Perkins, T. M. Knox, Frank Grande.
(ISBN: 0-918680-57-3)   paper $6.95 + $3 s&h)

Iran; In Celebration of the 2500th Anniversary of the Founding of the Persian Empire by Cyrus The Great. Vol II, No. 1. Spring 1971. Spec. Ed. Javad Haidari. Contrib.: Peter Chelkowski, Richard C. Clark, Javad Haidari, William L. Hanaway, Jr., Hasan Javadi, Mohammad Ali Jazayery, Ernst Rose, George M. Wickens, Donald N. Wilber, John d. Yohannan.
(ISBN: 0-918680-58-1)   paper $6.95 + $3 s&h)

Black Africa. Vol. II, No. 2. Fall 1971. Spec. Ed. Albert S. Gérard. Contrib.: Adeboye Babalola, Lyndon Harries, Janheinz Jahn, Daniel P. Kunene, Bernth Lindfors, J. Mbelolo Ya Mpiku, Gerald M. Moser, John Povey, Harold Scheub, Alexander Neil Skinner, Clive Wake.
(ISBN: 0-918680-59-X)   paper $6.95 + $3 s&h)

Russia: The Spirit of Nationalism. Vol. III, No. 1, Spring 1972. Spec. Ed. Charles A. Moser. Contrib.: Robert L. Belknap, Deming Brown, Richard C. Clark, James M. Holquist, Rosette L. Lamont, Robert A. Maguire, Nicholas Oulianoff, Walter N. Vickery, Robert T. Whittaker.
(ISBN: 0-918690-60-3)   paper $6.95 + $3 s&h)

Shakespeare and England. Vol. III, No. 2, Fall 1972. Spec. Ed. James G. McManaway. Contrib.: Murial Clara Bradbrook, Richard C. Clark, Reginald W. Ingram, Eldred Durosini Jones, J. A. Lavin, Giorgio Melchiori, Kenneth Muir, T.J.B. Spencer, Marvin Spevack.
(ISBN: 0-918680-61-1)   paper $6.95 + $3 s&h)

Turkey: From Empire to Nation. Vol. IV, No. 1, Spring 1973. Spec. Ed. Talât Sait Halman. Contrib.: Metin And, Süheylâ Artemel, Bedia Turgay-Ahmad, Ilhan Basgöz, Kathleen R. F. Burrill, Bedia Turgay-Ahman,
(ISBN: 0-918680-62-X)   (remainder) paper $ 4.95 + $3 s&h)

The France of Claudel. Vol. IV, No. 2, Fall 1973. Spec. Ed. Henri Peyre. Contrib.: Jean-Louis Barrault, Richard. C. clark, James. R. Lawler, Moses M. Nagy, Maurice Pinguet, Leopold Senghor.
(ISBN: 0-918680-63-8)   (remainder) paper $ 4.95 + $3 s&h)

The Multinational Literature of Yugoslavia. Vol. V, No. 1, Spring 1974. Spec. Ed. Albert B. Lord. Contrib.: Thomas J. Butler, Mary Putney Coote, Svetozar Koljevic, Blaze Koneski, John Loud, Aleksander Nejgebauer, Anne Paolucci, Henry Paolucci, Josip Torbarina.
(0-918680-64-6)   paper $ 4.95 + $3 s&h)

Greece: The Modern Voice. Vol. V, No. 2, Fall 1974. Spec. Ed. Peter A. Mackridge.Contrib.: Peter Bien, Edmund Keeley, Christopher Robinson, Katerina Anghelaki Rooke, Philip Sherrard, Mario Vitti.
(ISBN: 0-918680-65-4)   paper $6.95 + $3 s&h)

China's Literary Image. Vol. VI, No. 1, Spring 1975. Spec. Ed. Paul K. T. Sih. Contrib.: Eugene Ching, Richard C. Clark, Dell R. Hales, C. T. Hsia, Paul K. T. Sih, Richard Hsiuh Yang, Yen Yuan-Shu.
(ISBN: 0-918680-66-2)   paper $6.95 + $3 s&h)

Canada. Vol. 7, 1976. Spec. Ed. Richard J. Schoeck. Contrib.: R. G. Collins, Dorothy Livesay, Anne Paolucci, Henry Paolucci, Richard J. Schoeck, Philip Stratford, Ronald Benedetto Bignone Sutherland.
(ISBN: 0-918680-67-0)   paper $6.95 + $3 s&h)

Holland. Vol. 8, 1977. Spec. Ed. Frank J. Warnke. Contrib.: Bard H. Bakker, E. M. Beekman, Richard C. Clark, Egbert Krispyn, Fred J. Nichols, Johan Snapper, Henrietta Ten Harmsel, Frank J. Warnke.
(ISBN: 0-918680-68-9)   paper $6.95 + $3 s&h)

German Expressionism. Vol. 9, 1978. Spec. Ed. Victor Lange. Contrib.: M. Anderle, Armin Arnold, Richard C. Clark, Manfred Durzak, Victor Lange
(ISBN: 0-918680-69-7)   paper $6.95 + $3 s&h)

India. Vol. 10, 1980; Second printing 1984. Spec. Ed. Ronald Warwick. Contrib.: K. K. Chatterjee, Richard Clark, Prabhu S. Guptara, P. Lal, Alastair Niven, Vasant A. Shahane, William Walsh, Ronald Warwick.
(ISBN: 0-918680-20-0)   paper $6.95 + $3 s&h)

Australia. Vol. 11, 1982. Spec. Ed. L. A. C. Dobrez. Contrib.: Ronald H. Berndt, Manning Clark, Richard C. Clark, John Colmer, Livio Dobrez, H. P. Heseltine, Brian Kiernan, Anne Paolucci, Henry Paolucci,
(ISBN: 0-918680-16-6)   paper $6.95 + $3 s&h)

Norway. Vol. 12, 1983. Spec. Ed. Sverre Lyngstad. Contrib.: Edvard Beyer, Richard C. Clark, Janet Garton, John M. Hoberman, Leif Longum, Sverre Lyngstad, Rolf N. Nettum, Henry Paolucci, Janet E. Rasmussen,
(ISBN: 0-918680-17-4)   paper $6.95 + $3 s&h)

Armenia. Vol 13, 1984. Spec. Ed. Vahe Oshagan. Contrib.: Elena Alexanian, James Etmekjian, Levon Hakhverdian, Vrej Nersessian, Varak Nersissian, Vahe Oshagan, Anne Paolucci, Henry Paolucci, Nishan Parlakian,
(ISBN: 0-918680-77-8)   paper $6.95 + $3 s&h)
0-918680-22-0   cloth $12.00 + $3 s&h)

Pirandello. Vol. 14, 1987. Spec. Ed. Anne Paolucci. Contrib.: Jana O'Keefe Bazzoni, Victor Carrabino, Antonio Illiano, Umberto Mariani, Moses M. Nagy, Anne Paolucci, Mary T. Reynolds, Jennifer Stone, Franco Zangrilli
(ISBN: 0-918680-27-1)   paper $6.95 + $3 s&h)

Comparative Literary Theory: New Perspectives. Vol.15, 1989. Spec. Ed. Anne Paolucci. Contrib.: Albert S. Gérard, Bruce King, John J. Deeney, Norman Simms, Anne Paolucci, Henry Paolucci.
(ISBN: 0-918680-24-7)   paper $6.95 + $3 s&h)

Columbus, America, and The World. Vol. 16, 1992. Spec. Eds. Anne Paolucci & Henry Paolucci. Contrib.: Dino Bigongiari, Frank J. Coppa, Marie-Lise Gazarian Gautier, John K. Gillespie, Frank D. Grande, Foster Provost, O. Carlos Stoetzer
(ISBN: 0-918680-33-6)   paper $14.95 + $3 s&h)

Hungarian Literature. Vol. 17, 1993. Spec. Ed. Enikö Molnár Basa. Contrib.: George F. Cushing, Péter Dávidházi, , Béla Oinigáts, László Rónay, György E. Szonyi.
(ISBN: 0-918680-35-2)   paper $14.95 + $3 s&h)

Japan: A Literary Overview. Vol. 18, 1993. Spec. Ed. John K. Gillespie. Contrib: John K. Gillespie, Phillip T. Harries, Chieko Irie Mulhern, Edward Putzar, Makoto Ueda, Janet A. Walker.
(ISBN: 0-918680-23-9)   paper $14.95 + $3 s&h)

Native American Antiquities and Linguistics. Vol. 19, 1995. Justin Winsor. Part I of III. Spec. Eds. Anne Paolucci & Henry Paolucci.
(ISBN: 0-918680-49-2)   paper $25.00 + $3 s&h)

Cultures of the Aztecs, Mayas, and Incas. Vol. 20, 1996. Justin Winsor & C. R. Markham. Part II of III. Spec. Eds. Anne & Henry Paolucci.
(ISBN: 0-918680-50-6)   paper $25.00 + $3 s&h)

Early Spanish, French, and English Encounters with the American Indians. Vol. 21, 1997. Justin Winsor & George E. Ellis. Part III of III. Spec. Eds. Anne & Henry Paolucci
(ISBN: 0-918680-54-9)   paper $25.00 + $3 s&h)

Romanticism in its Modern Aspects, Vol. 1, New Series (Review of National Literature and World Report), 1998. Spec. Ed. Virgil Nemoianu, World Report: Early Discussions On Expanding Comparative Literary Studies, Ed. Anne Paolucci.
(ISBN: 0-918680-73-5)   paper $40.00 + $3 s&h)

Literature As a Unifying Cultural Force. Vol. 2, New Series, 1999. Ed. Anne Paolucci. World Report: Comparative Studies and Non-Western Literatures: A Retrospective, Ed. Anne Paolucci
(ISBN: 0-918680-78-6)   paper $40.00 + $3 s&h)

Italy: Fiction, Theater, Poetry, Film Since 1950. Vol. 3 New Series, 2000. Spec. Ed. Robert S. Dombroski. Contrib.: Joseph Farrell, Peter Hainsworth, Charles Klopp, John Picchione, Rinaldina Russell, Joseph Francese, Ellen Nerenberg, Peter Bondanella. Ed. Anne Paolucci
(ISBN: 0-918680-90-5)   paper $40.00 + $3 s&h)

COUNCIL on NATIONAL LITERATURES

PUBLISHER OF

REVIEW OF NATIONAL LITERATURES

and *CNL / WORLD REPORT*

COUNCIL ON NATIONAL LITERATURES / WORLD REPORT.
(ISSN: 0145-6783) Series Editor: Anne Paolucci.
A forum for scholars concerned with comparative literary study of the established, emergent, and neglected national literatures that make up the written and artistic legacy of the diverse contemporary peoples of the world.

Quarterly World Report 1977 through 1984 published as. Limited availability of back issues.
(Q.W.R. ISSN: 0145-6881) paper $2.50 + $3 s&h)

Problems in National Literary Identity and the Writer as Social Critic. Selected papers of the fourth annual NDEA Seminar on Foreign Area Studies, Columbia University, February 1980. Contrib.: Donald J. Puchala, Salim A. Salim, Bernth Lindfors, Robin Jared Lewis, Elena Klepikova, Frank Warnke, Robert Black.
(ISBN: 0-918680-11-5, 1980 paper $4.95 + $3 s&h)

New Literary Continents. Selected papers of the Fifth NDEA Seminar on Foreign Area Studies. Sponsored by the School of International Affairs, Columbia University. Contrib.: Anne Paolucci, Caroline Eckhardt, Norman Simms, Rosette Lamont, Marilyn Gaddis Rose, Edmund Keeley.
(ISBN: 0-918680-25-5, 1984 paper $4.95 + $3 s&h)

What Price Glory — in Translation? New Series, Vol. I. Contrib.: Marilyn Gaddis Rose, Norman Simms, Elizabeth Welt Trahan.
(ISBN: 0-918680-38-7, 1987 paper $4.95 + $3 s&h)

Comparative Literature and International Studies. Vol. II. Contrib.: Elizabeth Welt Trahan, Jeanne Smoot, P. E. Firchow, Anne Paolucci, Judith Roumani, Jayana Sheth, Katharina M. Wilson.
(ISBN: 0-918680-39-5, 1987 paper $4.95 + $3 s&h)

The Doctor of Arts Degree: Re-Assessing Teaching and Research Priorities. Vol. IV. Contrib.: Anne Paolucci, Willard Gingerich, Jo Anne Hecker, David L. Wheeler, Martin Kanes, Richard W. Bailey, William C. Woodson, Frank Ginanni, Frank Coppa, George Groman, Bruce Martin.
(ISBN: 0-918680-42-5, 1989 paper $4.95 + $3 s&h)

Selected Papers on Columbus and His Time. Ed. Anne Paolucci/Henry Paolucci. Contrib.: A. Paolucci, Frank J. Coppa, Theodore J. Cachey, Jr., Nishan Parlakian, N. Paolucci, Charles Weathers Bump.
(ISBN: 0-918680-40-9, 1989 paper $4.95 + $3 s&h)

Modern Views of Columbus and His Time. (Essays, Poems, Reprints.) Ed. Anne Paolucci/Henry Paolucci. Contrib.: A. Paolucci, Richard Gambino, C. F. Kelly, Marie-Lise Gazarian, Franklin C. Cacciutto, George Maritime, H. Paolucci, Claudia. L.Bushman, Ken Gambone, Herbert B. Adams, Charles Weathers Bump.
(ISBN: 0-918680-46-8, 1990 paper $4.95 + $3 s&h)

Multicultural Perspectives: New Approaches. Vol. VI. Contrib.: Carrol F. Coates, Nishan Parlakian, Juliusz Tyszka, Anne Paolucci, Willard Gingerich, Frank Cacciutto (w. 13 postcard size reproductions of original portraits by Constance Del Vecchio Maltese.)
(ISBN: 0-918680-52-2, 1993 paper $4.95 + $3 s&h)

Toward the 21st Century: New Directions. Vol. VII. (Special anniversary issue commemorating the 20th anniversary of the founding of Council on National Literatures - 1974-1994; and the 10th anniversary of *CNL/World Report* - 1984-1994.) Contrib.: Anne Paolucci, Richard C. Clark.
World Report of Books (R.C. Clark, Ed.)
 Greenwood Press: Geoffrey Ribbans, *History and Fiction in Galdós Narratives*; Kairamu Welsh-Asante, ed. *The African Aesthetic, Keeper of the Traditions.*
 Indiana Univ. Press: Jeffrey D. Mason, *Melodrama and the Myth of America.*
 Intercultural Press: Ari B. Siletz, *The Mullah With No Legs and Other Stories*; K.B. Rao, *Husband, Lover, Holy Man.*
 Louisiana State Univ. Press: Bilge Karasu, *Night*; Martin M. Simecka, *The Night of the Frog* (trans. Peter Petro.)
 Stanford Univ. Press: Fernando Alegria, *Allende: A Novel*, (trans. Frank Jenney)
 The Univ. of Washington Press: *The Bread of Salt and Other Stories*, N.V.M. Gonzalez.
— also —
 RNL, CNL/WR, CNL Conferences and publications: Book Reviews and Notices.
 "Shakespeare and the World": (Shakespeare Summerfest, 1981)
(ISBN: 0-918680-48-4, 1994) paper $4.95 + $3 s&h)

Latin America As Its Literature. Vol. VIII. (Selected papers of the XIVth Congress of the International Comparative Literature Association - Univ. of Alberta, August 1994.) Spec. Eds. Maria Elena De Valdés, Mario J. Valdés, and Richard Young. Contrib: Eduardo Coutinho, Roseanna Mueller, Leyla Perone-Moises, Luz Aurora Pimentel, Maria Elena De Valdés, Maria Do Carmo Campos, Tania Franco Carvahal, Maria I. Palleiro, Claudine Potvin, Tomo Virk, Daniel Castillo Durante, Amarylli Chanady, Renato Cordeiro Gomes, George Lang, Richard A. Young.
(ISBN: 0-918680-55-7, 1995 paper $4.95 + $3 s&h)

Multicomparative Theory, Definitions, Realities. Vol. IX.. (This volume is dedicated to the memory of Victor Lange, 7/31/08 - 6/29/96.) Spec. Ed. Virgil Nemoiano. Contrib.: Qian Zhongwen, Gerald Gillespie, Virgil Nemoiano, Tania Franco Carvahal, Anne Paolucci, Ersu Ding, Frederick Turner, Edward J. Mullen.
(ISBN: 0-918680-53-0, 1996 paper: $15.00 + $3 s&h)

ORDER FORM

All payments in US Dollars; Prepayment preferred; Invoices on request. Makes checks payable to: Council on National Literatures. Mail payments and correspondence to: Griffon House Publications, P.O. Box 468, Smyrna, DE 19806.
Tel/Fax: 302-659-1791 [griffonhse@aol.com]

Item	Title	ISBN	Qty	Price	s&h	Total
				$	$	$
					Total	$

THE PIRANDELLO SOCIETY OF AMERICA

Nishan Parlakian, President

GRIFFON HOUSE PUBLICATIONS
TEL/FAX: 302-659-1791 / griffonhse@aol.com

PSA

Anne Paolucci, Editor

P.O. BOX 468,
SMYRNA, DE 19977

THE OFFICIAL PUBLICATION OF THE PIRANDELLO SOCIETY OF AMERICA (ISSN: 1042-4822)
Published by: Council on National Literatures

VOLUME 1 (1985/1986) • *The Pirandello Society of America – 25th Anniversary Celebration.* • Contributors: Franco Zangrilli, Umberto Mariani, • Book Review: *Pirandello Studies, I, 1985,* Report on the AAIS/Pirandello Program, Tampa, April 1095. Giuseppe Faustini.

VOLUME 2 (1986/1987) • *Pirandello and The French Connection,* Proceedings of the MLA/PSA Annual Meeting, Chicago, 1985. • Contributors: Philip A. Fulvi, Moses M. Nagy. • Forum for Members. Book Reviews: *Pirandello in guanti gialli* (A. Costantini); *Metapsichica e letteratura in Pirandello* (G. W. Anderson); *L'arte novellistica di Pirandello* (G. Faustini). **[Out of Stock / Out of Print]**

VOLUME 3 (1987/1988) Contributors: John Gillespie, Philip Fulvi, Marie-Lise Gazarian Gautier, Victor Carrabino. • Book Reviews: *Pirandello e il teatro del suo tempo; Pirandello e il teatro; Pirandello pittore.*

VOLUME IV (1988/1989) Contributors: Kathryn Wylie, Anne Paolucci, Jana O'Keefe Bazzoni, Giovanni Bussino, Giuseppe Faustini.

VOLUME V (1989/1990) • Special Presentation by Joseph Maselli to the PSA: MLA/PSA Meeting, December 1988, New Orleans. Contributors: Maria Rosaria Vitti-Alexander, Nishan Parlakian, Philip A. Fulvi, Anne Paolucci.

VOLUME VI (1990/1991) • *PIRANDELLO AND COMMEDIA DELL'ARTE.* Contributors: John DiGaetani, Eric Bentley, Mark Spergel, Nishan Parlakian.

VOLUME VII (1991-1992) • 70th Anniversary Special (1921-1991): Pirandello's *Six Characters in Search of An Author.* Contributors: Matthew Roudané, Leslie Kane, Martin J. Jacobi, John DiGaetani, Nishan Parlakian. • Theater Review: *Henry IV* in London's West End. **[Out of Stock / Out of Print]**

VOLUME VIII (1992/1993) • *PIRANDELLO AND EDWARD ALBEE.* Contributors: *The "Pirandellian" Albee,* Matthew Roudané; *Pirandello: Leader of the Absurd,* Anne Paolucci; *Theater of the Grotesque: Meyerhold, Pirandello, and Albee,* Susan Haedicke; *The Pirandellian Author in Search of His Audience: Albee's "The Man Who Had Three Arms,* Anne Paolucci; *Pirandello, Albee, and Ayckbourn: An Absurdist Tradition,* John DiGaetani.

VOLUME IX (1992/1993) • *PIRANDELLO, SAROYAN, AND THE NEW YORK STAGE.* Contributors: Pirandello in a Bind, Anne Paolucci; *Pirandello, Saroyan, and the Absurd,* Nishan Parlakian; *"Chu Chin Chow": Music and Lyrics used in "Six Characters",* Eric Bentley; *Thoughts on Teaching Pirandello,* Zoë C. Kaplan.

VOLUME X (1994/1995) • *GIORGIO STREHLER IN NEW YORK. "THE MOUNTAIN GIANTS.* Contributors: *Into the New Century,* Anne Paolucci; *An Evening with Georgio Strehler,* E. Petriella-Bonomo; • Articles by: Giorgio Strehler, Mel Gussow, Nina DaVinci Nichols, Mary Talbot, Linda Winer. • Reviews by Enzo Ficile, Clive Barnes, Nina DaVince Nichols, Ben Brantley, Mario Fratti. • Letter from Pirandello to Vittorini (Courtesy Eric Bentley).

VOLUME XI (1995/1996) • *PIRANDELLO IN GERMANY. Pirandello, Nietzsche and The Good Mask,* Daniela Bini. • *On And Off The Rialto,* La Cronista. • *Pirandello in Germany (1924-1930) and "Tonight We Improvise,"* Jane House. • *Germany: The Biographical Connection,* John DiGaetani. • *Carteggi: Sulle Lettere di Pirandello a Marta Abba. Va in scena la polemica,* Tommaso Zerlina. Readings. • Produc-tions. • Conferences: Indiana Univ. theatre: Six Characters, James Fisher. • New York Theatre Workshop: Man, Beast, and Virtue, Michael Kowal. • Pirandello at Boston Collece, Nina DaVinci Nichols.

VOLUME XII (1996/1997) • *PIRANDELLO, SHAKESPEARE, AND MO-DERN TIMES.* • Presentations at PSA/MLA Meetings. • Notices, including a brief accouant of *PSA's* Anniversary Awards Dinner. • *Pirandello's theories of Comedy and Shakespeare's Clowns,* Maurice Charney. • *Tempest and Mountain Giants,* Nina DaVinci Nichols. *"Enrico IV," Pirandello's Cubist Quadro,* Rosana Vitale. Theatre Reviews: Hugo Weisgall's Opera of *Six Characters,* Manhattan School of Music: *"Six Characters in Search of an Opera,* Jon Messman. • *"The Pirandello Six, Singing but Still Dysfunctional,"* Allan Kozinn (*NY Times*). • *"Weisgall's neglected 'Six Characters' finds new life at the Lyric,"* John von Rhein (*Chicago Tribune*) • *"Opera: Pirandello's Plot,"* Howard Taubman (*NY Times*). • "Washington Critics Hail Weisgall Work," (*NY Times*). • "Six Characters in Search of an Author," Richard Gold-man (*The Music Quarterly*). • "Music: Weisgall's 'Six Characters'," (*NY Times*).

VOLUME XIII (1997/1998) • Commemorating the Society's 40th Anniversary. • FROM NARRATIVE TO DRAMA. • Presentations at PSA/MLA Meeting etc. • *Story to Play: Toward a Theory of Self-Adap-tation,* Robert S. Dombroski. • *Narrative in Pirandello's Plays,* Anne Paolucci. • *"The Players" Hosts PSA's 40th Anniversary Dinner.* • *Aspects of Italian Futurism in Pirandello's* "Tonight We Improvise," David S. Escoffery. *Reenvisioning Pirandello for the Contemporary Stage: Critical and Directional Interventions,* Jana O'Keefe Bazzoni. • *Pirandellian Themes in Paolo Pappa's "Le parole al Buio,"* Giuliana Sanguinetti Katz. • Theatre Notes and Reviews.

VOLUME XIV (1998-1999) • *PIRANDELLO IN TRANSLATION.* • Presentations at PSA/MLA Meetings, etc. • *Pirandello's Women Writer and the Birth Metaphor: Problems in Translation,* Mary Ann Witt. • *Translating Pirandello into the 21st Century: Literary, Historical and Linguistic Challenges,* Martha King. • *The Influence of Pirandello in Latin America,* James J. Troiano. • Annual Awards Dinner, November 30, 1999, honoring Benito Ortolani. • Productions: *The Freak of Nature: Pirandello's One-Act Plays,* Nina DaVinci Nichols, etc.

ORDERS FOR PSA

Single Copies   Vol. I thru XI – $15 (Individuals)   • $30 (Libraries)
From Vol. XII – $20 (Individuals)   • $35 (Libraries)
Add $3.00 for s&h (surface) / Add $2.00 for US AirMail or $5.00 for International
Prepayment preferred — Invoice supplied on request
All payments should be made out to:

Council on National Literatures

Mail orders and payments to:
GRIFFON HOUSE PUBLICATIONS
P.O. BOX 468, SMYRNA, DE 19977
Tel/Fax: 302-659-1791 / griffonhse@aol.com